Lecture Notes in
Global-
Local Policy
Interactions

World Scientific Lecture Notes in Economics and Policy

ISSN: 2630-4872

Series Editor: Ariel Dinar *(University of California, Riverside, USA)*

The World Scientific Lecture Notes in Economics and Policy series is aimed to produce lecture note texts for a wide range of economics disciplines, both theoretical and applied at the undergraduate and graduate levels. Contributors to the series are highly ranked and experienced professors of economics who see in publication of their lectures a mission to disseminate the teaching of economics in an affordable manner to students and other readers interested in enriching their knowledge of economic topics. The series was formerly titled World Scientific Lecture Notes in Economics.

Published:

For the complete list of volumes in this series, please visit
www.worldscientific.com/series/wslnep

World Scientific Lecture Notes in Economics and Policy – Vol. 12

Lecture Notes in Global-Local Policy Interactions

Ariel Dinar
University of California, Riverside, USA

With Annex contributions by:
Jessica Bradford
Edgar Castelan
Jorge Gavino
Jacquelyn González
Adam Jantz
Yang Li
Fortino Morales III
Michael Parmer

World Scientific

NEW JERSEY • LONDON • SINGAPORE • BEIJING • SHANGHAI • HONG KONG • TAIPEI • CHENNAI • TOKYO

Published by

World Scientific Publishing Co. Pte. Ltd.

5 Toh Tuck Link, Singapore 596224

USA office: 27 Warren Street, Suite 401-402, Hackensack, NJ 07601

UK office: 57 Shelton Street, Covent Garden, London WC2H 9HE

Library of Congress Control Number: 2022007582

British Library Cataloguing-in-Publication Data
A catalogue record for this book is available from the British Library.

World Scientific Lecture Notes in Economics and Policy — Vol. 12
LECTURE NOTES IN GLOBAL-LOCAL POLICY INTERACTIONS

ISBN 978-981-124-816-0 (hardcover)
ISBN 978-981-124-931-0 (paperback)
ISBN 978-981-124-817-7 (ebook for institutions)
ISBN 978-981-124-818-4 (ebook for individuals)

For any available supplementary material, please visit
https://www.worldscientific.com/worldscibooks/10.1142/12581#t=suppl

Desk Editors: Aanand Jayaraman/Yulin Jiang

Typeset by Stallion Press
Email: enquiries@stallionpress.com

Dedication

This book is dedicated to the students in the program Master of Public Policy (MPP) at the School of Public Policy, University of California, Riverside. Students who took this class under the difficult COVID-19 circumstances and, in particular, those students who found that certain global policies have a personal angle that reflects on their own life and experiences and selected those policies as a subject for their class projects.

About the Author

Ariel Dinar is a Distinguished Professor of Environmental Economics and Policy at the School of Public Policy, University of California, Riverside (UCR). He teaches courses on water policy, global–local policy interactions, management of international water, and micro-economics for public policy. His work addresses various aspects of economic and strategic behavior associated with management of water, land, and the environment. Dr. Dinar received his Ph.D. from the Hebrew University of Jerusalem. Since then he spent 15 years in the World Bank working on water and climate change economics and policy in a global context. In 2008, Dr. Dinar assumed a professorship at UCR. He founded the Water Science and Policy Center, which he directed until 2014. Dr. Dinar is a Fulbright Senior Specialist since 2003; an International Fellow of the Center for Agricultural Economic Research of the Hebrew University of Jerusalem, Israel, since November 2010; and was named a 2015 Fellow of the Agricultural and Applied Economics Association. He authored and co-authored nearly 250 publications in peer-reviewed journals, policy outlets, and book chapters. He co-authored and edited 30 books and textbooks. Dr. Dinar founded two technical journals (*Strategic Behavior and the Environment*, and *Water Economics and Policy*) for the latter one he serves at present as the Editor-in-Chief. He founded and serves as the Editor-in-Chief of the book series *Global Issues in Water Policy*.

Contents

Chapter 1

Introduction—Course Syllabus

Abstract

This chapter provides the motivation for the course and supporting documents that the lecturer and students will need to access. In preparing this chapter, I intentionally kept the structure I used for the syllabus of the course (offered in 2018 and 2020), with several modifications that allow easier understanding and use of the various components of the course.

1.1 Course Description

Recent developments in the world suggest strong relationships between local and global decisions, actions, and impacts. Global–local relationships are also associated with positive and negative externalities, which necessitate policy interventions. This course discusses the process of building and managing a global public policy and the interaction of public policies at the global and local (national) levels. (In this course: global policy $\equiv$ treaty $\equiv$ accord $\equiv$ agreement $\equiv$ convention.) We will learn about global negative externalities from under-regulation of various activities by one agent/country that affect the well-being of other agents/countries, and the design of policies (agreements) to reduce the impact of such externalities. We will also address the possible opposed interests to

1

global policies, of local actors and the (local) policies they established to tackle such externalities in their jurisdictions. We will introduce concepts and principles associated with conflict, negotiation, and cooperation, all of which are part of policy reform. We will explore the various extents to which the global–local interactions are related to selected policies. Policies discussed in class and assigned to students include: climate change, fisheries, water, health, trade, refugees, immigration, disability, deforestation, and desertification. We will discuss and compare the opportunities and challenges in establishing, implementing, and maintaining such policies.

1.2 Course Requirements

Students are required to attend all weekly classes; *be familiar with assigned reading material, participate actively in class discussions* for all weekly reading assignments; be ready to answer questions, and *lead one assigned discussion* of a part of a reading assignment; *respond* (team of several students, or individual students, depending on the size of the class) to weekly homework assignments (listed at the bottom of each week's course description); *prepare and present (same teams)* a final paper which reviews and analyzes, for a given global policy assigned to the team, several aspects such as the motivation for that policy, the processes leading to its consideration, its design and structure, the policy intervention mechanisms, the problems associated with its implementation (both technical and political), its interaction with local policies, and its effectiveness [the outline is presented in Section (1.5)].

This is a 10-week course. The last week is used for presentation of the final paper assignments that the students prepare (see Annex for examples). Material taught in this course is based on this book chapters and selected published books/papers/chapters that are referred to in the book. Weekly reading assignments (1–4 articles/ chapters per week) are also mentioned in each chapter.

1.3 Grading

1. Class attendance (5%)

   - Students who have to miss a class for job-related matters need to inform the instructor by email prior to the class. Only one class can be missed without penalty. Students have to submit their homework assignments on time even if they plan to miss a class.

2. Leading a short class discussion on a topic from one reading assignment (5%)

   - Students are expected to lead class discussion of one *assigned* component/topic of one reading assignment. Be ready to answer questions and provide explanations (no need to prepare a formal power-point presentation). The assigned component/ topic will be provided to the student by the instructor 1–2 weeks prior to the class.

3. Submission of homework assignments (30%)

   - Homework assignments (hard copies) of TYPED text have to be handed to the instructor by the beginning of the class. Late submissions will automatically be fined 10 points per hour (or part of it) of delay. Papers not turned in by the end of the class will get the grade of 0.
   - Homework text should not exceed two pages, typed in Times New Roman font, size 12, using 1.5 spaces.

4. Final paper (45%) and presentation (15%)

   - Presentation of final papers will take place during week 10. Each presentation will last 15–20 min and will engage the two team members. The presentation will be graded, based on the following: content, use of concepts from class, completion on time. Students will send their presentations to the instructor by 2 pm on the day of the class (on week 10).
   - Submission of final papers is expected by the day and time of the final exam, which will be announced by the instructor once

the exam day and time are known. Late submissions will be fined 10 points per day (or part of it) of delay.

- Final paper's structure is provided in Section (1.5).
- Final paper and presentation grades are assigned evenly to each member of the team.

1.4 Selection of Global Policy Case Studies

Students can select a global policy case for their final paper (that can be used also in some homework assignments) from the list in Table 1.1 Students can suggest also a global policy that is not listed in the table (but appears—bottom of Table 1.1—in the link to the list of Global treaties and processes, and in the link to United Nations Treaty Collection). However, for policies not listed among the global policies in Table 1.1 students have to obtain the consent of the instructor. Students have to bid on the global policy they selected during the first week of the class. Each student submits bids for three cases, ranked from 1–3, with 1 indicating highest interest and 3 indicating lowest interest (by *a date indicated by the instructor*). Bids will be awarded, based on a 'first bids, first being awarded' rule. Once the instructor has notified students about their cases, they can trade among themselves during the remainder of the week *and inform the instructor* about an exchange if it took place (by *a date indicated by the instructor*). Once a selection is finalized, students remain with their global policy case for the entire course.

1.5 Final Paper

Students will describe and analyze, in the Final Paper, all the following: the objectives of the *present version* of the global policy they selected; the motivation for establishing the policy (including previous versions of the policy); the politics and history involved in the process of reaching the policy; the structure of the policy and the institutions established to monitor and enforce it; the policy regulatory mechanisms; the problems associated with the policy implementation (both technical and political); to the role of local (state) interests in shaping the global policy; discussion about the stability of the policy; analysis of the effectiveness of the policy (including use of suggested indexes that measure effectiveness); and how that policy could benefit from features and experiences of other global policies (that have been discussed in class, and others researched by the student).

The final paper should not exceed 10 typed pages in Times New Roman font, size 12, 1.5 space, not including references, annexes, and tables (*to appear at the end of the document*). The Final Paper is expected in the ***inbox of the instructor's email*** by the end of the Final Exam time.

1.6 Sources for Major Global Policies

Table 1.1. Sample of Global Policies/Conventions/Treaties.

No.	Policy	Sample websites
1.	International Water **(Not for selection)**	Convention on the Law of the Non-Navigational Uses of International Watercourses 1997: http://legal.un.org/ilc/texts/instruments/english/conventions/8_3_1997.pdf
2.	Climate Change Policies **(Not for selection)**	United Nations Framework Convention on Climate Change Paris Agreement (2015): http://unfccc.int/paris_agreement/items/9485.php Kyoto Protocol (1997): http://unfccc.int/kyoto_protocol/items/2830.php
3.	High Seas Fisheries **(Not for selection)**	The United Nations 1995 fish stock agreement: http://www.un.org/depts/los/convention_agreements/convention_overview_fish_stocks.htm
4.	Health	Constitution of the World Health Organization: http://www.who.int/about/mission/en/ http://www.who.int/governance/eb/who_constitution_en.pdf

(*Continued*)

Table 1.1.   (*Continued*)

No.	Policy	Sample websites
5.	Trade	EFTA: http://www.efta.int/sites/default/files/documents/ legal-texts/efta-convention/Vaduz%20Convention %20Agreement.pdf Free Trade Administration: https://www.trade.gov/fta/ NAFTA: https://www.nafta-sec-alena.org/Home/Welcome NAFTA and CA: https://s.giannini.ucop.edu/uploads/giannini_public/ ee/d8/eed8ca94-8a7c-4f6c-99de-3101495f0b16/ v21n2_3.pdf GATT: https://www.wto.org/english/thewto_e/whatis_e/tif_e/ fact4_e.htm Uruguay Round: https://www.wto.org/english/thewto_e/whatis_e/tif_e/ fact5_e.htm Doha Round: https://www.wto.org/english/tratop_e/dda_e/dda_e.htm Bali Round: https://www.wto.org/english/thewto_e/minist_e/ mc9_e/balipackage_e.htm
6.	Terrorism	International Convention for the Suppression of the Financing of Terrorism: https://treaties.un.org/Pages/ViewDetails.aspx?src= IND&mtdsg_no=XVIII-11&chapter=_18&lang=en https://www.unodc.org/documents/treaties/Special/ 1999%20International%20Convention%20for%20the% 20Suppression%20of%20the%20Financing%20of%20 Terrorism.pdf
7.	Nuclear Weapons	Treaty on the Prohibition of Nuclear Weapons: http://undocs.org/A/CONF.229/2017/8 https://www.un.org/disarmament/ptnw/

Table 1.1. (*Continued*)

No.	Policy	Sample websites
8.	Chemical Weapons	Chemical Weapons Convention: https://www.un.org/disarmament/wmd/chemical/
9.	Biological Diversity	Convention on Biological Diversity: https://www.un.org/disarmament/wmd/chemical/ https://www.cbd.int/convention/text/
10.	Discrimination against Women	Convention on the Elimination of All Forms of Discrimination Against Women: http://www.un.org/womenwatch/daw/cedaw/cedaw.htm http://www.ohchr.org/Documents/Professional Interest/cedaw.pdf
11.	Law of the Sea	United Nations Convention on the Law of the Sea: http://www.un.org/depts/los/convention_agreements/texts/unclos/unclos_e.pdf
12.	Desertification	United Nations Convention to Combat Desertification: http://www2.unccd.int/convention/about-convention
13.	Deforestation	International Agreement to Protect World's Forests: http://www.un.org/apps/news/story.asp?NewsID=22389#.WfkMXhNSwY8
14.	Refugees	Convention on Refugees: http://www.unhcr.org/en-us/1951-refugee-convention.html http://www.unhcr.org/3b66c2aa10.pdf https://treaties.un.org/pages/ViewDetailsII.aspx?src=TREATY&mtdsg_no=V-2&chapter=5&Temp=mtdsg2&clang=_en
15.	The Iran Deal	https://obamawhitehouse.archives.gov/node/328996
16.	The North Korea Deal	https://www.armscontrol.org/factsheets/dprkchron

(*Continued*)

Table 1.1. (*Continued*)

No.	Policy	Sample websites
17.	Montreal Protocol on Ozone Depletion	http://ozone.unep.org/en/treaties-and-decisions/ montreal-protocol-substances-deplete-ozone-layer
	General Sources	
	List of global treaties and processes	https://en.wikipedia.org/wiki/List_of_treaties_by_ number_of_parties
	United Nations Treaty Collection	https://treaties.un.org/
	Useful links	https://blogs.un.org/blog/2012/09/24/most-ratified-international-treaties/
	Vienna Convention on the Law of Treaties	https://treaties.un.org/doc/publication/unts/ volume%201155/volume-1155-i-18232-english.pdf https://treaties.un.org/Pages/ViewDetailsIII. aspx?src=TREATY&mtdsg_no=XXIII-1& chapter=23&Temp=mtdsg3&clang=_en

1.7 Course Plan

1.7.1 *Week 1: Why global policies/treaties*

Introduction to the course, course structure, rules, requirements, grading, structure of the final paper. Two case videos to set the direction of the class. Globalization and externalities, state vs. federal in measuring global policy performance, cost–benefit analysis (CBA) as a tool for global policy performance. We will define a global policy. We will discuss the justification and motivation for global policies: why certain issues are included in a global treaty and others are not, why we see more global policies on environmental issues, and how global policies are developed.

Two cases—Videos:

1. Climate change: California vs. USA
2. Local and global water externalities

Reading:

Alemanno, A., 2013. Is there a Role for Cost-Benefit Analysis beyond the Nation-State? Lessons from International Regulatory Cooperation. In: Livermorem Michael, A. and Richard L. Revesz (Eds.), *The Globalization of Cost-Benefit Analysis in Environmental Policy.* Oxford University Press, pp. 104–122.

Darian-Smith, E. and Philip, C. M., 2017. The Global Turn. Chapter 2, *Why Is Global Studies Important?* University of California Press, pp. 29–54.

Lamy, S. L., John S. M., John, B., Steve, S., and Patricia O., 2017. *Introduction to Global Politics*, 4th edition. New York: Oxford University Press.

Homework 1 (Submission on week 2)*:

You are asked to search and identify two global policies/treaties/conventions (you can use the list in Table 1.1 as a departure point, but you can identify other global policies as well). Explain what is the motivation for each of these global policies: what are the reasons that each treaty has been negotiated and signed. Find information on the treaty establishment specifications (e.g., signature day, number of signatory states, how many countries ratified it by 2020, any amendments to the treaty—some treaties require annual or periodical meetings of the stakeholders for possible amendments). Summarize the information in a table. Suggest, based on the data you collected, a measure of possible attractiveness of each of the two treaties/policies to the community of countries around world.

All homework assignments can be submitted as a joint product of all team mates cooperating on the preparation of the final paper.

1.7.2 *Week 2: Concepts and principles of conflict*

This class and the classes of weeks 3 and 4 will focus on strategic behavior of agents involved in a conflict, and negotiation and cooperation processes—this is exactly the sequence leading to the establishment of a global policy.

The focus of this week's class is the principles and measurements of conflict. We will introduce the following concepts: definition of conflict; conflicts over natural resources; and how to measure conflicts. Example of a scale of levels of conflict:

from exchange of letters to war—basins at risks (BAR) as a measure of water conflicts is also covered. We will discuss unrelated relationships among the states, such as trade, diplomatic relations, and other exchanges as measures of conflict/ tension reduction.

We will introduce conflicts as games. Non-cooperative games in a matrix form. Concepts used will include: deterrence, threats, credible threats, payoffs, strategies, zero-sum game, chicken game, Nash equilibrium, prisoner's dilemma.

Reading:

(Recommended for week 2-4) Binmore, K., 2007. *Game Theory, A Very Short Introduction*. Oxford: Oxford University Press.

(Recommended for week 2-4) Shubik, M., 1982. *Game Theory in the Social Sciences: Concepts and Solutions*. Cambridge, MA: MIT Press.

Schelling, Thomas, C., 2003. *Chapter 1—The Retarded Science of International Strategy, The Strategy of Conflict*. Cambridge: Harvard University Press, pp. 3–20.

Homework 2 (Submission on Week 3):

In the global policy that you selected for your Final Paper, identify and discuss the main issues of contest between the various states (or blocks of states) involved, and the original positions of these states or blocks of states. For your consideration: it will be hard to analyze nearly 200 countries that are part of a global policy. You can observe (by doing research) a split in the interests/positions/etc ... and how sub-coalitions of countries are formed (for example, the EU in recent years–after its establishment–acts in one voice). You can also observe common interests of developed (industrial) vs. developing countries. In some cases, you will be able to see that countries are distributed in their 'favoritism' of the global policy by their perception of how they will be damaged due to their geographic situation (e.g., southern vs. northern hemisphere). Therefore, you can divide the group of states involved into subgroups, based on: (1) the conflictive issues and on (2) an index that you can develop and apply in order to measure the level of conflict on each said issue the global policy addresses.

1.7.3 *Week 3: Concepts and principles of negotiation*

We will discuss and demonstrate Concepts and Principles of Negotiation. We will cover basic negotiation aspects, such as 2-parties negotiating over one issue; two parties negotiating over several issues; and many parties negotiating over many issues. Concepts discussed will include: concessions, reservation value, zone of agreement, and issue linkage.

We will review how negotiations are made in the context of a global policy (using examples of the free trade agreements—the 'rounds', and the climate change negotiations—the 'conferences of the parties, COP') and what are the problems faced by the negotiating parties as the number of negotiators increases.

Reading:

Grzybowski, A., Stephen, C. M., and Richard, K. P., 2010. *Beyond International Water Law: Successfully Negotiating Mutual Gains Agreements for International Watercourses.* University of the Pacific, Scholarly Commons.

Michaelowa, K. and Axel, M., 2012. Negotiating Climate Change. *Climate Policy,* 12(5):527–533.

Raiffa, H., 1982. *Some Organizing Questions, Chapter 1, The Art and Science of Negotiation.* An Arbor: The University of Michigan Press, pp. 11–19.

Schelling, Thomas, C., 2003. *Chapter 2, An Essay on Bargaining, The Strategy of Conflict.* Cambridge: Harvard University Press, pp. 21–52.

Homework 3 (Submission on Week 4):

Describe the negotiation process of one global policy of your choice (either the one you selected for the final project, or any global policy from the list in Table 1.1 of the Syllabus, or any other one you can come up with). Describe the original positions of the parties (you can divide the parties into major blocks of states) and the positions at the final agreement. Describe what was given up by each of the parties and what was gained by each. Your analysis can be qualitative, using a matrix format.

Student Leading Class Discussion (for week 4):

1. The Columbia River Basin (Grzybowski *et al.*, 2010, pp. 149–151).
2. The Nile River Basin (Grzybowski *et al.*, 2010, pp. 151–152).

1.7.4 *Week 4: Concepts and principles of cooperation*

We will introduce terms such as global public 'bads', negative externalities, equity, self-enforcement, punishment, and monitoring. We will demonstrate the meaning of singleton coalitions, partial coalitions, and grand coalition. We will emphasize the importance of the concept of economies of scale and transaction costs in the creation of cooperative arrangements (agreements). Additional concepts used will include: Allocations, Core. We will demonstrate why big groups of agents may or may not lead to cooperative agreement, depending on realized gains and costs. We will talk about the possibility that some countries would want to withdraw (defect/disrupt) from the treaty or even not join it on the first place. This defines the term of stability of the policy—propensity to disrupt a treaty. We will use several examples of popular treaties/policies in recent years, such as the global climate change policy and the international water treaty.

Reading:

Axelrod, R., 1984. Chapter 1—*The Problem of Cooperation, The Evolution of Cooperation*. Basic Books, pp. 3–24.

Sadoff, C. and David, G., 2005. Cooperation on International Rivers. *Water International*, 30(4):1–8.

Homework 4 (Submission on week 5):

Examine the global policy you selected earlier, in Homework 3, to identify (potential and actual) cooperative gains and costs of engagement for certain countries or blocks of countries. Qualitatively explain/measure the gains from cooperation and the direct and indirect costs from being part of, and adhering to, that global policy.

1.7.5 *Week 5: Creation, implementation, and management of the 1997 Convention on the Law of the Non-Navigational Uses of International Watercourses*

We will focus on the history of developing and establishing the various frameworks leading finally to the 1997 Convention on the Law of the Non-Navigational Uses of International Watercourses. We will go through the various attempts and initiatives starting in the 1860s and how they have been evolving with the changes that took place in water uses around the world. In particular, we will review several concepts relevant to international water, such as: Upstream and Downstream riparian states, Sovereignty, No-harm rule, Equitable and reasonable utilization. We will try to explain the reasons for the unattractiveness of this global water treaty and to attempt to extrapolate from this to other global treaties. While the class will focus very closely only on the '1997 Convention on the Law of the Non-Navigational Uses of International Watercourses', *you will be requested in the assigned homework (#5) to refer also to the Climate Change policies. Therefore, pay attention to the required and recommended reading in the following list.*

Reading:

Dinar, A., Dinar, S., McCaffrey, S., and McKinney, D., 2013. *Chapter 3—The Development and Application of International Water Law, Bridges over Water.* pp. 63–85.

Gupta, J., 2010. A History of International Climate Change Policy. *Wiley Online Library*, 1:636–653.

Salman, M. and Salman, A., 2007. The United Nations Watercourses Convention Ten Years Later: Why has Its Entry into Force Proven Difficult? *Water International*, 32(1):1–15.

(*Recommended*) Schroeder, H., 2010. The History of International Climate Change Politics: Three decades of progress, process and procrastination. In: Maxwell T. Boykoff (Ed.), *The Politics of Climate Change: A Survey*. London: Routledge, Retrieved Online at https://books.google.com/books?hl=en&lr=&id=xHesAgAAQBAJ&oi=fnd&pg=PA26&dq=related:yedC2e LDV88_MM:scholar.google.com/&ots=GGRNKxTXL8&sig=3NjMMju8RJ 3g5fEtXjhPhVqr7x0#v=onepage&q&f=false on October 26, 2017.

van der Gaast, W., 2017. Climate Negotiation Factors: Design, Process and Tactics. Chapter 2. In: van der Gaast, Wytze (Ed.), *International Climate Negotiation Factors, Design, Process, Tactics*. Berlin: Springer.

Homework 5 (Submission on week 6):

Extend the history of the two global policies (water and climate change) beyond the years which the papers in the reading list reached. Contrast and compare the Convention on the Law of the Non-Navigational Uses of International Water and the Paris Accord on Climate Change. In your response describe the process, the politics, the stability (as you measure it), and the future prospect of each of these policies given trends in local as well as global economic and political situations and in global environmental changes.

   Also, start preparing your Final Paper and Presentation.

Student Leading Class Discussion (for week 6):

3. Tactical Factors for Climate Negotiations (van der Gaast, 2017, pp. 35–40).
4. 2008 and Beyond: Leadership During the Financial Crisis (Gupta, 2010, pp. 648–650).
5. Why are states Reluctant to Become Parties to the Convention (Salman, 2009, pp. 8–12).

1.7.6   *Weeks 6, 7, 8: Global policies—From theory to practice*

We will discuss during weeks 6, 7, and 8 the actual implementation of several global agreements such as the International Water Treaty, the Climate Change agreement (overflow from week 5), the High Seas Fishery agreements (and if time allows, also Trade Liberalization policies). Using these agreements, we will introduce and demonstrate the meaning of several important concepts such as: free riding, implementation costs (private, social), and punishment. We will use the clean development mechanism (CDM) of the Kyoto Protocol as an example of a policy with two objectives (reduction of global CO_2 emission and development of low-income countries), we will learn about the role of international organizations (IO) (e.g., World Bank, UNEP), and leading nations and/or groups of nations (e.g., EU), and we will use examples from various global policies about opposition blocks (EU vs. USA; developing countries vs. developed counties, etc.). This issue has been on the agenda of the fishery resource managers for a long time, and is gaining interest as the BREXIT of the UK takes effect. We will introduce also the political opposition to certain global agreements (e.g., Trade) by International NGOs concerned by possible impacts on the environment, conflicts among nations, etc.

Reading:

Week 6:

Connelly, J., Graham, S., David, B., and Clare, S., 1999. Chapter 7—Policy Principles and Instruments. In: Connelly *et al.* (Eds.), *Politics and the Environment—From Theory to Practice*, 3rd edition. New York: Routledge.

Connelly, J., Graham, S., David, B., and Clare, S., 1999. Chapter 5—Greening Global Governance. In: Connelly *et al.* (Eds.), *Politics and the Environment—From Theory to Practice*, 3rd edition. New York: Routledge.

Soroos, M. S., 2005. Gurrett Hardin and Tragedies of Global Commons. In: Dauvergne, Peter (Ed.), *Handbook of Global Environmental Politics*. Cheltenham: Edward Elgar.

Week 7:

Axelrod, M., 2017. Blocking Change: Facing the Drag of Status Quo Fisheries Institutions. *International Environmental Agreements*, 17:573–588.

Munro, Gordon, R., 2008. Chapter 2—Game Theory and the Development of Resource Management Policy—The Case of International Fisheries. In: Dinar, Ariel, Jose Albiac, and Joaquin Sanchez-Soriano (Eds.), *Game Theory and Policymaking in Natural Resources and the Environment*. London: Routledge.

Week 8:

Yamagata, Y., Jue Y., and Joseph G., 2017. State Power and Diffusion Process in the Ratification of Global Environmental Treaties, 1981–2008. *International Environmental Agreements*, 17:501–529.
Homework: Start/Continue preparing your Final Paper and Presentation.

Student Leading Class Discussion (for week 7):

6. Intro, Hardin's Thesis, The Concept of the Commons, Ownership of the Commons (Soroos, 2005, pp. 35–40).
7. Preventing Environmental Tragedies (Soroos, 2005, pp. 41–44).
8. Global Warming as a Tragedy of the Commons (Soroos, 2005, pp. 44–48).
9. The International Politics of Climate Change (Connelly *et al.*, 1999, Chapter 7, pp. 276–280).
10. Information (Connelly *et al.*, 1999, Chapter 5, pp. 194–200).

Student Leading Class Discussion (for week 8):

11. Individual (sub-coalition) Rationality Condition (Munro, 2008, pp. 25–27).
12. Prisoner's Dilemma (Munro, 2008, pp. 27–29).
13. Side Payments (Munro, 2008, pp. 29–36).

Student Leading Class Discussion (for week 9):

14. US Fisheries Negotiating Positions (Axelrod, 2017, pp. 578–581),
15. EU Activity in Fisheries Agreements (Axelrod, 2017, pp. 581–584),
16. State Power and Treaty Diffusion (Yamagata *et al.*, 2017, pp. 501–529).

1.7.7 *Week 9: Shaping global policies by international organizations and NGOs*

We will focus on the role of IOs in shaping global policies. As we already became aware of, several IOs such as the World Bank, the OECD, the World Health Organization, the World Trade Organization, the United Nations Development Programme, to name a few, have played major roles in initiating and framing several global policies. We will explore the motivation of and the strategies used by the IOs to develop and implement global policies, their own interests, and the conflicts created with states that were part of the development of those policies. We will also discuss the interactions between IOs and NGOs, both local and international.

Reading:

Fox, J. A. and Brown, L. D., (Eds.), 1998. *The Struggle for Accountability: The World Bank, NGOs, and Grassroots Movements.* Cambridge: Cambridge University Press.

Mahon, R., 2020. Transnational Care Chains as Seen by the OECD, the World Bank, and the IOM. In: Dolowitz, David, Magdalena Hadjiisky, and Romuald Normand (Eds.), *Shaping Policy Agendas, The Micro Politics of Economic International Organizations.* UK: Cheltenham.

Stilwell, J. and Nwabufo, O. O., 2006. Global Policy Outcomes: The Role of NGOs. *Graduate Journal of Political Science*, 3(1):27–48.

Tortajada, C., 2016. Nongovernmental Organizations and Influence on Global Public Policy. *Asia & The Pacific Policy Studies*, 3(2):266–274.

Homework: Continue preparing your Final Paper and Presentation.

1.7.8 Week 10: Presentations of final papers and class discussions

This weekly meeting will be dedicated to team presentations of the final papers. Each team will be allotted 15–20 minutes for the presentation. All presentations have to be ***emailed to the instructor by 2 pm on the day of the class*** so that they can be uploaded onto the system. Presentations will be made by order of the Global Policy selected. This meeting may last beyond the usual class time.

Chapter 2

Globalization and Global Policies

Abstract

This chapter deals with globalization and externalities. We will compare state vs. federal interests and impacts in measuring global policy performance. Special attention will be provided to cost–benefit analysis (CBA) as a tool for global policy performance. We will define a global policy. We will discuss the justification and motivation for global policies: why certain issues are included in a global treaty and others are not, why we see more global policies on environmental issues, and how global policies are developed.

2.1 Globalization Processes and the Need for Policy Interventions

Globalization is a process of interaction and integration among people, companies, and governments of different nations. The process is driven by several flow vectors of possible useful outcomes such as international trade, investments, and access. However, there are flow vectors of less useful, and even destructive, outcomes such as negative externalities, aimed resource destructions, pollution, and even terrorism. The globalization process is aided by information technology, by supporting institutions such as agreements or challenging institutions such as regulations and/or tariffs.

More precisely, societies across the globe have established gradually closer interactions over time (the big village), but recently, with the increased availability of communication and information technologies due to the drop in their cost and increased simplicity of operation, the trend has dramatically increased (Global Policy Forum, n.d.). The increased availability of technologies has made communication and flow of data and information among societies easier and faster. The increased rate of interaction (via trade, propaganda, influence, etc.) has led different societies around the world to be more interdependent on each other and more affected by each other. Influential multinational, or even global, corporations emerge, dealing with investments, production, commerce, and finance (to mention a few), and regional, or even global NGOs increase the process of sharing ideas and cultures (Pierre, 2013; Darian-Smith and Philip, 2017).

Several examples on the change of globalization extent over time, using several indicators, are offered by IMF (2008) and summarized in Table 2.1.

Is globalization good for society? Globalization affects many aspects of peoples' lives around the world, such as Environment, Culture, Political systems, Economic development and prosperity,

Table 2.1.   Representative indicators demonstrating increased globalization over time.

Indicator	Indicator units	Year; Value of indicator	Year; Value of indicator
Value of global trade	% of world GDP	1980; 42.1	2007; 62.1
Foreign direct investment	% of world GDP	1980; 6.5	2006; 31.8
Cross boarder telephone calls	Minutes per capita	1991; 7.3	2006; 28.8
Foreign workers	Million people	1965; 78 (2.4% of world population)	2005; 191 (3.0% of world population)

Source: IMF (2008).

and Human physical well-being (Lamy *et al.*, 2011). Globalization could be good in certain aspects, but could also be associated with risks to certain segments of society that cannot adequately deal with and adjust to globalization (Alemanno, 2013).

Globalization is associated with direct and indirect threats (US Office of the National Intelligence, 2018) to individual countries as well as to economic sectors, regions and to the global economy. One can identify the following threats: cyber threats that may affect strategic services such as electricity production or performance of institutions such as elections; weapons of mass destruction and proliferation such as biological, chemical and nuclear; terrorism that targets certain strata of the population, or the general population; or terrorism that focuses on strategic resources such as water terrorism (Veilleux and Dinar, 2019); counter intelligence and foreign denial deception; emerging and disruptive technologies; technology acquisition and economic competition; space and counter-space interventions; transnational organized crime; drug trafficking; human trafficking; environment and climate change; human displacement; health (infectious diseases such as measles and avian flu, and the recently occurring COVID-19 that is still—at the time of writing this book—affecting health in many countries and the global economy).

So, globalization could have both good and bad outcomes on various countries and their populations. The good outcomes, identified also by having positive externalities, are characterized by a potential for increased social welfare. In this case, a global policy would be concerned with how to regulate the global welfare flows so that the positive effects are maximal. The global policy could also be concerned with how to allocate the incremental benefits among all actors (sectors, regions, countries).

2.1.1 *The case of COVID-19*

As I am writing this book, the world faces the COVID-19 pandemic, which is a classic example for a global negative externality that affected the lives of so many all over the world. While at this stage, answers are scarce, we can only raise questions and try to provide intelligent answers.

1. How has the Coronavirus spread?
2. Have nations been prepared?
3. Is there a global institution that can coordinate responses and introduce a global policy to cope with COVID-19?
4. What has that organization actually done and was it relevant?
5. What are the local–global policy conflicts related to COVID-19 that we have witnessed?

The reader is invited to answer these five questions based on own search and reading. The bottom line is summarized in Figure 2.1 and the following discussion.

Globally, as of April 26, 2021 (the time of writing this chapter), there have been nearly 150 million confirmed cases of COVID-19, including nearly 3.2 million deaths, reported to the World Health Organization (WHO). The cumulative cases from January 22, 2020 to April 26, 2021 can be found in Figures 2.1 and 2.2.

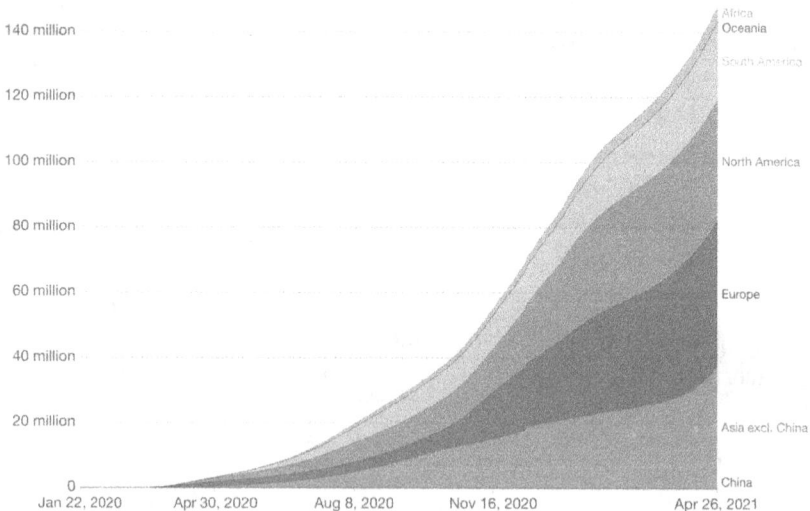

Figure 2.1. Cumulative confirmed COVID-19 cases in the world, January 2020–April 2021.

Source: https://ourworldindata.org/grapher/cumulative-covid-cases-region. Max *et al.* (2020).

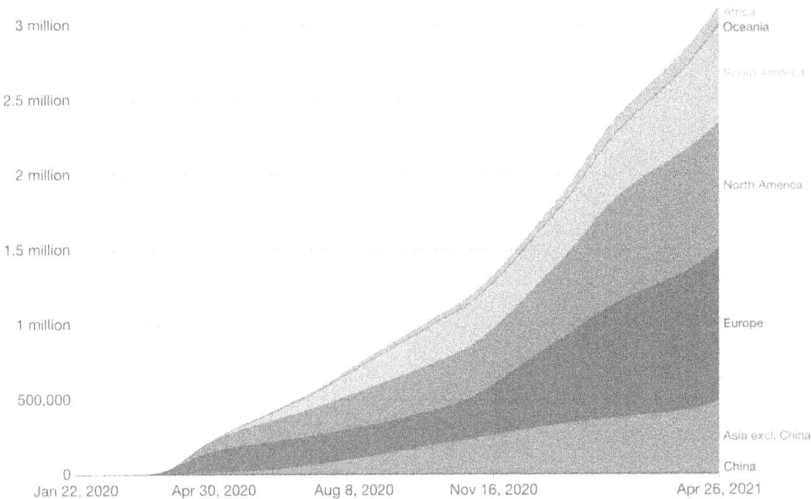

Figure 2.2. Cumulative confirmed COVID-19 deaths.
Source: https://ourworldindata.org/grapher/cumulative-covid-deaths-region.
Max *et al.* (2020).

As seen in Figure 2.1, the world has not yet found a solution to this serious negative externality. The number of confirmed cases is still increasing exponentially, even if a vaccine has been produced and administered. Another important observation is that the distribution of the effects (cases and deaths) is uneven across the continents in terms of cases per million people). This reflects the preparedness of countries, the resources available in different countries and the governance level of the countries.

Figure 2.2 shows that the number of deaths from COVID-19 is still on the rise worldwide, although the trend has declined on a continental basis. We do not present country-level data for Figures 2.1 and 2.2, but it is apparent that both the number of infected and the number of deaths vary tremendously by country, even on a basis of per million people.

With the availability of vaccination, it is also evident that globally the vaccine has not been equally administered in all countries (Figure 2.3).

Share of people who received at least one dose of COVID-19 vaccine

Share of the total population that received at least one vaccine dose. This may not equal the share that are fully vaccinated if the vaccine requires two doses.

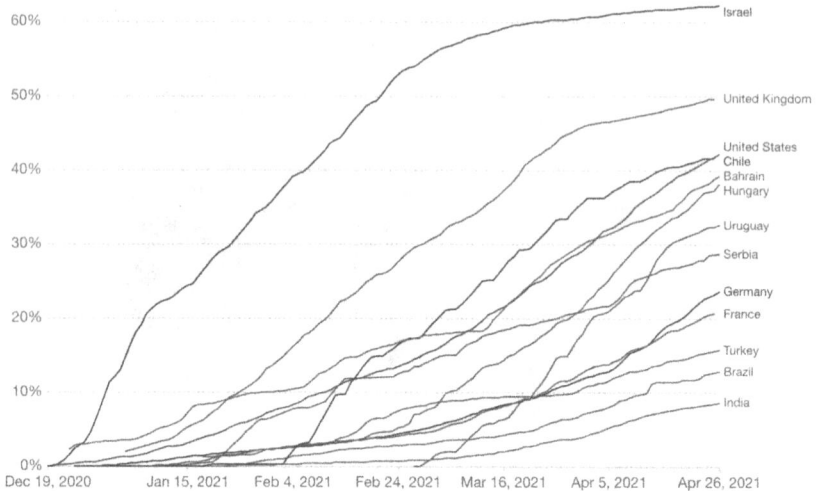

Figure 2.3. Share of people who received at least one dose of COVID-19 vaccine. *Source*: https://ourworldindata.org/covid-vaccinations. Max *et al.* (2020).

Figure 2.3 suggests that vaccination start day and share of vaccinated population differ dramatically by country, indicating the lack of equal access to vaccines across the globe. This suggests a lack of a global policy for distribution of the vaccine between developing and developed countries. After all, with the almost free move of people across continents, there is a high likelihood for negative externalities of infection by COVID-19.

Summarizing the information discussed above, it is clear that globalization has introduced several challenges that the world has not been prepared for. We have just looked at the number of infected, dead, and vaccinated. We have not compared the economic consequences, but it is clear that we could see economic effects that are similar to the distribution of infected, dead, and vaccinated. The big question is whether or not a global policy for addressing such a pandemic should be in place and who should be responsible for its preparation and administration. While our course will not address a global COVID-19 policy, the other global policies discussed and principles of their creation should suffice to establish a basic understanding of what constitutes the global–local policy interactions.

2.2 Why is Global Policy Needed?

Interactions between states, especially with globalization, make it more likely to lead to bad outcomes (or what we used to call in economics negative externalities). These negative externalities, if not regulated, may lead to reduced welfare that is not equally distributed across the various countries. The main questions that need to be addressed include the following:

- How can we regulate the global flows in order to reduce the volume of bads faced by various countries?
- How can we allocate the global incremental reductions of bads and costs of doing so acoss the world countries?

This is exactly the nature of global policies [In this course: global policy ≡ treaty ≡ accord ≡ agreement ≡ convention].

2.2.1 *Regulating effects of globalization and their impacts on the various actors*

As a result of global negative externalities, laws, economies, and social movements are adjusting/forming at the international level. Many politicians, academics, and journalists treat these trends as both inevitable and (on the whole) welcome. But for billions of the world's people, business-driven globalization means uprooting old ways of life and threatening livelihoods and cultures. The global social justice movement, itself a product of globalization, proposes an alternative path, more responsive to public needs. Intense political disputes will continue over globalization's meaning and its future direction.

A recent publication by United Nations (2009) quantifies the value of global coordination (global policies) for fiscal measures of financial stimuli undertaken by individual governments to

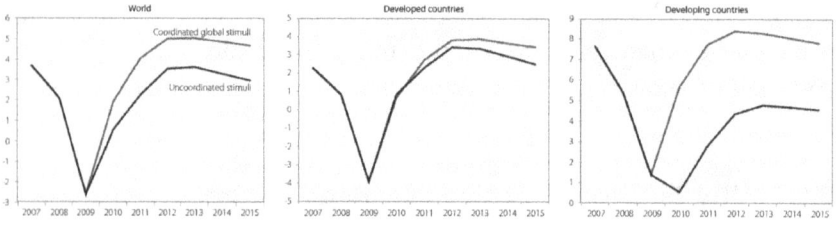

Figure 2.4. Simulations of economic recovery under coordinated and uncoordinated global stimulus policy interventions, 2009–2015.
Note: Vertical axis measures percentage change in economic growth.
Source: United Nations (2009).

recapitalize banks around the world (about $18 trillion) following the 2008 financial crisis. The findings of that global study suggest that without adequate coordination, the policy measures may not be effective. Without coordination the policy interventions will limit the multiplier effects of the stimuli, thus reducing the impact on global economic growth and employment. As can be seen from Figure 2.4, developing countries will be most affected (larger gap) from an uncoordinated global stimuli policy.

Conflicts also exist within countries. Two examples can be realized from the following links:

1. Climate change: California vs. USA, http://www.sacbee.com/news/politics-government/capitol-alert/article120928688.html.
2. Local and global water externalities, https://www.youtube.com/watch?v=P-TE1LHBhEE.

While global negative externalities range across and cover many instances, the list of existing global policies to address such negative externalities is handful and barely covers the needs to protect the world against them. The United Nations is the global agency that is in charge of producing such policies and the agency that archives the policies. A list of global policies can be found on a United Nations website: https://treaties.un.org/doc/source/events/2012/Treaties/list_global_english.pdf. But, how are global policies developed? Is there a general pattern that they follow?

2.3 The Vienna Convention on the Law of Treaties

The Vienna Convention on the Law of Treaties (VCLT) is a treaty concerning the international law on treaties between states. It was adopted on May 23, 1969, and opened for signature on May 23, 1969. The Convention entered into force on January 27, 1980. The VCLT has been ratified by (only) 115 states as of November 2017.

Some countries[1] that have not ratified the Convention, such as the United States, recognize parts of it as a restatement of customary law and binding upon them as such.

2.3.1 *Some basic concepts regarding global treaties— Signature, ratification, accession*

2.3.1.1 *Signature ad referendum*

A representative may sign a treaty *ad referendum*, i.e., under the condition that the signature is confirmed by her state. In this case, the signature becomes definitive once it is confirmed by the responsible organ [Art. 12 (2) (b), VCLT 1969].

2.3.1.2 *Signature subject to ratification, acceptance or approval*

Where the signature is subject to ratification, acceptance or approval, the signature does not establish the consent to be bound. However, it is a means of authentication and expresses the willingness of the signatory state to continue the treaty-making process. The signature qualifies the signatory state to proceed to ratification, acceptance or approval. It also creates an obligation to refrain, in good faith, from acts that would defeat the objective and the purpose of the treaty [Arts. 10 and 18, VCLT 1969].

2.4 Measuring Global Policy Attractiveness

I suggest to view global policies as innovations and their ratification by the various states as their adoption. Figure 2.5 shows the

---

[1] We use interchangeably the terms 'state' and 'country'.

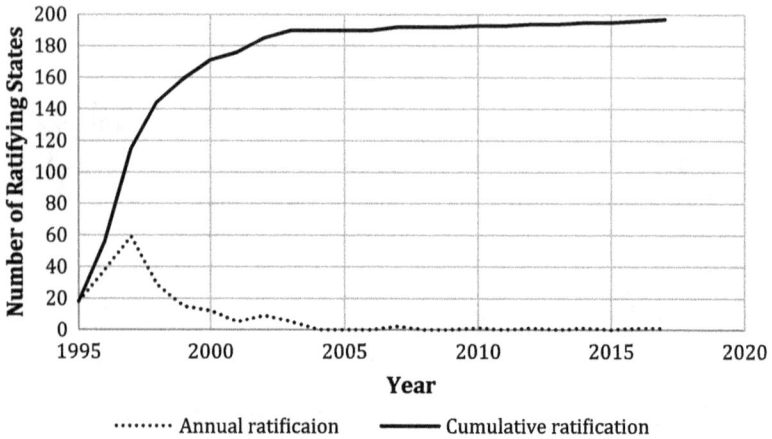

Figure 2.5. Annual and cumulative number of ratifications of UNCCD, 1995–2017.
Source: Author elaboration, using data in https://www.unccd.int/convention/about-convention/unccd-history (see also Annex A.6 in Chapter 6).

adoption/ratification pattern of the 1995 United Nations Convention to Combat Desertification (UNCCD). A more detailed discussion of this convention can be found in the Annex.

What does the shape of the adoption curve in Figure 2.5 tell us about the attractiveness of the UNCCD? The adoption curve tells us how fast the policy was ratified by the countries since its creation. Given that the number of states in the world is 195, we can immediately see that after 22 years the global policy was adopted by 195 states + 2 non-state entities, which is 100% of the countries in the world. This is one indicator to attractiveness. The more countries ratify the global policy, the more it is attractive. Another indicator for attractiveness is the speed by which the global policy was ratified. From Figure 2.5, we can see that by the year 2005 (10 years after the UNCCD was signed) most countries ratified it. The shorter it takes to reach the ceiling of the ratification share, the more attractive is the global policy. Just as a comparison, the Paris Accord, signed in 2015, has been ratified in 2021 (6 years after its signature) by 195 states.

Once a global policy is activated, there still might be difficulties in its implementation. Countries may not follow the rules which they agreed to, thus leading to a non-effective policy. Such situations are met with punishments by the international community.

2.5 How is a Global Policy Enforced?

A treaty may have incorporated into its own text enforcement provisions, such as arbitration of disputes, or referral to the International Court of Justice (ICJ). However, some treaties may not specifically include such enforcement mechanisms, which necessitates other measures to be used.

So, how can this unwritten law be enforced?

In an international system where there is no overarching authoritative enforcer, punishment for non-compliance functions differ. States are more likely to fear tactics used by other states, such as reciprocity, collective action, and shaming (Yamagata *et al.*, 2017).

2.5.1 *Reciprocity*

Reciprocity is a type of enforcement by which states are assured that if they offend another state, the other state will respond by returning the same behavior.

Guarantees of reciprocal reactions encourage states to think twice about which of their actions they would like imposed upon them:

- During peace periods, states may 'return' their ambassadors home for consultation, which is a severe diplomatic move, or call the other country's ambassador for 'a reprimand meeting'. A reciprocal action is expected.
- During a war, one state will refrain from killing the prisoners of another state because it does not want the other state to kill its own prisoners.

In a trade dispute, one state will be reluctant to impose high tariffs on another state's goods because the other state could do the same in return (USA and CHINA Trade war).

2.5.2 *Collective action*

Through collective action, several states act together against one state to produce what is usually considered a punitive result. For example, Iraq's 1990 invasion of Kuwait was opposed by most states, and they organized through the United Nations a resolution to condemn it and to initiate joint military action to remove Iraq from Kuwait. Similarly, the United Nations imposed joint economic sanctions, such as restrictions on trade, on South Africa in the 1980s to force that country to end the practice of racial segregation known as Apartheid.

2.5.3 *Shaming*

Shaming is also known as the 'name and shame' approach.

The following link includes a video clip of the US ambassador to the United Nations Nikki Haley in a speech where she names and shames Russia for its alleged help to President Bashar Assad against his people: https://www.ynet.co.il/articles/0,7340,L-5225591,00. html#autoplay.

Most states dislike negative publicity and will actively try to avoid being named and shamed, so the threat of shaming a state with public statements regarding their offending behavior is often an effective enforcement mechanism.

This method is particularly effective in the field of human rights where states, not wanting to intervene directly in the domestic affairs of another state, may use media attention to highlight violations of international law. In turn, negative public attention may serve as a catalyst to having an international organization address the issue; it may align international grassroots movements on an issue; or it may give a state the political will needed from its populace to authorize further action.

References

Alemanno, A., 2013. Is there a Role for Cost-Benefit Analysis beyond the Nation-State? Lessons from International Regulatory Cooperation. In: Livermorem Michael, A. and Richard L. Revesz (Eds.), *The Globalization of Cost-Benefit Analysis in Environmental Policy*. Oxford University Press, pp. 104–122.

Darian-Smith, E. and Philip, C. M., 2017. Chapter 2—Why Is Global Studies Important? *The Global Turn*. University of California Press, pp. 29–54.

Global Policy Forum, n.d. *Globalization.* https://www.globalpolicy.org/globalization.html, Accessed on August 23, 2019.

IMF (International Monetary Fund) 2008. *Globalization: A brief Overview.* Issues Brief 02/08, May. https://www.imf.org/external/np/exr/ib/2008/pdf/053008.pdf. Accessed on August 23, 2019.

Lamy, S. L., John, S. M., John, B., Steve, S., and Patricia, O., 2011. *Introduction to Global Politics*, 4th edition. London: Oxford University Press.

Max, R., Hannah, R., Esteban, O.-O., and Joe H., 2020. Coronavirus Pandemic (COVID-19). Published online at OurWorldInData.org. Retrieved from: https://ourworldindata.org/coronavirus [Online Resource].

Pierre, J., 2013. *Globalization and Governance.* CheltenhamL Edward Elgar.

US Office of the National Intelligence, 2018. Statement for the Record Worldwide Threat Assessment of the US Intelligence Community https://www.dni.gov/files/documents/Newsroom/Testimonies/2018-ATA—Unclassified-SSCI.pdf.

United Nations, 2009. *Global Policy Model: An Application. Coordinated and Uncoordinated Policy Measures as the Global Financial Crisis Intensifies.* Policy and Analysis Division Department of Economic and Social Affairs. New York: United Nations.

Veilleux, J. and Dinar, S., 2019. A Global Analysis of Water-Related Terrorism, 1970–2016, *Terrorism and Political Violence*, DOI: 10.1080/09546553.2019.1599863.

Yamagata, Y., Jue, Y., and Joseph G., 2017. State Power and Diffusion Processes in the Ratification of Global Environmental Treaties, 1981–2008. *International Environmental Agreements*, 17:501–529.

Chapter 3

Concepts and Principles of Conflict

Abstract

This chapter focuses on strategic behavior of agents involved in a conflict, as part of a process leading from conflict through negotiation to cooperation, which is the sequence leading to the establishment of a global policy. The focus of this week's class is the principles and measurements of conflict. We will introduce the following concepts: definition of conflict; conflicts over natural resources; and how to measure conflicts. An example of a range of the level of conflict, using basins at risk (BARs) work, is also provided starting with exchange of letters to war. We will discuss unrelated relationships among the states, such as trade, diplomatic relations, and other exchanges as measures of conflict/tension reduction. We will introduce conflicts as games. Non-cooperative games in a matrix form. Concepts used will include the following: deterrence, threats, credible threats, payoffs, strategies, zero-sum game, Chicken game, Nash equilibrium, Prisoner's dilemma.

3.1 What is a Conflict?

Many people associate the word 'conflict' with war or physical interactions between two or more opponents. While it is true that war is a type of conflict, not all conflicts are wars. Webster's dictionary provides two lines of definitions for the word conflict: first, conflict is defined as fight, battle, war. A second definition for conflict is 'having a competitive or opposing action'. Therefore, 'conflict' may have meanings ranging from 'opposed interests' to 'war'. In simple terms, 'conflict' means disagreement on something.

Several examples (taken from: http://www.merriam-webster. com/dictionary/conflict) include: the violent conflicts in the Middle East between different parties in the region, the possible conflict between parties in the parliament over the country's budget, to name a few. In the case of global policy issues, we can identify situations where conflicts prevented parties to sign the agreement, and we can also observe situations where conflicts rose after signing a global policy agreement leading one or more signatory countries to defect from the agreement.

3.2 Handling the Conflict

As suggested by Schelling (2003: Chapter 1), maneuvering through conflicts is an art that includes short- and long-term considerations. We as analysts of the conflict would like to understand how the actors involved actually conduct themselves through the conflict situation. Understanding of the appropriate moves may provide a benchmark for an appropriate strategy for each actor, and helps control and affect the behavior of the other parties to the conflict. Some of the conflict characteristics (variables) could be controllable by the actors or by mediators. Knowing how some of such variables may affect the behavior of the parties could allow the development of successful strategies to get out of, or to improve the status of some of the actors in, the conflict.

3.2.1 *Rational vs. actual behavior*

We may observe two types of behavior on the part of the actors— rational and actual. Rational behavior, which is driven by sensible calculations of advantages, based on explicit and internally con- sistent value system on the part of the actors is most likely not common. Assuming such type of behavior would lead to very limited applicability of the results. It can lead to an optimal benchmark, which is certainly not a realistic one.

Assuming actual behavior of the actors would lead to a good approximation of reality, but any attempt of generalizing it, in order to develop theories that might be applicable to any situation (and not a particular one), runs the risk of being irrelevant. Therefore, judgmental consideration is needed to find the appropriate mix between rational vs. actual behavior of each of the actors. In doing so, we need to refer to the principles we discussed earlier in the chapter and derive the various aspects of the strategy of conflict and its interpretation. We need to remember that such strategy (1) may not be necessarily an efficient application of force but rather exploitation of potential force; (2) may not be necessarily looking at the actors as enemies who dislike each other but rather partners who distrust or disagree with each other; and (3) may not consider division of gains and losses between/among the actors but rather consider the possibility that certain outcomes are worse/better for certain actors or all.

Under such a strategy, for example, international conflicts are not "constant-sum game" but rather "variable-sum game" because there is a common interest in reaching outcomes that are mutually advantageous. Such a strategy is heavily affected by the interdependency between the actors, namely, the ability to maneuver of one actor depends to an important degree on the choices or decisions that the other participants make.

What are the tools that actors can use in the process of dealing with conflict? Several approaches are known, including deterrence, credible threat, and threat efficacy.

Deterrence is a strategy of discouraging a certain action on the part of the opponent party through instilling doubt or fear of the consequences. It is the use of threats by one party to convince another party to refrain from initiating some course of action. Deterrence is relevant among 'friends' as it is relevant among 'enemies'. For example, during the Cuban missile crisis of 1962, it became clear that Washington was ready to defend its core security interests, leading the Soviet Union to withdraw the missiles it had started to deploy in Cuba. Deterrence may fail if the opponent's interest in achieving a certain objective is higher than the party exerting discouragement.

The threats may not be credible, which means that the threatening party may not be able to execute the threats (Allison and Zelikow, 1999). In this case we observe a reputation problem.

Credible threats are a well-known concept in conflict situations. Deterrence may not be effective if the threats regarding the consequences would not be credible on the part of the opponent party. The level of credibility of the threats may depend on the costs and risks associated with fulfillment of the threat for the party making it. For example, situations of direct deterrence often center on territorial conflicts between neighboring states in which the major powers do not directly intervene. In the Arab-Israeli conflict, Israel has relied on its own military forces to attempt deterrence against hostile Arab neighbors. For example, since the end of the Six-Day War of 1967, in which Israel occupied the Golan Heights, Israel has generally been successful in its efforts to deter Syria from attempting to retake the Golan by force of arms. In October of 1973, however, Israeli policies of general and then immediate deterrence failed as Syria launched a large-scale attack against Israeli forces in the Golan Heights (Huth, 1999).

The threat efficacy may depend on the available alternatives to the deterred party once the threat is fulfilled. For example, the expulsion of the Iraqi occupation army from Kuwait in 1991 became necessary because US diplomacy, including powerful threats of force, failed. While the US demonstrated its military capabilities and willingness to utilize force if necessary to expel the Iraqi military from Kuwait, mobilizing half a million US soldiers, sailors, and air men and women to the region, including a coalition of military alliance, as it fell short of achieving compliance with US demands and the Iraqi troops had to be expelled by force of arms. The US was not able to accomplish its goals through threats alone (Blechman and Cofman Wittes, 2000).

3.3   Conflicts as Games

The dynamics of a conflict suggests an iterative process, where one party acts and the other party responds (or not). This dynamic nature can be represented, using game theory framework. We will use the Cold War and its crises between the USA (West) and USSR (East). The story is well known and we will not repeat it here. However, we will use the story and the strategic behavior of the West and the East to convert the conflict and its outcome to game theory modeling.

3.3.1 *The two parties' separate game schedule*

In the process of our exercise, let East be represented by E and West be represented by M. Let us also assume (for simplicity) that E and M agreed to transform their back and forth chasing of each other into a game of coin showing (not flipping). Each of them shows the coin at the same time. M wins if both coins show the same face. E wins if the two coins show different faces. The game is presented in Figure 3.1. The symbols 'W' and 'L' mean win and loss, respectively.

As can be seen from Figure 3.1, M wins when both his and E's coins show either 'head' or 'tail', and E wins when his coin shows 'tail' and M's coin shows 'head', or when his coin shows 'head' and M's coin shows 'tail'. Using the same rationale M loses when his coin shows 'tail' and E's coin shows 'head' or when his coin shows 'head' and E's coin shows 'tail'. E loses when his and M's coins show 'tail' or 'head' at the same time. The game is played in several rounds and the winner will be the party that won most of the rounds.

The two matrix schedules of the game can be combined into one-matrix-includes-all as is shown in Figure 3.2.

West		Head	Tail
	Head	W	L
	Tail	L	W

East		
	Head	Tail
Head	L	W
Tail	W	L

Figure 3.1. The 'East–West' game schedules for West (left panel) and East (right panel).

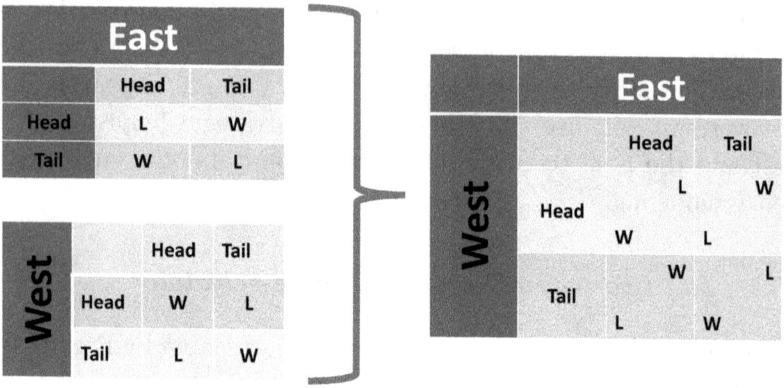

Figure 3.2. Conversion of the one-player game schedule matrix into a two-players schedule matrix.

As shown in Figure 3.2, all the information from the separate individual game matrix schedules have been compressed into one matrix schedule that is interpreted as follows: each cell with game outcomes includes the outcomes for each player. For example, the cell that corresponds to the strategy 'head' selected by M and 'head' selected by E shows the outcome 'W' for M and the outcome 'L' for East. And the cell that corresponds to the strategy 'head' selected by M and 'tail' selected by E shows the outcome 'L' for M and the outcome 'W' for East.

3.3.2 *Zero-sum games*

The game between M and E is defined as a zero-sum game. This means that the gain to one party is exactly the loss to the other party. In other words, if M gets W then E must get L. In other words, one player's gain is the other player' loss, which translates to W + L = 0 (or $W = -L$). Examples of zero-sum games include the medieval days fight of 'Duel', that doesn't end until only one fighter remains alive; or the fights between animals over territory or a female—a territory can be controlled only by one of the animals, and the female animal can be coupled only with one male animal.

3.3.3 *Games expressed in monetary values*

While winning these games is important, we are more interested in the monetary meaning of winning or losing. Winning the game (W) or losing the game (L) could also (but not necessarily) be expressed in monetary values to M and E. W and L are the outcomes of the conflict/game to each player and are called payoffs. Payoff means that the player has a monetary outcome at the end of each turn, and therefore, also at the end of the game.

Remember that each of the players has two options: Showing the 'head' or showing the 'tail'. These options are called strategies because each of the players may select among 'head' and 'tail' in a particular sequence. For example, one strategy could be that a player decides to select only 'tail' along the entire sequence of the game. Another strategy could be for that player to select 'head' and 'tail' in alternate turns. Yet another strategy could be that one player selects in a given turn exactly what the opponent player selected in the previous turn.

With monetary outcomes in the game, we can expect a certain behavior of the players. We expect and assume that the players are 'rational' with regards to the payoff, meaning that they prefer higher payoff over lower payoffs. This categorizes the players as 'payoff maximizers'. Payoff maximizing may not be the motivating pattern behind certain players. For example, states involved in conflicts may have other motivating patterns than monetary payoffs. We can easily see states with interest in regional influence rather than payoff maximization. Let us keep this in mind, while we analyze the conflict management strategies.

To express the outcomes of the game in monetary values we need to assign a value to W and a value to L, keeping in mind that the sum should be equal to zero (when dealing with zero-sum games). Therefore, if we award winners with \$1, we have to charge losers with $-\$1$ so that $W + L = 1 - 1 = 0$. We could select another value, say \$5 to award winners and charge losers. In that case $W + L = 5 - 5 = 0$. Figure 3.3 presents the game for the \$5 value we assigned the winner and $-\$5$ we charged the loser.

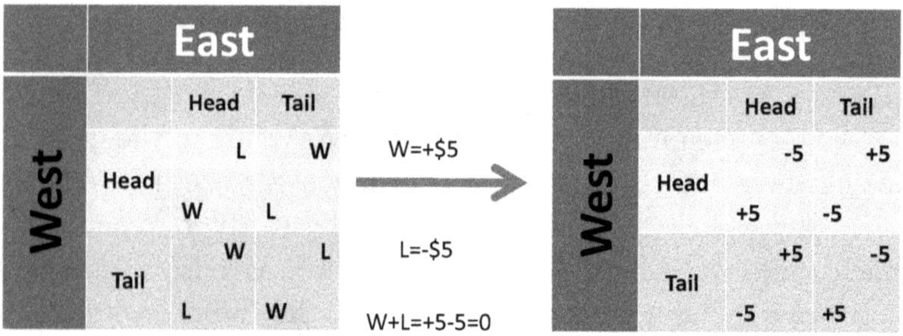

Figure 3.3. Conversion of the two-players letter schedule matrix to a numeric schedule.

3.3.4 *The Chicken game*

Life is not a zero-sum game and thus the zero-sum game we applied to the case of E and M is not a good representation of real life. A game structure that fits more real-life situations is the Chicken game. You may remember the movie *Rebel Without A Cause*, starring James Dean. That movie was about two people driving cars toward each other's direction in a narrow road to see who will be the first one to chicken out (slow down) and let the other pass. This game represents many international conflicts between two states, such as the USSR–USA missile conflict during the cold war.

In the movie *Rebel Without A Cause* the two teenagers can select between two strategies—Slow and Speed. The consequences could be as follows:

If both of them speed up (Speed–Speed): both may be killed or injured. If both of them slow down (Slow–Slow): both will be able to go across each other. If one of them speeds and the other slows (Speed–Slow): the one that selected the Slow strategy allowed the opponent to cross the narrow road and be the Winner, while the slowing player is called Chicken—a very stigmatized title among teenagers.

Let us now present the case of M and E assuming that the nature of their conflict is represented by a Chicken game and expressed in monetary units (Figure 3.4).

How do we read the (made-up) values in the different cells? If both E and M slow down or, using the issues they conflicted over,

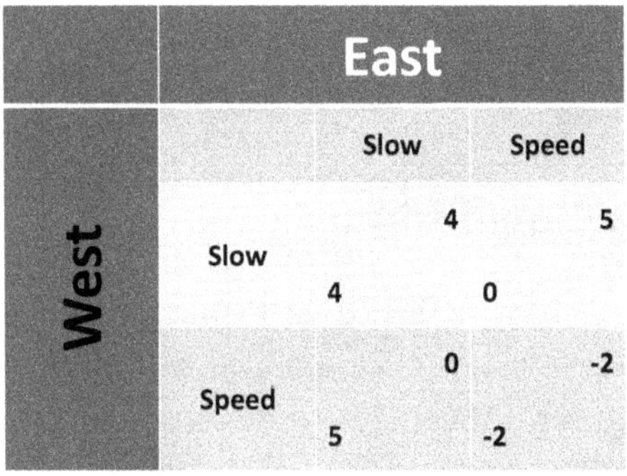

Figure 3.4. The Chicken game between West and East.

if both had agreed to a certain compromise, each would get a monetary outcome (payoff) of four units. If both M and E would speed, namely if they will remain stubborn and stick to their original plan, they will crash and injure themselves, or even die. In this case, the outcome would be the worst outcome they can expect. Both will lose. For simplicity, we assigned similar losses to each, but we could as well assign differential losses, depending on the opportunity cost from losses to each of them. The result would be similar anyway. If E slows and M speeds, the outcome would be 0 and 5 to E and M, respectively, and similarly (using the same values), if E speeds and M slows, the outcome would be 5 and 0 to E and M. The player that slows and the player that speeds are not injured, but the speeding player gets the glory and admiration from the crowd watching the race.

Inspecting the different cells of the game schedule suggests that the total joint outcome of both players $(4 + 4 = 8)$ is highest when both slow, it is the lowest $(-2 + (-2) = -4)$ when both speed, and is somewhere in the middle if one speeds and one slows $(0 + 5 = 5$, and $5 + 0 = 5)$. The highest total outcome/payoff for both players is when both slow $(+8)$, the lowest outcome/payoff for both players is when both speed (-4), and the somewhat medium outcome $(+5)$ is when one speeds and the other slows. Why don't both agree to slow? Remember that for later on. What motivates our players are their individual maximal gains (5 and 5) so that they are motivated by some irrational objective that can be harmful and detrimental for each of them.

3.4 The Nash Equilibrium

Nash Equilibrium (NE) is a concept taken from game theory. An NE is a set of strategies, one for each player that would be stable if nobody has a unilateral incentive to deviate from their own strategy. That is, NE has the property that each player's choice is his or her best response to the choices of the other $n - 1$ players (in the case of n parties).

Let us apply the NE concept to the game between East and West as expressed in the Chicken game in Figure 3.4. If M knew that E was going to choose Slow, he would maximize his payoff by choosing Speed. If M knew that E was going to choose Speed, he would maximize his payoff by choosing Slow. Using the same rationale if E knew that M was going to choose Slow, he would maximize his payoff by choosing Speed. If E knew that M was going to choose Speed, he would maximize his payoff by choosing Slow. These relationships are presented in Figure 3.5 on the diagonal line connecting the 5-0-0-5 payoff values.

For payoff-maximizing players: The two strategies identified by M and E in the cells along the marked line are called NE:

For E [M(slow) → E(speed)]; for M [E(slow) → M(speed)];
for E [M(speed) → E(slow)]; and for M [E(speed) → M(slow)].

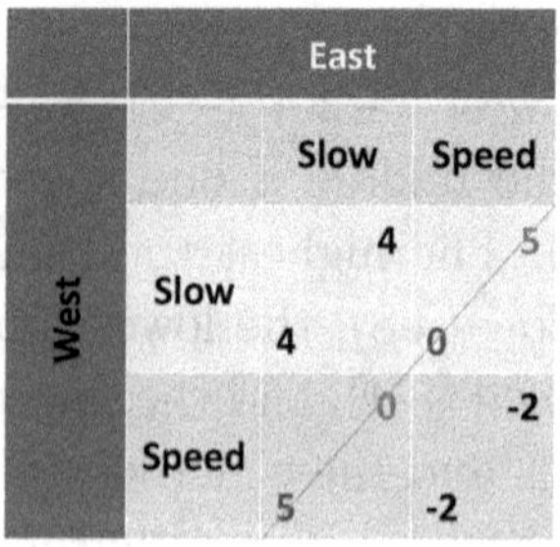

Figure 3.5. The NE of the East and West Chicken game.

Therefore, if each player has chosen a strategy and no player can benefit by changing his or her strategy while the other players keep theirs unchanged, then the current set of strategy choices and the corresponding payoffs constitute an NE.

So far, we discussed abstract conflict situations and demonstrated ways they are addressed, using a couple of game theory tools. In the remainder of the chapter, we depart from West and East. We employ more applied real-world cases that resemble the conflicts associated with water scarcity. We first present the BAR scale for measuring conflict and cooperation in international river basins around the world. Then we apply economic principles to evaluate a water conflict among two agent-states. Through that example we introduce the Prisoner's dilemma game[1] and how its outcome can be improved for both parties.

3.5   Water as a Conflicting Resource

Let us start with some background information on water, scarcity, and conflict. Water doesn't recognize political boundaries. As such it can flow across territories reflecting scarcities in some regions and abundance in others.

The most controversial aspect of water resources is their level of scarcity, which is considered by many as the source for conflict. Indeed, scarcity is important, but is not sufficient in explaining conflict among riparian states. Additional aspects that must be taken into account for explaining conflict are the geography of the basin—whether or not the river is a cross-border one or a border creator one. The geography of the river basin dictates the level of interdependencies among the parties that share the basin. The parties that share a water source act differently regarding

---

[1]The Prisoner's dilemma game is a paradox where two parties acting in their own self-interests do not produce the optimal outcome. The typical Prisoner's dilemma describes two jailed individuals who committed a crime, are put in two separate cells, and are interrogated. Both choose to protect themselves at the expense of the other participant. As a result, both find themselves in a worse state than if they had cooperated with each other in the interrogation process.

the water: they may have different interests, they may have different utilization plans for the water, and these and other aspects create different incentives to cooperate. Some additional considerations that explain level of conflict or cooperation over shared water include (but are not necessarily restricted to) relative power of the parties involved (military, economic, political), existing protracted conflict among the parties and the relationship between that protracted conflict and the water conflict, and the effect of domestic politics in each of the states on the nature and level of the conflict with the other state.

3.5.1 *Determining water conflict intensity and cooperation potential*

In the context of international waters, where interdependency among the riparian states is intrinsic to the physical river shape, cooperation is more efficient than unilateral action and conflict. However, in many cases we still can see that conflict prevails. We can define the intensity of the conflict depending on:

- the level of scarcity;
- the degree of mutual dependence (not necessarily only water) between the two states;
- historical/geographical/rights-based differences of water ownership among the parties;
- existing of a protracted conflict;
- existence of alternative sources of water (or other resources that can be linked) to a negotiated agreement; and
- the relative power of the parties (military/economic/political).

An index of the level of conflict (or cooperation) has been suggested by Wolf *et al.* (2003) for the case of international waters between dyads of states in the basin. The index (Table 3.1) ranges from −7 (war or highest level of the conflict) to +7 (creation of one state or highest level of cooperation).

The BAR index was derived by Wolf *et al.* (2003), using a compiled dataset of every reported conflictive or cooperative interaction between two or more countries, which involved water as a scarce

Table 3.1. The BAR index of conflict-cooperation in international river basins.

Index value	Description of the conflict/cooperation
-7	Formal war
-6	Extensive military acts
-5	Small-scale military acts
-4	Political/military hostile acts
-3	Diplomatic/economic hostile acts
-2	Strong/official verbal hostility
-1	Mild/unofficial verbal hostility
0	Neutral, non-significant acts
1	Mild verbal support
2	Official verbal support
3	Cultural, scientific agreement support
4	Non-military economic, technological industrial agreement
5	Military, economic, strategic support
6	International water treaty
7	Unification into one nation

and/or consumable resource or as a quantity to be managed. Water was the driver of each of the recorded events.

3.6 Developing a Groundwater Prisoner's Dilemma Game[2]

While the values used in the games of this chapter so far were made up, we turn now to developing a case of a Prisoner's dilemma game that has an economic background and all the outcome/payoff values are derived logically from a conflict over water.

3.6.1 *The basis for the conflict between the countries using the aquifer water*

Assume two countries, A and B, that share a groundwater aquifer (see Figure 3.6). We do include several simplifying assumptions, such

---

[2] After Dinar *et al.* (2013).

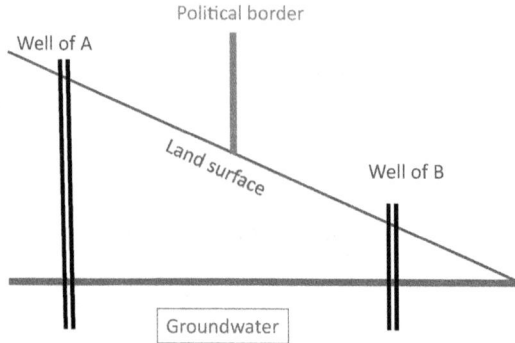

Figure 3.6.   The region described in the groundwater conflict.

Table 3.2.   The demand schedule for water in the international market (four points on the demand function).

P ($\$/m^3$)	Q (billion m^3)
32	2
16	4
9	6
5	8

as each country has its own well from which water from the aquifer is pumped; due to landscape position, the water level under Country A is far deeper to reach than that of Country B. Thus, the cost of pumping for A far exceeds that of B; and the economies of A and B depend on the water that is pumped from the joint aquifer. Each country sells the water in the international market and uses the proceeds to buy goods for consumption by the population. There is a border with no exchange of information between A and B.

Since A and B sell their water in the international market, they both face the same demand function for water by international consumers. The demand schedule is presented in Table 3.2.

The values in Table 3.2 help us calculate the revenue that each country can get by selling a given quantity of water in the international market. As we can see from the table, the demand for water is very in-elastic. Small quantities (Q) can be sold for a very high price (P) per unit sold, and the price drops very dramatically when the quantities sold increase. For simplicity we will assume that the pumping strategies of countries A and B are similar, but refer only to the first two rows in Table 3.2. What motivates the countries in pumping groundwater is the net revenue from selling water. They consider too the pumping cost that each of them faces. The net benefit from the pumping of groundwater is the difference between the revenue from sales and the pumping cost.

Revenue can be calculated (as will be shown in what follows) from Table 3.2. Pumping costs are known to be $0.6/\mathrm{m}^3$ for A and $0.2/\mathrm{m}^3$ for B.

3.6.2 *The Prisoner's dilemma matrix game*

The question we need to answer is whether or not the two countries would know how to work together and increase their individual outcomes, or that each will look just on their objective and find themselves in a worse situation. To answer this question, we need to populate the matrix in Figure 3.7.

As indicated earlier, each country can consider two pumping strategies (2 and 4 billion m^3/year). With the data we already have we can now populate the Xs and Ys in the different cells of the matrix,

			Country B		
			Water Pumping strategy (billions of m³/year)		
			2		4
Country A	Water Pumping strategy (billions of m³/year)	2	X1 Y1		X2 Y2
		4	X3 Y3		X4 Y4

Figure 3.7. The Prisoner's dilemma game between Countries A and B over the groundwater aquifer.

Source: Dinar *et al.* (2013).

which will allow us to identify an optimal strategy and whether or not conflictive or cooperative outcomes would prevail.

The values X and Y in Figure 3.7 are the payoff for each country from selecting a certain strategy. The payoff is calculated as Payoff = (quantity of water pumped and sold) × (price per unit of water pumped and sold) − (pumping cost per unit pumped) × (quantity pumped). Be aware that if Country A selects strategy 2 and Country B selects strategy 2, the total amount of water to be sold in the international market would be $(2 + 2 =)4$ billion m^3. We will demonstrate the calculation of one strategy, but the calculation principles are similar to each strategy combination.

For Country A, pumping and selling 2 billion m^3 and for Country B, pumping and selling 2 billion m^3, the following would be the case (all monetary values are in billions of dollars):

- Price (for $2 + 2$ billion cubic meters) $= 16$
- Pumping $cost_A = 0.6/m^3$
- $Quantity_A = 2\,m^3$
- $Payoff_A = (16) \times (2) - (0.6) \times (2) = 32 - 1.2 = 30.8$
- Pumping $cost_B = 0.2/m^3$
- $Quantity_B = 2\,m^3$
- $Payoff_B = (16) \times (2) - (0.2) \times (2) = 32 - 0.4 = 31.6$

The complete game matrix with all calculated values is presented in Figure 3.8.

			Country B			
			Water Pumping strategy (billions of m³/year)			
			2		4	
Country A	Water Pumping strategy (billions of m³/year)	2	30.8		16.8	
				31.6		35.2
		4	33.6		17.6	
				17.6		19.2

Figure 3.8.   The strategy/payoff matrix of the water pumping Prisoner's dilemma game.

Source: Dinar *et al.* (2013).

From analyzing the payoffs in Figure 3.8 it is clear that Country A will always chose strategy 4 because the payoff to that country will be the highest (33.6) and Country B will always chose strategy 4 because the payoff to that country will also be the highest (35.2), but if both A and B chose strategy 4, they will end up in the lower right quadrant where Country A gets 17.6 and Country B gets 19.2. This is the lowest payoff that Countries A and B could get. This game is called a Prisoner's dilemma game because the parties will always find themselves in the worst situation if they do not coordinate their actions.

3.6.3 *How to escape from a Prisoner's dilemma outcome?*

As it is obvious from Figure 3.8, the conflict between the two countries leads to the worst outcome for each of them. One aspect that characterizes a conflict with a Prisoner's dilemma outcome is the asymmetry of information to each of the parties (remember our assumption of a border between the countries with no information being shared). Another aspect that leads to a Prisoner's dilemma outcome is the fact that each of the parties attempts to maximize its own benefits without taking into consideration the other party. These two aspects lead to a dead loss to both parties.

What can the parties do to elevate their situation? The parties could approach a skilled mediator to help them remove the wall/border between them. This may include establishing diplomatic relations between them. Removing the wall is a necessary condition for moving away from a situation of no communication. Another condition that has to take place is that the two parties have to look at the whole rather than the individual outcome. Figure 3.9 presents the joint outcome in each cell (in center), which is the sum of the payoff to Country A plus the payoff to Country B. The center values in Figure 3.9 suggest that Strategy 2 for Country A and Strategy 2 for Country B are the most preferred, while Strategy 4 for Country A and Strategy 4 for Country B are the least preferred.

			Country B			
			Water Pumping strategy (billions of m³/year)			
			2		4	
Country A	Water Pumping strategy (billions of m³/year)	2	30.8 62.4 31.6		16.8 52.0 35.2	
		4	33.6 51.2 17.6		17.6 36.8 19.2	

Figure 3.9.   Changing a water pumping Prisoner's dilemma game to cooperation game.

Source: Dinar *et al.* (2013).

Our goal now is to find new outcomes for Country A and for Country B that will be attractive enough to move them away from the conflicting situation to a cooperative situation. Looking at the joint payoffs (62.4, 52.0, 51.2, 36.8) and looking at the alternatives they face when not cooperating, we can design a new allocation of the payoffs. The new allocation will certainly refer to the highest joint payoff (62.4), rather than to any other payoff (52.0, 51.2, and 36.8). So how should the payoff 62.4 be distributed?

Let us say that Country A gets Ca and Country B gets Cb such that Ca + Cb = 62.4. This must be one condition for the allocation of the highest joint payoff. What additional conditions should be introduced? Let us look at the worst payoff in the lower, right quadrant of the matrix in Figure 3.9. Country A would not agree to have less than what it had in the Prisoner's dilemma payoff and the same goes for Country B. Therefore, Ca ≥ 17.6 and Cb ≥ 19.2. Using these constraints we can realize that there are many ways to allocate the 62.4 payoff between A and B, mainly because 62.4−(17.6+19.4) = 25.4 ≫ 0. This means that there is a big surplus to allocate to A and B beyond what might be their minimum request. How to allocate the surplus of 25.4 between A and B is subject to additional considerations. Several ideas could include an equal allocation of that difference to each (12.7), or allocation relative to each country's best alternative payoff in other cells (e.g., 33.6 for A and 35.2 for B suggest 48.8% to A and 51.2% to B). We will discuss these considerations in more details when reaching Chapter 5.

References

Allison, G. and Zelikow, P., 1999. *Essence of Decision: Explaining the Cuban Missile Crisis*, 2nd edition. New York: Pearson Longman.

Blechman, B. M. and Cofman Wittes, T., 2000. Defining Moment: The Threat and Use of Force in American Foreign Policy Since 1989. In: Stern, Paul C. and Daniel Druckman (Eds.), *International Conflict Resolution After the Cold War*. Washington DC: National Academies Press, pp. 90–122.

Dinar, A., Dinar, S., McCaffrey, S., and McKinney, D., 2013. *Bridges over Water: Understanding Transboundary Water Conflicts, Negotiation and Cooperation*, 2nd edition. Singapore: World Scientific Publishers.

Huth, P. K., 1999. Deterrence and International Conflict: Empirical Findings and Theoretical Debates. *Annual Review of Political Science*, 2:25–48.

Schelling, T. C., 2003. Chapter 1—The Retarded Science of International Strategy. *The Strategy of Conflict*. Cambridge: Harvard University Press, pp. 3–20.

Shubik, M., 1982. *Game Theory in the Social Sciences: Concepts and Solutions*. Cambridge, MA: MIT Press.

Wolf, A. T., Aaron, T., Yoffe. S. B., and Giordano, M., 2003. International Waters: Identifying Basins at Risk. *Water Policy*, 5:29–60.

Chapter 4

Concepts and Principles of Negotiation

Abstract

In this chapter, we discuss and demonstrate Concepts and Principles of Negotiation. We will cover basic negotiation issues, such as two-party negotiating over one issue; two-party negotiating over several issues; and many parties negotiating over many issues, which is common in international negotiations over policies. Concepts discussed will include: concessions, reservation value, zone of agreement; issue linkage; best alternative to a negotiated agreement, and the problems faced by the negotiating parties as the number of negotiators increases.

We will review how negotiations are made in the context of a global policy (using examples of the free trade agreements concept of the 'rounds', and the climate change negotiations concept of the 'conferences of the parties' (COP)).

4.1 Negotiation Background

Negotiation (or bargaining) is the process that may allow parties at the stage of conflict to move towards agreement (cooperation), depending on the success of the negotiation process. In the context of our class, negotiation is part of a process in which parties (states) engage in signing a global policy and have opposed interests over some of the aspects of that policy. Negotiation is a process which takes into account many of the attributes of the parties involved. It is quite possible that the negotiation process will lead to one party winning, or all parties feeling that they have won. This depends on the departing points and the relative power, influence, and negotiation skills of the parties involved. Schelling (2003) defines the bargaining power as being determined by the ability to fool and bluff, the outcome of being weak and disorganized, and the ability to exert credible threat on the opponent party(ies).

In addition to the qualifications of the negotiating parties, some institutional and structural characteristics of the negotiation process may make the commitment tactics easy or difficult to use. What is commitment? As we will see in what follows, negotiators have reservation values (beyond which the party will not move). This is called commitment, and it is quite affected by the nature and level of existing institutions that affect the negotiation process. Institutions that characterize the negotiation process include: the use of a bargaining agent, whether or not the negotiation takes place in secrecy vs. publicity, whether or not there are intersecting negotiations, whether or not these are continuous or one-time negotiations, whether or not the negotiation is regulated by a restrictive agenda; and whether or not the negotiations include the possibility of compensation. This list is not necessarily a complete list of institutions that characterize and affect the negotiation, but rather an indicative list.

We will follow the structure suggested by Raiffa (2000), which is very relevant for the structure of our class. The concepts covered in our class will include:

- Monolithic party;
- Repetitive negotiation;
- Issue linkage;
- 'Expanding the cake';
- Best Alternative To a Negotiated Agreement (BATNA);
- Benefit-Sharing;
- Reservation (commitment) price/position/value;

- (Potential) Zone of Agreement (P-ZOA); and
- Concession.

4.2 Negotiating Parties and Concepts

We can expect a big difference between conflicts/negotiations involving two parties and those that involve more than two parties. For example, the Columbia River negotiation between the USA and Canada (two parties) as compared with the Law of the Sea that involved 114 countries, or the Paris Agreement on Climate Change that involved 195 countries +2 Observers. No matter how many parties are involved, the questions that are always asked are: 'are the parties well defined?', 'does each country speak in one voice?', 'are there subgroups such as sectors (hydropower, agriculture,..., Industry)?', 'are there regions (north, south, valleys, mountains)?', 'Are there classes of citizens (poor, rich) engaged?' In this section, we discuss concepts that explain the nature of the negotiation. Some of these concepts are also demonstrated more technically in Section 4.3.

4.2.1 *Monolithic parties*

We can also find that there is a dynamics of forming and splitting parties/coalitions during the process of negotiation, depending on the interests and the opportunities as the dynamics of negotiation develops.

At times, during the negotiation process, the parties are on the same side and hold the same views, but each may put different weights on different issues. At times, during the negotiation process, the parties are on different sides and remain on these sides for the duration of the process. In some cases, separate agreements have to be cut, on different issues, between the parties in the negotiation.

4.2.2 *Repetitive negotiations*

One-time negotiations among parties may yield different outcomes than negotiations that are repetitive. For example, one-time negotiation over the issue of allocation of a flow of water in a shared river may yield an outcome that is less cooperative than periodical (annual, biennial, every n-years) negotiations (and results from elements such as cheating, power, etc.).

When the negotiation is repetitive, such as negotiating every year over the allocation of the flow of water or the annual climate change negotiations conference of the parties (COP), then each country is more concerned about their reputation, and the negotiation is performed in a more cooperative and considerate manner. However, this may not be the case if the countries are heterogeneous, for example, if the information over the water flow is associated with asymmetry, that is, if one country has information on the nature of the flow that is not available to the other country, the repetition will allow it to act in order to accumulate long-term rewards.

4.2.3 *Expanding the cake*

When there are several issues to be jointly determined through negotiation, the parties have an opportunity to considerably 'expand the cake' by including several issues to be negotiated simultaneously. In such cases, the negotiating parties have first to decide on the set of issues, which by itself is an issue for negotiation.

For example, the agenda is well described in the case of the peace agreement between Jordan and Israel (Haddadin, 2000), which by itself is an issue for negotiation. In the case of the Paris Agreement, issues included: technology transfer, compensation to developing countries, commitment on % reduction in greenhouse gases (GHGs).

4.2.4 *Issue linkage*

Linkages are often used to break impasses in negotiations. Even if the negotiation on one issue started in isolation from negotiations on another issue, linking may have a desirable effect (land and water in negotiations between Jordan and Israel, and other issues/work permits in negotiations between Israel and the Palestinian Authority). For example, linking the negotiation over allocation of the river flow to negotiations over economic cooperation that are going on between the countries (USA–Mexico on the Rio Grande: linking

Rio Grande and Colorado rivers, linking storage abroad). Repetitive negotiation can also link an allocation in year t to allocation in year $t - 1$ (e.g., seasonality, such as the case between India and Bangladesh on the Ganges at Farakkah). We will demonstrate in a graph the opportunity in issue linkage later in the chapter.

4.2.5 *Linkage vs. expanding the cake*

We have introduced two concepts of the negotiation analysis—issue linkage and expanding the cake. These two aspects are similar in certain attributes, but differ significantly, and should be rather explained to prevent confusion.

Linkage is based on conditionality of concessions, in the sense that not all parties are interested in all linked issues. For linkage to work, Party A will take more on issue 1 and Party B will take more on issue 2 (in the case that there are two issues). Preferences regarding each issue of each negotiating party have to be orthogonal to each other.

Expanding the cake, on the other hand, introduces issues that all parties have an interest in developing. And therefore, all parties view all issues as affecting their interests in the same way, resulting in higher value placed on more issues included in the negotiation.

4.2.6 *Time constraints and time-related costs*

It is often seen that one party to the negotiation might be more time stressed than the others. Therefore, some party's strategy might be to delay the negotiation as much as possible, or even indefinitely. For example, if the *status quo* portrays a situation in which the allocation of the disputed resource is extremely uneven, the party that holds more than its potential negotiated share may adopt tactics that lead to a delay in the negotiation and, thus, sticking to the *status quo*.

One example could be Egypt's behavior in the Nile negotiations (until recently), which presented delays to any arrangements that were considered in the negotiation between the Nile basin riparian states.

4.2.7 *Best alternative to a negotiated agreement—description*

Parties to the negotiation need to compare possible outcomes of the negotiation process to possible outcomes to themselves if they elect not to participate (and accept) the negotiated agreement. That alternative that each party secures is called BATNA. Sometimes the BATNA is simply the *status quo*, which could be a good enough alternative for some of the parties. Sometimes, if possible to secure, the alternative to a negotiated agreement could be an agreement with a subset of the parties involved (usually called partial coalition)—in the case of a multi-party negotiation. A more technical presentation will be provided later in the chapter (Section 4.4).

4.2.8 *Are negotiated agreements binding?*

The immediate answer is that international negotiated agreements are not binding in the broad sense as is explained in what follows.

International agreements are documented in Treaties. Experience so far suggests that most of treaties are stable, and if not, they are opened for further negotiation at the consent of all parties. However, there are also examples of parties disrupting unilaterally from an international agreement, such as the cases of the USA leaving the Climate Change treaty and the 'Iran deal' in 2017, following the Trump presidency. In addition, international agreements can also be modified, such as the long-term treaties between the USA and Mexico on the Rio Grande, or even the Climate Change treaty during the COP annual meetings.

4.3 Quantitative Representation of Negotiation and Measurement of Positions

In the following, we introduce several simple models of portraying negotiations with qualitative and quantitative means of measuring and evaluating the negotiation process.

4.3.1 *Negotiation between two parties on one issue*

We refer to a bargaining/negotiation process, where the parties involved have opposed interests over the negotiated issue. For example:

1. Buyer and seller of a good in a market have opposed views over the level of the negotiated price (low and high, respectively).
2. Regulator and a polluting firm have opposed views over the level of the standard (high and low, respectively).
3. Two riparian countries have opposed views over the flow allocation (each wants more than less, and because the flow is fixed, the more one gets, the less remains for the other).
4. The irrigation and the hydropower sectors that negotiate over the regime of release of water that is stored behind the dam (agriculture wants the water during the summer, and hydropower wants the water during the winter).

So, the negotiated issue is not always price, or quantity, but may take various forms, such as timing. However, in the example that we discuss in the class, we stick, at least for now, to a negotiated price. The two parties involved are monolithic, the negotiation process is a one-time shot, and the particular bargaining process is not linked to any other bargaining. These conditions will hold also in the next example.

4.3.1.1 *Negotiating the price of water behind a dam*

Two countries find out that a joint use of the water in a river, that both are riparian to, is a good investment on both sides. Naturally, they consider a dam to be located on the jurisdiction of the upstream country, situated in a mountainous landscape. The downstream country is more economically developed, and may use the water, or electricity produced, more efficiently. As a matter of fact, the upstream country may not be able to use all the water or all of the electricity produced. Both countries agreed that the water, or the electricity produced by the upstream country, would be sold at a special price to the downstream country. The subject of this analysis is the negotiation over that particular water unit price.

The upstream wants the price to be as high as possible, and the downstream country wants it to be as low as possible. Each party to the negotiation tried to determine its BATNA (BATNA—will be addressed later in the chapter) by both evaluating the no agreement situation, where the dam may be built and the water or electricity will not be sold to the downstream country. The way that the parties establish each one's zone of agreement is by determining the reservation price, which is the price each would like to obtain. Using Figure 4.1, we can evaluate the negotiation process and determine the likelihood of reaching an agreement.

The upstream party (seller) has a reservation price, s, which is the minimum they will be willing to settle for. Any agreeable price $x^* < s$ represents a situation, for the upstream, that is worth less than no agreement. If the agreed upon price $x^* > s$, than $x^* - s$ is the upstream surplus.

The downstream party (buyer) has its reservation price at b that represents the maximum value it is willing to pay. Therefore, any negotiated price $x^* > b$ represents for the downstream party an outcome that is inferior to no agreement. If the agreed upon price $x^* < b$, then $x^* - b$ is the downstream surplus. If the reservation

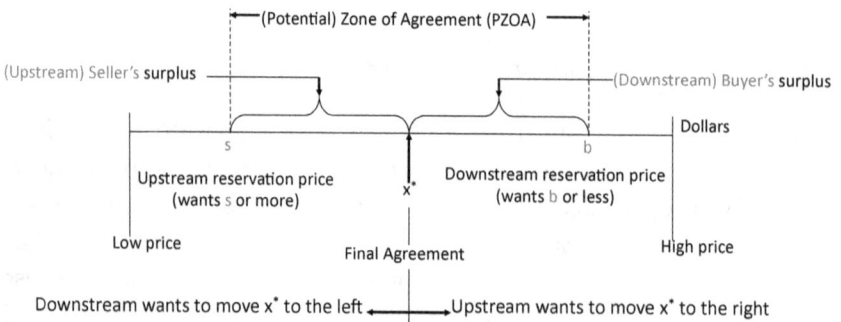

Figure 4.1.   The downstream (buyer)/upstream (seller) negotiation over the price of water behind the dam.

Source: Modified from Dinar *et al.* (2013: Figure 7.1).

prices are such that $b < s$, there is no zone of agreement. But if $b > s$, then the potential zone of agreement is the range $[b, s]$, where $s < x^* > b$.

However, even in this case, the parties may not be able to agree on a price x^* that will fall in the potential zone of agreement. Why? Simply because neither of the negotiators has been able to consent to the price that is seen favorably by the other party.

What additional factors other than the reservation price (known only to each party) affect the final agreed price? Some of these factors include: who is the party that opens the series of offers (Does the downstream suggest the first offer or is it the upstream party that makes the first offer?).

1. The party's capacity to make concessions, mainly at the beginning of the process, where the parties are far from each other in the space P-ZOA. The larger the difference $(|x^* \gg i; i = b \text{ or } s|)$, the easier it is to make concessions.
2. Asymmetry of information. Can the downstream party estimate the cost of the dam and extrapolate to the reservation price of the upstream? Or vice versa, can the upstream party estimate the demand function of the downstream for water and derive the price reservation value of the downstream party?

We can consider several possible scenarios:

a. Each party knows the other's reservation price;
b. One party knows the other's reservation price; and
c. Each party has probabilistic information about the other's reservation price.

Factors affecting final agreement:

- Big and few vs. small and many concessions. These strategies can be seen in Figure 4.2.
- Time limit to reach a contract price (Is the upstream bounded by loans to build the dam? Any payment schedule that makes the negotiation subject to time constraints? Is the downstream party

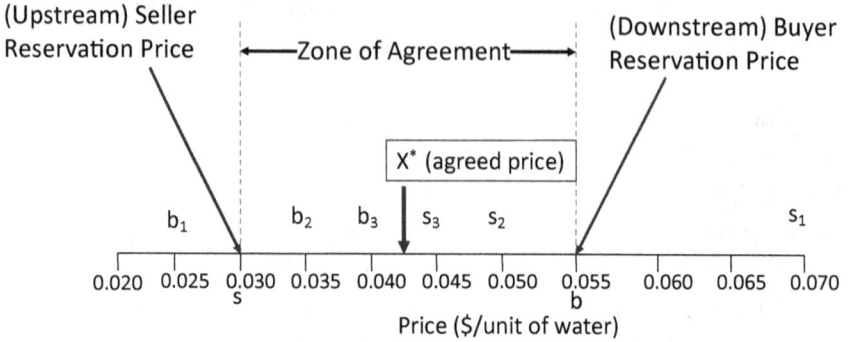

Figure 4.2. The negotiation steps diagram.

Source: Adapted from Raiffa (2000: Figure 3).

engaged in any development programs that put it under pressure to obtain additional water or electricity and makes its position weaker?).

- Existence of other alternatives (Can the upstream sell the electricity/water to someone else, or use it domestically? Can the downstream obtain water/electricity from another source, and for how much?) or BATNA.

4.3.2   *Negotiation between two parties over several issues (integrative bargaining)*

When more than one issue is introduced into the negotiation among two parties, a new dimension is added into the negotiation process— the possibility that the parties will not be strictly opponents (such as in the case with one issue that is likely to be a constant-sum).

With several issues to be negotiated, the parties can 'expand the cake'/'link issues' that they can divide.

Using our example in the previous section, assume that the upstream and the downstream countries are engaged in two separate negotiations. One negotiation is over the price of the water/electricity behind the dam, and the other is over the time of release of the water (winter or summer).

First Issue: Price

On the first issue, the price per unit of water/electricity, the upstream will not settle on a value lower than $0.12 per unit of water, and the downstream cannot afford paying more than $0.08 per unit of water.

Therefore, there is no ZOA between the upstream and the downstream over the price issue (Figure 4.3).

Second Issue: Time of Release

On the second issue, the time of release of the water behind the dam, the upstream, using it mainly for hydropower generation, cannot settle on releasing the water later than February. The downstream, which uses the water mainly for irrigation, cannot settle on having the water earlier than May. Again, for this issue, there is no ZOA (Figure 4.3).

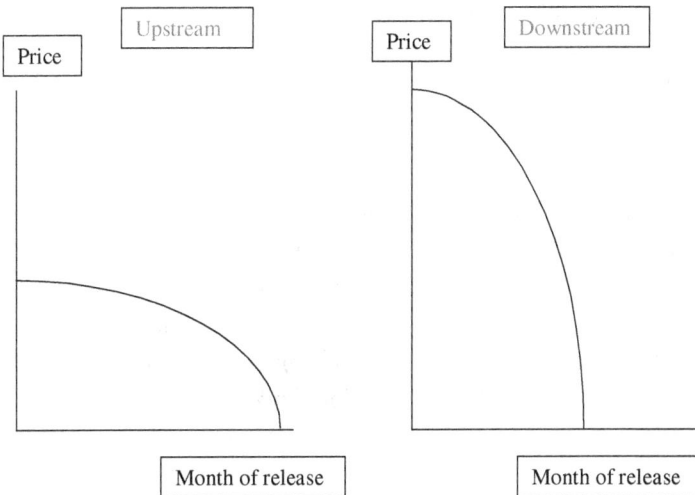

Figure 4.3.   Tradeoff/substitution curves for the negotiation.

Two Parties, Two Issues Simultaneously

So, if the two issues are negotiated separately, the parties may end up with no agreement (deadlock) across the issues on the negotiation table.

What may happen if the two issues are linked and are negotiated simultaneously?

To answer this question we would need to have more information on the characteristics of the two parties and on the physical and economic nature of the two issues.

However, some general observations can be made, and they are provided as follows.

We introduce now the familiar terms of tradeoff and concession:

Each party has a preference/rating/weights by which they can evaluate the relative value (in terms of utility/benefits) from being closer to the reservation value, or being above/below the unacceptable value of the particular issue that is negotiated.

A tradeoff/substitution relationship can be depicted between the issues under negotiation.

Once a tradeoff relationship is obtained, concessions made by the parties can be added to the negotiation, and a ZOA can more easily be found.

Tradeoff/substitution curves for the negotiation:

Using a numerical example, assume that the upstream and the downstream countries are engaged in two separate negotiations. One negotiation is over the price of the water/electricity behind the dam, and the other is over the time of the release of the water.

On the first issue, the price per unit of water/electricity, the upstream will not settle on a value lower than $0.12 per unit of water, and the downstream cannot afford paying more than $0.08 per unit of water. Therefore, there is no ZOA between the upstream and the downstream over the price issue.

On the second issue, the time of release of the water behind the dam, the upstream, using it mainly for hydropower generation, cannot settle on releasing the water later than February. The downstream, which uses the water mainly for irrigation, cannot settle on having the water earlier than May. Again, for this issue, there is no ZOA.

So, if the two issues are negotiated separately, the parties may end up with no agreement across the issues on the negotiation table.

Linkage to the two issues, may most likely lead to better chances for a ZOA, depending on the characteristics of the parties and on technical aspects associated with the two issues to be negotiated. However, some general observations can be made, and they are provided as follows. We introduce now the familiar terms of tradeoff and concession.

- Each party has a preference/rating/weights in which they can evaluate the relative value (in terms of utility/benefits) from being closer to the reservation value, or being above/below the unacceptable value of the particular issue that is negotiated.
- A tradeoff/substitution relationship can be depicted between the issues under negotiation.
- Once a tradeoff relationship is obtained, concessions made by the parties can be added the negotiation, and a ZOA can more easily be found (Figure 4.4).

4.3.3 *Many parties, many issues*

In moving from two-party to multi-party negotiations, we submit ourselves to major analytical difficulties, resulting mainly from numerous interactions among the parties, although the basic approach in this case is similar to that in two-party negotiation.
What are some of the issues that we need to pay attention to?

- The parties are not always well defined, or organized.
- Some of the parties, once organized, might shift and split apart during negotiation.
- The monolithic nature of parties may not hold.

We attempt to describe the dynamics of the parties' positions as the negotiation process evolves. Drawing on Raiffa (1982), a

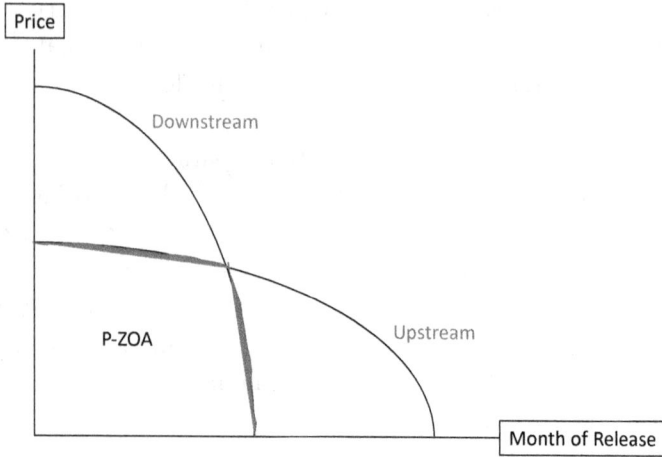

Figure 4.4.   Tradeoff/substitution curves for the linked negotiation and P-ZOA.

global negotiation process may be characterized by many parties and many issues. Generally, the parties to an international negotiation process may represent domestic interests of government agencies, business sector, and local NGOs. In addition, there are also interests of international NGOs, and international agencies such as World Trade Organization, the UN, the World Bank, which also affect the process. If the history of the negotiation processes is documented, then the interim offers (or positions) and counter-offers may reveal a certain pattern from which projections about the likelihood of reaching an agreement within a limited period, and the nature of the agreement, may be estimated. The initial set of issues discussed in the negotiation may be relatively wide. However, over the course of the negotiation process, one may observe that for some parties the relative importance of some of the issues has changed, and some issues even have become irrelevant.

In a multi-party, multi-issue situation, it is harder to predict in early stages what the results are going to look like because of the phenomena described above. Note that the time horizon of a multi-party, multi-issue case might not be the same as that of a two-party-one-issue negotiation.

While the analytical framework presented above is useful in that it provides a general framework for assessing the dynamics of a negotiation process, it does not provide quantitative measures to express the 'values' each party possesses *vis a vis* each negotiated issue. A great deal of the empirical work has to do with measuring 'position values' at each stage of the negotiation process.

What happens during the negotiation process?

- Coalitions change;
- Relative importance of issues change;
- Possibility of bringing in new issues; and
- Possibility of bringing in new parties.

Examples:

- Climate change negotiations;
- The Exxon Valdez Oil Spill (parties, issues); and
- The Nile River Basin (parties, issues).

As we mentioned earlier, in the case of many parties, the analytical tools to describe and explain the negotiation dynamics is much more complicated.

- The parties have agreed upon the issues to be negotiated and on the possible resolution levels for each issue.
- Each party uses a confidential additive scoring system to rank the issues and the possible resolution levels.
- Each party has already examined the negotiation space and scored its BATNA (to be discussed in length later in the chapter).

For each negotiated issue, a party has to have an idea on what would be if it doesn't come to an agreement with the other parties on that issue. Of all these states of the world that occur in case of not reaching an agreement, the party can find the most favorite one—the BATNA [minimum security level requested by the party: reservation value, *status quo*]. Then the parties can negotiate a compromise agreement (Figure 4.5).

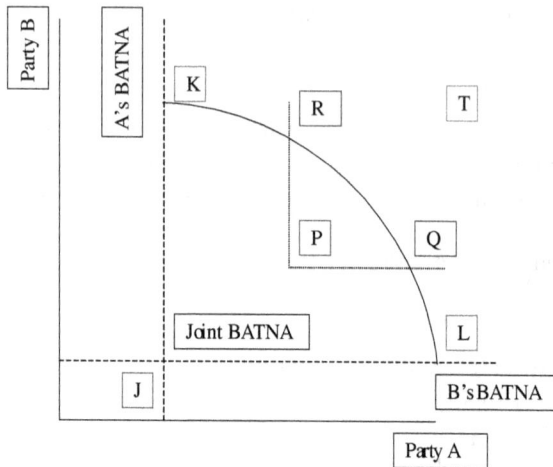

Figure 4.5.   Joint evaluation of negotiated outcomes.
Source: Modified from Keeney & Raiffa (in Young, 1991).

4.4 Best Alternative to a Negotiated Agreement—Technical Representation

BATNAs are confidential and are not shared among the parties in the negotiation. Each party has to prepare a BATNA for each issue and for negotiation with each opponent.

Because the negotiation process is associated with transaction cost and other related complications, each party can calculate the minimum value of the negotiated issue that will make a negotiated agreement ≻ BATNA.

This may mean a comprehensive or partial agreement:

1. With all negotiated parties; and
2. On all negotiated issues.

The point J represents the BATNA scores of A and B. Point P represents the outcome of one pair of negotiations. Q-R is the arc of efficient outcomes associated with the outcome P. K-R-Q-L is the possible outcome frontier. No outcome is possible to its right.

How do parties select their preferred outcomes? How do 'mediators' evaluate the negotiation likelihood? We introduce now several approaches that have been used in the literature in order to answer such questions. Most of the examples refer to the field of water negotiations.

4.5 The Strategic Management Process

Different strategies will be needed for different stakeholders, depending on their importance (power), and positions *vis-a-vis* a given issue. Nutt and Backoff (1992) propose a two-by-two matrix (Figure 4.6) where the vertical axis represents stakeholders' position on supporting (0 to +5) or opposing (−5 to 0) a course of action on an issue; and the horizontal axis represents the power or capacity of the stakeholder to implement its position.

The use of the Strategic Management Process (SMP) is demonstrated with an application to a multi-state, multi-issue negotiation on the Nile river basin (Egypt, Rwanda, Sudan, Tanzania, Uganda, Zaire, Ethiopia Kenya, Burundi, and Eritrea), taken from Alemu (1995) and was later further developed in Dinar and Alemu (2000). The parties include 10 riparian states and one international organization, all having stakes in the issues of the basin. The analysis focused on two issues:

1. [A]-Settlement of the equitable entitlement of the basin water; and
2. [B]-Promotion of region-wide cooperation in all aspects.

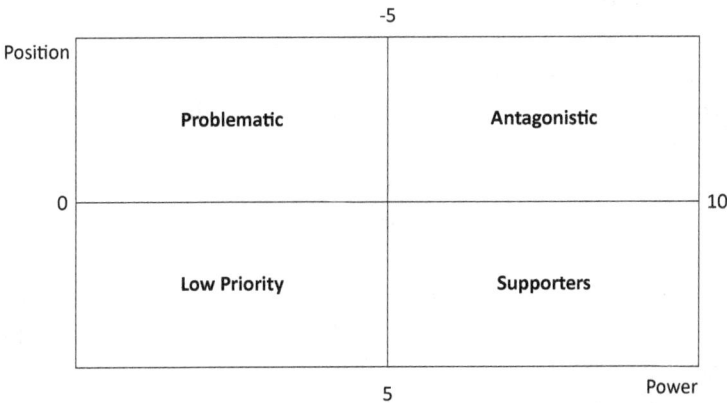

Figure 4.6.   The Strategic Management Process matrix.

Table 4.1.   Strategic Management Process (SMP) values for issue position and power.

	Parties' grades			
	[A]-Settlement of the equitable entitlement of the basin water		[B]-Promotion of region-wide cooperation in all aspects	
Party	Y-Position	X-Importance/ power	Y-Position	X-Importance/ power
1	2.0	3.0	0.0	6.0
2	−5.0	9.0	5.0	8.0
3	3.0	4.0	−3.0	6.0
4	4.0	7.0	−5.0	7.5
5	2.0	4.0	−1.0	6.0
6	2.5	3.0	0.0	6.5
7	−4.0	8.0	4.0	6.0
8	3.0	5.0	−0.5	6.5
9	2.5	6.0	−2.0	7.0
10	0.0	5.0	0.0	8.0
11	2.5	3.5	−1.5	6.0

Source: Alemu (1995).

Table 4.1 depicts the values assigned to each issue in regard to X—Importance/Power, and Y—Position. Intentionally, no attempt is made to explain how these values have been arrived at. The interested reader can find out more about it in Dinar and Alemu (2000).

The values for X and Y of issues A and B are plotted in the SMP matrix in Figures 4.7 and 4.8.

What can we learn from the results of the SMP analysis as presented in the two figures?

We could learn more if we have the match between the diamonds and the actual parties (names of the states). But this would need a much more detailed analysis for which we do not have space at this point. However, it is clear that reaching a consensus or a majority agreement on issue A is impossible if it is negotiated separately. We can also see that the two parties that were opposed (antagonists) to issue A are supporters of issue B and the parties for which issue A was a 'low priority' moved to the 'antagonistic' quadrate in issue B.

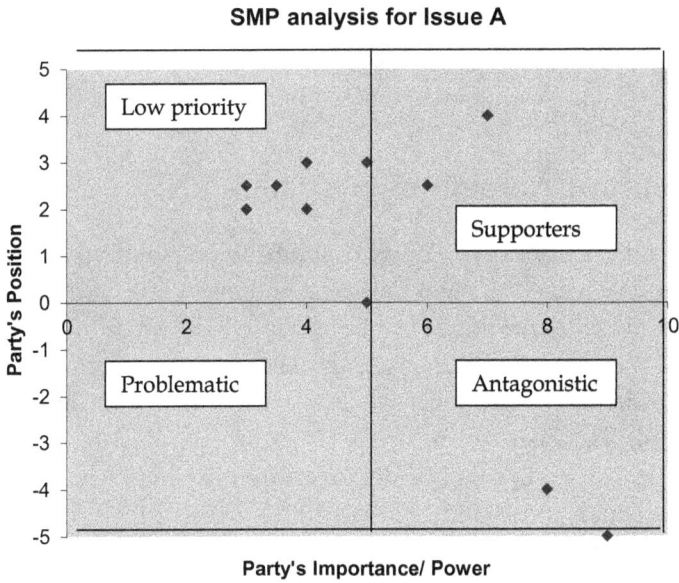

Figure 4.7.   SMP analysis for issue A.
Source: Modified from Alemu (1995).

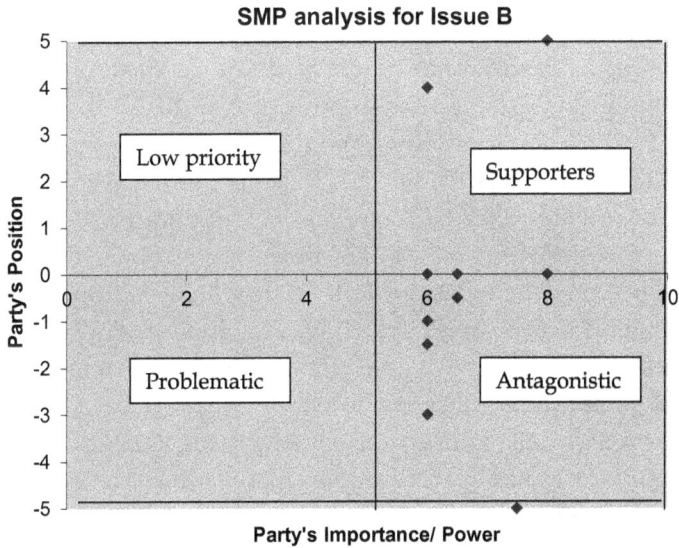

Figure 4.8.   SMP analysis for issue B.
Sources: Modified from Alemu (1995).

Therefore, combining the two issues (A+B) and/or adding new issues of interest to the parties may change the distribution of the parties in the SMP analysis.

4.6 Political Accounting System

Coplin and Oleary (1976, 1994) evaluate issue positions, power over issues, and salience attached to issues, and provide an ordinal ranking of likelihood to agree on a set of negotiated issues.

The metrics used for each of the three parameters are as follows: Issues (−3 through +3), Power (0 through 3), and Salience (0 through 3). Calculations are a bit more complicated than in the case of the SMP. They will be demonstrated in the following example, based on Dinar and Wolf (1994a,b, 1997) where a Potential Regional Water Market in the western Middle East involving Ethiopia, Egypt, Sudan, Israel, West Bank, and Gaza, was considered.

The possibility of having water transfers in the form of a water market (WM) and a market for irrigation technology, where excess water will be traded for a price to be set in a market for water, was evaluated. The different standpoints concerning a possible WM and consequent water diversions depend on individual relationships as well as on attitudes towards 'target entities.'

To summarize the political positions of each of the players, the Political Accounting System (PAS) was used. Each player's political attitude (Issue, Power, and Salience) were ranked for the two scenarios: (a) Nile water to Gaza, and (b) Nile water to Israel. Issue Position is scored from −3 to +3, reflecting strongly negative and strongly positive attitudes towards each scenario, respectively (for the rationale for the specific ranking, see Dinar and Wolf (1994a)). In the case of hydrologic disputes, power can include riparian position and legal strength as reflected in a water sharing treaty, as well as the more traditional military and political aspects, and is ranked from 0 to 3 to reflect increasing levels of power. Issue Salience is, simply, the importance of a proposal, and it is also rated from 0 to 3 to show increasing salience. Multiplication, carried out horizontally, provides a reading of an entity's overall position. Finally, summation

Table 4.2. PAS for Nile water diversion under two scenarios.

	Position	Power	Salience	Total
Scenario a—Nile water to Gaza				
Riparian				
Egypt	+2	2	3	+12
Sudan	+2	2	2	+8
Ethiopia	+1	3	2	+6
Targets				
Israel	+1	2	3	+6
West Bank	+2	1	2	+4
Gaza	+3	1	3	+9
Total				**+45**
Scenario b—Nile water to Israel				
Riparian				
Egypt	+1	2	3	+6
Sudan	−2	2	2	−8
Ethiopia	−1	3	2	−6
Targets				
Israel	+2	2	3	ǀ 12
West Bank	−1	1	1	−1
Gaza	−1	1	1	−1
Total				**+2**

over each player's total allows the comparison of different scenarios, with higher numbers suggesting greater relative viability.

Relative rankings for each entity are suggested by the previous discussion of their likely concerns over a water market and transfer. The total for each party summed across the parties provides the relative likelihood of the issue/scenario on the negotiating table. The results of this analysis (Table 4.2) reveal the unlikeliness of scenario (b) as compared to scenario (a).

References

Alemu, S., 1995. Problem Definition and Stakeholder Analysis of the Nile River Basin. Paper Presented at the *3rd Annual Nile 2002 Conference*, Arusha, Tanzania, February 13–15, 1995.

Coplin, W. and O'Leary, M., 1976. *Everyman's Prince: A Guide to Understanding Your Political Problems*. New York: Duxbury Press.

Coplin, W. and O'Leary, M. (Eds.), 1994. *The Handbook of Country and Political Risk Analysis*. Syracuse, NY: Political Risk Services.

Dinar, A. and Wolf, A., 1994a. International Markets for Water and the Potential for Regional Cooperation: Economic and Political Perspectives in the Western Middle East. *Economic Development and Cultural Change*, 43(1):43–66.

Dinar, A. and Wolf, A., 1994b. Economic Potential and Political Considerations of Regional Water Trade: The Western Middle East Example. *Resources and Energy Economics*, 16:335–356.

Dinar, A. and Wolf, A., 1997. Economic and Political Considerations in Regional Cooperation Models. *Agricultural and Resource Economics Review*, 26(1): 7–22.

Dinar, A. and Alemu, S., 2000. The Process of Negotiation Over International Water Disputes: The Case of the Nile Basin. *International Negotiation*, 5:331–356.

Haddadin, M., 2000. Negotiated Resolution of the Jordan-Israel Water Conflict. *International Negotiation*, 5(2):263–288.

Keeney, R. L. and Raiffa, H., 1991. Structuring and Analyzing Values for Multiple-Issue Negotiations. In: Young, P. H. (Ed.), *Negotiation Analysis*. Ann Arbor: The University of Michigan Press.

Nutt, P. C. and Backoff, R. W., 1992. *Strategic Management of Public and Third-Sector Organizations: A Handbook for Leaders*. San Francisco, CA: Jossey-Bass Publishers.

Raiffa, H., 2000. *The Art and Science of Negotiation*. Ann Arbor: The University of Michigan Press.

Schelling, T. C., 2003. *The Strategy of Conflict*. Cambridge: Harvard University Press.

Chapter 5

Domestic Interests and International Negotiations*

Abstract

The focus of this lecture is on the interaction between domestic interests and the direction which the international negotiations take. It is well recognized that domestic interest may derail international negotiations or support them. The ability of states to sign and ratify a global policy will be the result of a domestic negotiation as well. The chapter describes the interaction between domestic interest groups and the state representatives in the international negotiations and predicts different outcomes under different power relations that take place.

5.1 Introduction

The heart of this chapter is around the question what constitutes cooperation among countries, what drives countries to cooperate, and what affects a country's behavior in the international arena. We dwell on and extrapolate from the approach in Milner (1997), and use for that purpose the model by Milner and Rosendorf (1997).

We used to think (and even assumed for simplicity) in our analyses of international negotiations by a state as a unified organ that

---

*Modified from Milner (1997) and Milner and Rosendorf (1997).

'talks in one voice'. Then, when it comes to cooperation, the actors representing the voice of a state adjust their behavior to the actual or anticipated preferences of others, through a process of policy coordination. Policy coordination in turn implies that each state's policies have been adjusted so that their negative consequences on the other states are reduced.

Cooperation/agreement can thus be conceived as a process of exchange. Cooperation among nations is a specific type of exchange. It involves the adjustment of one state's policies in return for, or anticipation of, the adjustment of other states' policies so both end up better of. Exchange here refers to the mutual accommodation of nations' policies rather than the economists focus on goods and services.

International cooperation necessitates domestic and international policy coordination. Four different levels of policy coordination are distinguished, each representing greater levels of political commitment.

1. Exchange of information to facilitate tacit policy coordination;
2. The negotiation of specific policy 'deals' on a one-time basis;
3. The establishment of a set of rules, guiding policy choice; and
4. The surrender of national policy instruments to form a larger policy community.

While level (1), the lesser policy coordination extent, allows nations, or riparian states in the case of international river basins, to keep their domestic policies intact, but reduces the likelihood of externalities to other riparian states via the creation of symmetric information structures, level (4) is the highest policy coordination instrument. In the case of international river basins, this is equivalent to the creation of an international river basin authority, or a region/basin-wide action plan, that has the authority to dictate relevant policies at the national level. A good example for policy coordination level (1) is the India–Bangladesh pre-1996 Ganges agreement status. An example for policy coordination level (4) is the combination of the Danube Action Plan Agreement of 1994 coupled with the EU Water Directive, which was adopted by all EU members, many of which are also the riparian states of the Danube River Basin.

So far in the discussion we assume that the decision of a riparian state to engage in international policy dialogue is done in a sterilized environment (the one-voice model). However, cooperative agreements create winners and losers also domestically, and therefore, they create supporters and opponents to the agreement or part of it by many segments domestically. The internal struggle between these groups shapes the possibility and nature of international cooperative agreements. For example, during the negotiation that led to the 1994 Jordan–Israel Water agreement, groups of special interest in both Israel and Jordan, via their access to information and by using their domestic power, affected both the pace and the direction of the negotiation process (Haddadin, 2000).

A simple convergence process between domestic and international interests is presented in Figure 5.1.

What happens during such a negotiation process? We may expect coalitions change, change in relative importance of issues, possibility of bringing in new issues, and possibility of bringing in new parties, or leaving some of the parties. If ideal, the domestic

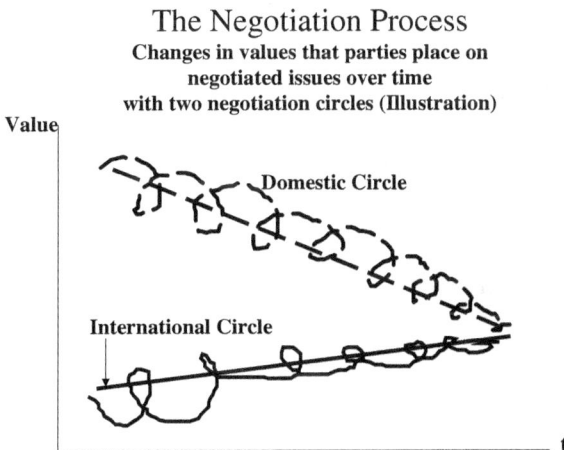

Figure 5.1.   The domestic–international convergence negotiation process.

and international processes could converge and the state involved in the international and domestic negotiations would ratify the global/ international policy.

5.2 Analytical Framework

States are not unitary actors. They can be strictly hierarchical (dictatorships), polyarchic (parliamentary regimes), and there are states where their domestic politics are characterized as anarchy. In this model, states are polyarchic, composed of actors with varying preferences, who share power over decision-making. The struggle for political power domestically is critical for them. The survival of the state is an important value for decision-makers, but most decisions do not directly concern the state's survival. Once we leave the world of unitary actors and strict hierarchy, the behavior of states changes. International politics and internal policy become part of the domestic struggle for power and the search for internal compromise.

Three major factors that affect a state's placement on the hierarchy–anarchy continuum are:

1. The policy preferences of domestic actors;
2. The institutions for power sharing among the domestic actors; and
3. The distribution of information among the domestic actors.

The distribution of power and information among domestic groups and the divergence among their preferences defines the extent of polyarchy.

1. Polyarchy assumes that actors' preferences differ ('not talking in the same voice'). If players have the same preferences, power and information do not matter. The extent to which preferences differ is an important variable;
2. Decision-making must be shared. If one actor controls the decision-making process, we are back to the unitary actor model where hierarchy prevails; and

3. The relevant processes have to be transparent and relevant information has to be shared. If controlled by one actor, we are again in the hierarchical model.

Three groups of domestic actors will be part of this model: the executive (the prime minister or the president), the legislator, and interest groups.

In the model it is assumed that each of the three groups, namely, the executive, the legislator, and the interest groups, are unitary (see explanation in Milner, 1997: 34) and rational. (These two assumptions are problematic, especially when it applies to the legislature and the interest groups.) Policy preferences of domestic actors are derived from their basic interests, which are captured in their utility functions, which they attempt to maximize. For example, political actors' basic interests are to retain office, and social actors' basic interests are to maximize their net income. For all, more is better over less.

Executives have to worry about two factors: the overall economy and the preferences of interest groups that support them—voters tend to punish and reward incumbents in retrospect. Executives will thus try to choose policies that optimize both the state of the national economy and the interests of their interest-group supporters. Policies entailed by international cooperation will only be chosen if they fit this criterion.

Legislators usually vote for or against an international agreement proposed by the executive. Since they are assumed to be rational (in regard to their own utility function), they will approve a treaty only if it will improve their likelihood to retain office in the next elections. Given the unitary assumption regarding the legislator, we refer to the median legislator in the parliament. As political actors, both the executive and the legislator are assumed to have similar interests, although they may prefer different policies to maximize these interests. Because in a parliamentary system the legislator usually chooses the executive, differences in preferences between these two actors are less likely. Take for example a parliament that is controlled by a party that represents agricultural regions in the country. When an international water treaty is proposed, agricultural interests that are not secured by such a treaty will not pass.

There are many interest groups and each is assumed to be unitary and rational as well. (The internal politics within an interest group is discussed in the collective action literature.) Here it is assumed that each interest group behaves as a unit that reflects the median members' preferences. Interest groups, as rational organs, attempt at maximizing their members' income (their preferences can be reduced to a single dimension). Hence, interest groups will support (oppose) policies entailed by international cooperation that promote (detract from) this interest. Take for example the agricultural lobby and its preferences in regard to an international water treaty. The main, if not the only, motive of the agricultural sector is to secure all necessary water, presently utilized by farmers. In case of a country with less than needed water resources for agricultural production at present, the agricultural interest groups' preference is a treaty that will allow more water in the future for irrigation.

The model addresses also situations of divided governments where policy preferences vary between the executive and the legislators. We will not address this here, but the reader can find it in Milner (1997: 37–42).

Policy preferences of political actors are in the domestic (unilateral) as well as the international (multilateral) domains. Domestic, unilateral policy choices have much more effect on the country' economy than do international cooperative ones. Although acknowledging the primacy of domestic policy tools for influencing the national economy, international cooperative efforts are sometimes chosen, not to replace domestic, unilateral policy. International cooperative policy may not be as efficient as a domestic unilateral one, but some times more electorally beneficial to political leaders.

The central reason for political actors (policymakers) to choose multilateral policy depends on:

1. The degree of the nation's openness (integration into the world economy); and
2. The type of externalities that country's policies generate.

Openness is associated with greater impact of other countries' policies on the home country. When through its choice of policies a foreign country generates costs or benefits for another country or other countries that are not included in the foreign country's calculation of the optimality of the policy, we can speak of externalities. Externalities generate demand for cooperation.

The externalities generated by the other countries' policies tend to grow in importance as an economy is opened. As these externalities rise, ceteris paribus, so do the gains from cooperation, and hence so do the incentives for it.

If countries' economies are tightly woven together through trade and capital flow, they may not be able to achieve their economic goals without other states' help. If rates of growth, employment, and/or inflation in one state depend on the policies chosen in other states, then politicians' re-election hopes are tied to the behavior of these foreign countries.

Cooperation is frequently desired to change the policies of other countries; either to prevent them from adopting some policy they intend to or to push them to adopt a policy that they would not otherwise adopt. If political leaders in Country A with an open economy believe that Country B will adopt policies that generate negative externalities for A's economy, then Country A may hope to block Country B from doing so. International coordination (multilateral treaty) may be a way to prevent Country B from unilaterally imposing negative externalities on A and thus from hurting Country A's leaders' electoral chances. Country A may have to give up something in return, but this may be worth the price of binding B. A similar reasoning holds when Country A wants Country B to adopt a particular policy that generates positive externalities for A, but Country B is not keen about it.

Political actors may also seek international cooperation to avoid domestic political problems. However, international cooperation may be decayed domestically. Powerful groups within a country may be able to prevent the adoption of policies they dislike in a domestic (unilateral) setting, even when political actors like them. Multilateral cooperation (international coordination) may allow political actors to overcome this opposition and adopt policies that they otherwise could not. International cooperation may also allow political leaders to bind themselves, thus 'locking in' their preferred policies. International cooperation may be one way for political actors to commit themselves to not doing something.

It can be argued that interest of political leaders (their 'demand for'—as the term used by Milner (1997: 47)) in international cooperation varies by issue area, which in turn rests on policy instruments involved. Several issue areas that can be considered for international cooperation include: trade and industrial policy (tariffs, quotas, and subsidies); monetary policy (money supply); exchange rate policy; and fiscal policy (public expenditure and taxes). Additional issues that have been subject to international cooperation include Arms control, or trans-boundary resources such as Fishery and Water treaties.

The central variables differentiating issue areas are: the nature and extent of externalities that other countries' policies may impose on the home country, and the nature and the extent of benefits that the country's own unilateral use of the policy instrument can provide domestically (Table 5.1).

Cooperation costs are taken into account as well. Costs include (1) direct losses associated with giving up unilateral use of the instrument/resource; and (2) the effect of foreign countries' retaliation against the home country for its unilateral use of the policy instrument/resource.

Table 5.1. Qualitative identification of political demand for international cooperation.[a]

	Low externalities	High externalities
High home benefits	No/least demand	Some demand
Low home benefits	Some demand	High demand

Note: [a]We need of course to remember that a country's level of economic openness influences the home benefits it derives from a policy instrument/resource, because it reduces the effectiveness of unilateral policies, and it affects the level of impact of retaliation—countries with closed economies will not be able to retaliate and will have a minimal impact of retaliation by other countries.

Therefore, the political actor in each country plugs into their utility function the following two factors: (1) the net home benefits to the actor from using the instrument/resource unilaterally (the benefits to the economy and to the interest groups minus the cost of retaliation, if any); and (2) the net external cost imposed on the home country by foreign countries when they use the policy instrument/ resource.

The model that is being presented reveals how domestic and international factors interact to shape cooperation between two nations, by means of ratifying a treaty. The model varies the level of polyarchy to show its impact on the international negotiations.

5.3 The Analytical Model

The model explains the impact of the structure of domestic politics (preferences, power, information) on international cooperation (signing treaties). The model addresses two aspects: (a) the structures of domestic preferences; and (b) the domestic distribution of information.

Four sets of players participate in a two-level international game between a home country and a foreign country:

1. The political executive of the home country;
2. A foreign country executive;
3. The legislator of the home country; and
4. Interest groups within the home country.

First, the model demonstrates the effect that different structures of domestic preferences have on international cooperation. These features of domestic politics cannot be ignored when we examine the likely terms of an international cooperation agreement. Differences include:

• Legislator or executive is the most hawkish internally; and
• Big diversion between preferences of the executive and the legislator.

The results of the model contradict the common belief about the role of structure and information, that is, the more united domestically, the better the outcome of the internationally negotiated agreement. 'Thomas Schelling conjecture' suggests that internal division may create international advantages for that country. For example, take a situation where farmers are demonstrating and rioting in the streets against a water treaty that may make concessions to the foreign country resulting in restrictions on their water quotas. The foreign country negotiators may be aware of this situation and think that pushing on this issue too much may result in collapse of the entire set of issues under negotiation. Thus, the negotiator for the domestic country may be able to avoid making concessions in this area and thus, secure a 'better' treaty internationally.

Actually, domestic differences can work to the advantage or disadvantage of the domestic country. The net effect depends on the configuration of domestic factorial interests, their power in internal negotiations, and the nature of the external bargain—whether it divides a fixed cake or attempts to enlarge the cake.

The model shows the conditions under which divided government affects the likelihood of international treaty and when it improves the divided side's bargaining power.

Second, the model examines the effects of different distributions of information among the domestic actors. Rather than assuming that information is perfectly distributed to all actors, some are assumed to have better access to information than others. A common belief is that lack of full information either at the international or at the domestic level hinders cooperation. Incomplete information—and the misinterpretation of information—is the central source of conflict. Stein argues that misinterpretation is often the result of incomplete information (Stein, 1990: 58). The model, however, shows that under certain conditions incomplete information, domestically, may not be harmful to international cooperation.

5.3.1   *Model (technical) assumptions*

5.3.1.1   *Players and their preferences*

There are four sets of players: the foreign country, F, specified as a unitary actor; the executive of the home country (president, or prime minister), P (called the proposer), the legislator, C (called the chooser), and the domestic interest groups, E (called endorsers in the asymmetric information case).

All players are utility maximizers, each attempts to obtain a policy (outcome of the international negotiation) as close as possible to its most preferred point—its ideal point.

The policy space is uni-dimensional—one issue to be considered in the negotiation process. A player's utility decreases linearly and symmetrically as the implemented treaty/policy deviates from the ideal.

The domestic political players are P and C. The ideal point on their utility function reflects the policy that perfectly balances the many preferences of their constituents so that their chances of reelection are maximized. The optimal/ideal policies of P and C may differ. Since most legislatures operate by majority rule, the preferred policy of the median member of the legislature becomes that of the entire parliament. The legislator and the executive seek to maximize the likelihood of their reelection by maintaining the overall economy at a satisfactory level and by serving their respective constituencies while in office.

The foreign country, F, is a unitary player—a dictator or an executive elected by a majority rule. Its ideal policy is that preferred by the median voter.

The ideal points/policies for F, P, and C are f, p, and c, respectively.

5.3.1.2 *The international level game*

There are two players, F and P, in the international game. The rationale for having two players only in the international game is that in most international negotiations, although there are many committees involved, they provide input to the executives. The final stage of the negotiations includes the two executives only. The model is a Nash Bargaining Solution (NBS), which was discussed in class earlier. The outcome of the model is nondictatorial in that neither bargainer can enforce their will without the consent of the other. The solution is symmetric (if the parties are identical, the outcome would be of identical shares). The solution is also Pareto optimal. An NBS will be struck by rational players if and only if it gives each a utility at least as large as they could guarantee in the absence of a treaty, and if there is no other agreement that they both would prefer. While the NBS is a good model for the international game, it is less useful for the domestic analysis.

5.3.1.3 *The domestic level: The agenda setter model*

The game is a version of the agenda-setter, take-it-or-leave-it bargaining game. There are two agenda setters, F and P. In most countries, executives and legislator share decision-making powers. In the home country the executive branch, P, has the power to initiate international policies, to negotiate it with foreign executives, and to implement the foreign policy. The executive branch, however, will need a confidence/ratification vote from the legislative branch, C. Different parliamentary structures will lead to different interactions between P and C.

If a domestic group(s) is essential in implementing the international treaty, then the executive must have the 'approval' of that domestic group (or groups). For example, if a water treaty includes water standards on the shared river, which necessitate cooperation of the industry, that is one of the biggest polluters, the executive would need to have the support of the industry in the treaty. This may be associated with some political cost to the legislator.

If the negotiated treaty could hurt large or important segments in the country, domestic complaints will call the legislature to consider stringent forms of ratification. The more domestically contentious the agreement is, the more likely the executive will face a more formal or stringent vote of ratification. Domestic ratification will shape executives' behavior in the international negotiations.

5.3.1.4 *Sequence of moves*

The sequence of moves in the game reflects the interaction of the international and domestic games. In period 1 the home executive, P, negotiates with the foreign executive, over a policy choice, and an agreement, called agreement a, is reached and proposed for ratification. In period 2 the legislature, C, ratifies or rejects the proposed agreement. If the agreement is rejected by the legislature, the *status quo*, q, becomes the outcome, meaning no international cooperation. That ends the game in the complete information environment.

5.3.2 The outcomes

5.3.2.1 International negotiations without domestic politics

Figure 5.2 depicts the outcome of an international game with two players P and F, without any domestic politics. The game assumes complete and symmetric information. The ideal points of P and F are p and f, respectively, and are known as the *status quo*, q. Each state is a unitary, rational actor. We assume that P and F have no domestic considerations that are not factored into their ideal points. The horizontal axis depicts all the possible values of the *status quo*, q. The vertical axis represents a continuum of policy outcomes on a single issue. We assume that all ideal points of P and F, as well as the outcome of the negotiation, a, are in that range. The thick line represents the equilibrium policy choice—the outcome of the negotiation.

How is the equilibrium in the NBS found? We will distinguish between several levels of the values of p, f, and q.

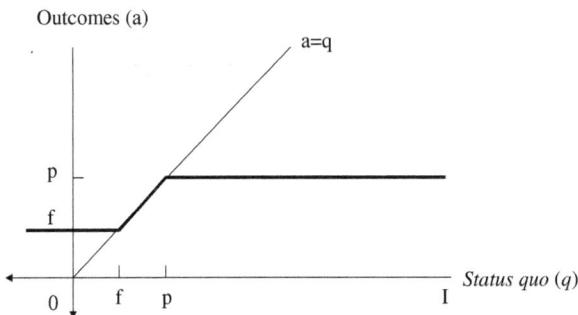

Figure 5.2.   The international game with no domestic politics.
Source: Milner and Resendorff (1997).

When $f < q < p$, the *status quo* is always the outcome. No treaty is the result of the negotiation because a mutually preferred bargain is not possible. This is similar to the case of having an empty core in cooperative game theory, or the case of having an empty P-ZOA (potential zone of agreement).

When q takes any other value, mutually preferred bargains can be made. The cooperative agreement will always be in the range [f, p]. The exact location of the agreement, a, in the range [f, p] will be dictated by the location of q.

When $q > p > f$, then p is the cooperative equilibrium. When $q < f < p$, then f is the equilibrium. The player with their ideal point placed closest to the *status quo* exerts greater influence. As in Raiffa's model of negotiation (Raiffa, 2000) that we discussed in a previous class, the actor with the best alternative to the agreement has greater leverage. The *status quo* should be thought here as the outcome when negotiations fail, and not necessarily the *ex-ante status quo*.

As the difference between p and f grows, two implications follow:

1. The area of no agreement grows, so cooperation becomes less likely; and
2. The actors are forced to accept more extreme outcomes.

When $q < p < f$, then F will accept P's ideal point, which is now much further away.

We can see that the outcome of no agreement is frequently arrived at in the case of complete information. Therefore, incomplete or asymmetric information among the parties is not necessary for failure of cooperation among nations. Unitary actors are also not a guarantee of cooperation.

5.3.2.2 *Domestic politics and complete, symmetric information*

Figure 5.3 introduces domestic politics in it simplest form. Assume a polyarchic state by adding a ratification game. A parliament, C, must ratify any agreement negotiated internationally. C is portrayed as a unitary voter, representing the median voter in the parliament.

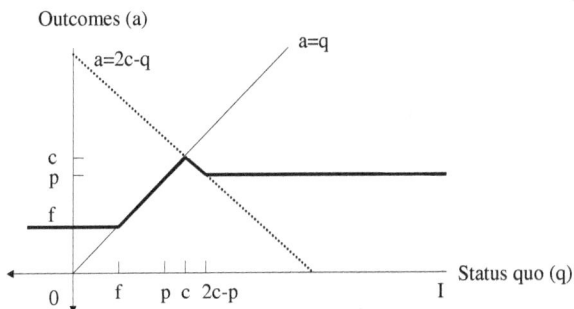

Figure 5.3. The international game with domestic politics and complete information, $p < c$.

Source: Milner and Resendorff (1997).

The legislature must either accept or reject the proposed agreement, and return to the *status quo*.

We maintain the assumption about full symmetric information. P, F, and C all know one another's preferences and the nature of the proposed agreement.

Legislators seek to maximize their electoral prospects, and thus their preferences depend on the weighted sum of the preferences of the interest groups—their constituents. The preferences of the interest groups thus help shape the median legislator's ideal point. Legislators may loose or gain electoral support, depending on the distance of the median legislator's ideal point from that of the interest groups. Loosing or gaining electoral support can be expressed in monetary values. Therefore, the legislator would favor a policy/treaty that balances preferences of all related interest groups—in the case of water: agriculture, urban users, environment, etc.

The outcome of the ratification game in the case where the executive ideal point is closer to that of the foreign country than is the legislature's ideal point, that is, $f < p < c$, the legislature is a hawk because its ideal point differs most from the foreign executive.

The vertical axis in Figure 5.3 represents the ideal points of the players and the proposed agreement. The horizontal axis represents the position of the *status quo*. The thick line shows the equilibrium agreement reached along the vertical axis. It demonstrates when

Outcomes (a)

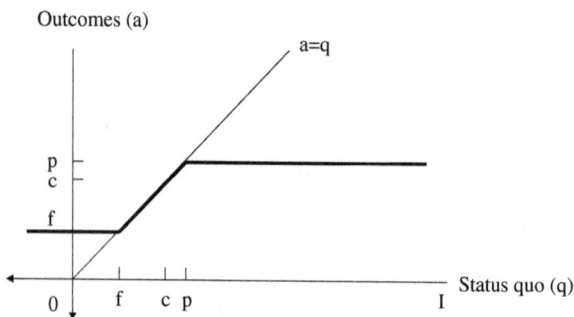

Figure 5.4. The international game with domestic politics and complete information, $p > c$.

Source: Milner and Rosendorf (1997).

cooperation is possible and whose preferences are most closely adhered by any agreement when the structure of preferences is such that the legislature is extremely nationalist or hawkish.

Figure 5.4 shows the outcome when the structure of preferences is altered and now the executive is most hawkish ($f < c < p$). That is, the legislature ideal point is closer to that of the foreign country than that of the executive of the domestic country. As before, the structure of the domestic politics affects the ratification game and hence the cooperative outcome.

When the executive is the most hawkish (Figure 5.4), domestic politics has no effect on the international negotiations. The equilibrium points in Figures 5.2 and 5.4 are exactly the same. When $f < c < p$, the legislature cannot exercise any constraint on the executive in the domestic ratification game. This is true even if the *status quo* is closest to the legislature's ideal point. The executive's autonomy is maximized when he or she are a hawk.

For example, when the *status quo* is between f and c ($f < q < c < p$), no agreement must be the outcome, for neither C nor P will move to F's side of the *status quo*, and vice versa. When the *status quo* is between p and c ($f < c < q < p$), the legislature (C) is still without influence since P will never accept any proposal less than the *status quo*.

When preferences domestically are structured $f < p < c$, domestic politics plays a significant role. Figures 5.2 and 5.3 show the conditions under which international politics continues to dominate. Figure 5.3 assumes $p < c$. When $q < f$, the equilibrium is always f because F is not assumed to have any domestic politics. Once this assumption is released, then the area $q < f$ is affected by domestic pressure. Generally, domestic politics has no influence only when the *status quo* lies between p and f, or is extreme. When $q > (2c–p)$, then p is the equilibrium. Hence if the *status quo* (or no agreement point) takes an extreme value (far from p or f), there are few constraints on the international negotiators. The legislature, C, is again unable to influence the negotiations. In addition, if q is between p and f, the *status quo* is the outcome, as in the international game. Under these circumstances, the domestic political/ratification game has little effect.

Under what conditions do domestic politics matter? Consider the case that q is between p and c. If P and F negotiate to the point p, C will reject such an agreement and implement the *status quo* since q is closer to c than p is. Hence, for P and F to extract ratification they must offer q or better. The best ratification agreement then is q, which is offered and accepted. So, no cooperation is the outcome when the *status quo* is between p and c. P and F are unable to cooperate to realize the joint gains available under the international game.

What happens if the *status quo* is closer to c $(f < p < c < q)$, but not too extreme (e.g., $c < q < [2c–q]$)? For every $q > c$ there is a point $(2c–q)$ to the left of c that C finds indifferent to q. That is, the utility to C is indifferent between q and $2c–q$. Therefore, we allow C to accept an offer of $2c–q$ if it is made. Now P and F, both, prefer $2c–q$ to q when $q > c$. So P and F offer $2q–c$, an agreement that C will accept. In this region in the game, then, domestic politics exercises a substantial constraint on international negotiations. The negotiators will offer a cooperative agreement that is ratifiable, but it is one that they don't like as much.

Comparison of the international game and the domestic politics game shows what happens when polyarchy is introduced in it most basic form. When legislature and executive share decision-making power in a ratification game, there are three findings.

First, international agreement is less likely when domestic politics are involved. With domestic politics there is a range $(p < q < c)$ where the *status quo* is the outcome although mutual gains for the international negotiations simultaneously exist and remain unexploited. The range where q is the outcome expands when the legislature and executive share decision-making power. Hence, the presence of domestic political tension makes international cooperation less likely than in the international game. Shifting and differing interests of domestic stakeholders will reflect on how states formulate their initial position over a given issue (Iklé, 1964: 122).

Second, in the range $c < q < (2c–p)$, the preferences of the legislature, C, have an impact on the nature of the international agreement. In this interval, C's indifference point $(2c–q)$ becomes the equilibrium rather than q, as is the case with no domestic politics. P and F find it necessary to compromise for there is no way to bypass the constraint imposed by the legislature, C. P and F would prefer the outcome in Figure 5.1, where NBS is P's ideal point, but in this range C can threat to opt for the *status quo* instead of the proposal preferred by P and F. Domestic power sharing changes the terms of the agreement; the terms will reflect C's preferences more closely. Power to define the outcome of an international negotiation thus depends not only on states' balance of capabilities but also on their domestic politics.

Third, as the *status quo* moves further and further from c, the legislature's influence over the negotiations weakens. When $q > (2c–p)$, C loses all influence over the outcome; the international negotiators will no longer feel constrained by the legislature, and they will turn to their unconstrained NBS. C's threat to chose the *status quo* instead of the proposal that P and F prefer becomes incredible at this point. This underlines the importance of the *status quo*, or the reversion point. As in the international negotiations, the actor closest to the *status quo* has greater leverage but only up to a certain point. When the *status quo* becomes extreme, but is still closest to the legislature, the executive gains influence, mainly because of his/her agenda-setting power.

5.3.2.3 *Domestic politics with asymmetric information*

In a polyarchy, asymmetric information is likely to exist, which increases the likelihood of ratification failure. Some players will not

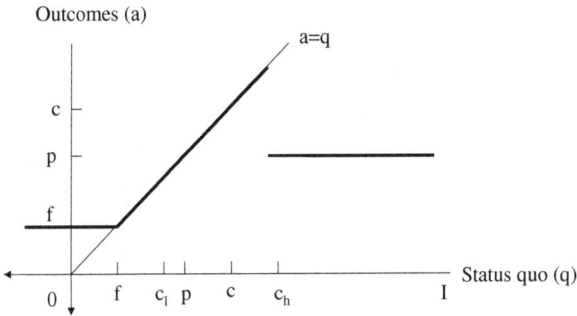

Figure 5.5. The international game with domestic politics and incomplete information.

Source: Milner and Rosendorf (1997).

be fully informed; others will have private information. The less informed group must worry about being exploited and hence will often reject agreements that have been concluded by the better-informed players. Asymmetric information may create inefficiencies as well as political advantages (Figure 5.5).

Here we assume that the legislature is not fully informed about the nature of the agreement that P and F have negotiated. C does not know F's preferences with certainty, but P and F are fully informed. They have private information on the nature of the agreement (which is reasonable since they negotiated it without C). In reality, it may happen that some legislators have information on the agreement and some don't. The median legislator, however, is not a policy expert. They are constrained by time and resources and depend heavily on interest groups and political parties for clues on how to vote. This assumption implies asymmetry of information domestically.

Lacking the executive's information about the agreement, C will accept any offer that is an improvement over the *status quo*; we call the set of acceptable offers C's preferred-to set. For example, if $c < q$ the preferred-to set is $(2c{-}q,q)$. C doesn't know where any offer that has been made actually lies. C can only estimate its location. If C believes that there is a large enough probability that the agreement offered for ratification lies in its preferred-to set, it will chose not to ratify.

How do P and F respond to this behavior? For given prior beliefs and locations of p and f, the international negotiators know in advance if any offer is going to be accepted or rejected. If C is a 'convenient' legislature and ratifies everything, then P and F are not constrained and will offer their NBS for ratification, as in the international game with no domestic politics. If on the other hand, C is a hostile legislature and rejects everything, it will also reject P and F's proposal, and the *status quo* will prevail.

What does the addition of asymmetric information mean for cooperation? If the *status quo* point, q, is close to c, then it is unlikely that the offer lies in C's preferred-to set. Hence, for any beliefs there is an interval of qs around c, in which case C always rejects the offer. However, for qs outside this interval around c, there may be indeed a high enough probability that the offer is in the preferred-to set and C will accept it. This is most likely when q lies far from c, making the preferred-to set very large. Hence, for extreme qs, C is likely to accept the offer, and for qs around c, rejection is most likely.

In Figure 5.5, we can see the equilibrium outcomes. The *status quo* outcome occurs whenever C rejects the offer (here, in the range between c_l and c_h) and therefore, P and F select q. In Figure 5.3, the set of *status quo* points is [f, c], compared with the set of *status quo* points in Figure 5.2, [f, p].

Whereas failure to cooperate was possible for some values of q, when there was complete information domestically, the inclusion of the assumption of asymmetric information makes cooperation even less likely. The region in which cooperation fails to occur expands even further.

When the legislature is less informed, it has less impact, there are no circumstances under which C can influence the proposal made by P and F. P and F always offer their NBS, irrespective of C, and C behaves accordingly—leading to the outcome of the *status quo*.

5.4   General Conclusions

We can distinguish between two situations of domestic politics: (1) complete, symmetric information, and (2) asymmetric information.

In the case of domestic politics with complete, symmetric information, the actor closest to the *status quo* has greater leverage but only up to a certain point. In the case of domestic politics with asymmetric information, when the legislature is less informed, it has less impact, there are no circumstances under which C can influence the proposal made by P and F. P and F always offer their NBS, irrespective of C, and C behaves accordingly—leading to the outcome of the *status quo*.

References

Haddadin, M., 2000. Negotiated Resolution of the Jordan-Israel Water Conflict. *International Negotiation*, 5(2):263–288.

Iklé, F. C., 1964. *How Nations Negotiate*. New York: Harper & Row.

Milner, H. V., 1997. *Interests, Institutions and Information, Domestic Politics and International Relations*. Princeton: Princeton University Press.

Milner, H. V. and Rosendorf, P. B., 1997. A Model of the Two Level Game. In: Milner, Helen V. (Ed.), *Interests, Institutions and Information, Domestic Politics and International Relations*. Princeton: Princeton University Press.

Stein, A., 1990. *Why Nations Cooperate?* Ithaca: Cornell University Press.

Chapter 6

Concepts and Principles
of Cooperation

Abstract

In this chapter, we discuss the notion of cooperation in the context of
global policies and review several game theoretic approaches to conflict
and cooperation between several players. Concepts to be discussed
during this lecture include: allocation, characteristic function, coalition,
grand coalition, partial coalitions, non-cooperative coalitions, defection, egoism, individual rationality, group rationality, efficiency, Nash–
Harsanyi solution, power, Prisoner's dilemma, propensity to disrupt,
Shapley Value, status quo, the core, and value.

6.1 Principles of Cooperation

Under what conditions will cooperation emerge in a world of egoists
without a central authority imposing it? While we are aware of
the way international relations take place and the United Nations'
role in setting such relations, still, we know that nations interact
without a central authority, on issues such as national security and
international trade. We compare nations to individuals and find many
similarities, which lead to understanding how they may act in setting
global policies (agreements, treaties).

According to Axelrod (1985), agents (nations, individuals) cooperate not because they are concerned about the welfare of others
(patronage), but only because they are interested in their own

good (egoism). They expect to benefit from what they do with the other party (or parties). Examples may include: helping a colleague and expecting some 'in kind' in return, or the behavior behind the statement 'how many times shall I invite my colleague for dinner without being invited by her?' or the case where an official leaks news to a journalist in return for a favorable coverage, which is well experienced in many countries.

The pursuit of self-interest by agents leads to the poorest outcomes for all (Prisoner's dilemma), which, in other words means that a self-interest-motivated behavior may not necessarily lead to a cooperative outcome. Since we mentioned the Prisoner's dilemma (PD), let us start by presenting a PD game and then discuss how one can pull oneself out from such a situation.

6.1.1 *A (symmetric) Prisoner's dilemma game*

We start by describing an interaction between two agents (Figure 6.1), which is a simplification of the situation in the case of global policies. However, what we learn from the case of two agents can be easily extended without loss of generality to a game among a larger group of agents.

For the specific design of the game in Figure 6.1, it pays for the Column Player to defect if she thinks that the Row Player will cooperate $(T > R)$. It also pays for the Column Player to defect if she thinks that the Row Player will defect $(P > S)$. Similarly, for the

		Column Player	
		Cooperate	Defect
Row Player	Cooperate	R=3; R=3 Reward for mutual cooperation	S=0; T=5 Sucker's payoff (S), and Temptation (T) to defect
	Defect	T=5; S=0 Temptation (T) to defect, and Sucker's payoff (S)	P=1; P=1 Punishment (P) for mutual defection

Figure 6.1.   A symmetric Prisoner's dilemma game with two agents.

Row Player it pays to defect if she thinks that the Column Player will cooperate $(T > S)$. And the Row Player will be better of Cooperating if she believed that the Column Player will cooperate $(R > S)$.

It the verbal analysis so far, the agents introduce only individual rationality considerations. Individual rationality leads to a worse outcome for both agents—PD, where most likely they will find themselves in lowest payoff/outcome possible (in a Defect–Defect combination). For a two-agent PD game to hold, the relationships between the payoffs require (1) $T > R > P > S$ and (2) $R > (T + S)/2$.

Is there an alternative for agents in a PD setting? Can they move out of the trap that they will end up in with the Defect–Defect situation?

6.1.2 *How to get out of PD?*

There is no mechanism to enforce threats or commitments on the agents. The agents have all possible strategies available to select from. But there is no way to forecast an agent's next move, therefore, history matters and learning from history (of the relations between the agents) would be a key to developing future ways out of PD.

There are several restrictions that have to be taken into account. There is no way to eliminate other agents' behavior, just defect or cooperate on the next move. There is no way to change payoffs in the table. Therefore, the agents have to make the future matter. Let the agents interact indefinite number of times without knowing when the last interaction will take place. By allowing the agents to interact indefinitely we introduce degrees of freedom and options to their strategies. The ability of an agent to remember allows the history of the interactions to be taken into account in an agent's strategy.

One of the best examples of long-term interactions in the field of global policy negotiations are the Conferences of the Parties (COPs) in managing the climate change conventions. The first COP took place in 1995 in Berlin, Germany, and the recent COP took place in 2021 in Glasgow, Scotland. These rounds of meetings among the stakeholders to the climate change global agreements are a good demonstration of the effectiveness of this recurring mechanism and its impact on the willingness of the agents to move away from individual rationality considerations alone.

What does such a mechanism introduce and how does it support cooperative behavior? By having the recurring meetings, the agents adjust their behavior as if they face a discount rate affecting present decisions on future actions. Cooperation may emerge if players know that they will meet again in the future. But the future is less important than the present: future payoffs are valued less than present payoffs. Thus, the next payoff is less important unless future payoffs are discounted in such a way that future moves and payoffs will be regarded such that they still matter.

So far, the PD game we considered was a symmetric one. But this would not always be the case. We rather would face situations where the PD game is not symmetric. How would such a structure affect the outcome of the game?

6.1.3 *A (non-symmetric) Prisoner's Dilemma game*

Figure 6.2 presents a non-symmetric PD game. We change the setting a bit compared to Figure 6.1, but the principles are the same.

Let us re-introduce the concept of Nash Equilibrium (from Chapter 3). So, what is the Nash Equilibrium of this game? It is the line connecting (4, 0) and (0, 5), which suggests a strategy for cooperation. Under the PD game rules, Player 2 will always select Defect, expecting to get the maximum 5 units of payoff. The same is true for Player 1 who will always select Defect, expecting to get the maximum of 4 units of payoff. However, when both select Defect, they

		Player 2	
		Cooperate	Defect
Player 1	Cooperate	2, 3	0, 5
	Defect	4, 0	1, 1

Figure 6.2. A non-symmetric Prisoner's dilemma game.

will end up in the cell 'Defect; Defect' (1; 1), which is the worst total payoff for both $(1 + 1 = 2)$. If they could move away from the 'Defect; Defect' both could gain and then consider sharing the total gain.

So, how could a strategy for cooperation be initiated among the two agents? Let us imagine that the agents can talk to each other (this is one of the changes to the PD 'rules' that we have to make in order to allow for possible cooperation). Here is a suggested strategy by Player 2: 'My dear friend "Player 1," I do not know how much your payoff will be, but I am willing to give you half of my payoff if you agree to cooperate.' Let us examine this 'offer'. The total payoff for Player 1 + Player 2 is the highest in two cells Cooperate; Cooperate $= (2 + 3 = 5)$ and Cooperate; Defect $= (0 + 5 = 5)$. All other cells lead to lower total payoffs, and especially lower payoff to Player 2. So, if Player 2 can convince Player 1 to cooperate, then Player 1 gets $2 + 1.5$ $(= 3/2) = 3.5$ and Player 2 will get $3/2 = 1.5$. Both get a total of 5, but the re-distribution now favors Player 1. Player 2 is still better off with 3.5; 1.5 (Cooperate; Cooperate) compared with 4; 0 (Defect; Cooperate), which are the two preferred strategies for Player 2.

6.1.4 *How can we foster better cooperation (summary)?*

To summarize and generalize the conversion of non-cooperation to cooperation, let us list what we have discussed, and also add a couple of new ideas:

- Repeated interactions among the agents;
- Verbal communications and direct links among the agents; and
- If possible, introduce direct influence by a third party recognized by the agents.

6.2 Types of Cooperative Games and How Joint Cost/Gains are Shared

As we realized from the offer made by Player 2 to Player 1 in the PD game in Section 6.1.3, cooperation might be likely if one agent (in our case, Player 2) has sufficient gains to share with the other party(ies) and still be better off compared to the *status quo*. Later on we will transfer this rule to simple equations, but in the meantime let us describe situations where either games dealing with joint costs or joint gains allow for a cooperative arrangement.

Let us start with an agreement that concludes with spending funds by the agents and what is at stake is the sharing of the joint cost among the agents. Each agent can participate in the project that ends up with a joint facility to produce a good that all agents are interested in, or, alternatively, each agent can produce the good on their own, without the others. Assuming economies of scales, we can expect that the average cost per unit of the good produced in the joint facility will be the lowest when the joint facility will be the largest (e.g., including all the agents).

Examples for sharing costs of a joint facility include: a jointly funded water treatment facility, a jointly funded hydropower dam, a joint regional development project, or in the case of a global policy, the operation of a global policy on pollution monitoring agreement with transaction costs that decrease on average when more agents join the agreement.

Likewise, there are situations when agents do not share costs but rather gains. Examples for sharing joint gains include sharing net benefits from any joint project, such as joint development and management of a joint aquifer to support agricultural activity by each of the agents. Such projects could include global agreement to curb climate change negative effects around the world, or gains from global agreement for free trade, or a global agreement to fight terrorism, which affects many countries.

6.3 Games and Cooperative Arrangements

We use principles from Cooperative Game Theory (CGT). We already defined Game Theory earlier in this chapter as the study of human conflict and cooperation within a competitive situation. It is the science of strategy, or at least the optimal decision-making of independent and competing actors in a strategic setting. Therefore, we would need to introduce several assumptions and definitions to help us move on with the development of the relationships we need.

Our first assumption is that the agents involved (either individuals or states) are economically rational players. This means that agents are profit maximizers, and the decision of each player to join a given coalition is voluntary. We define the agents' behavior as rational. We distinguish between different levels of rationality and efficiency as is explained in what follows. Here again we introduce the concept of *status quo*. Status quo represents the original situation an agent faces. Since we convert the way we measure an agent's improvement to value, we compare everything to money. We use an incremental comparison where the agent compares payoff at a new situation to the payoff at a previous situation (*status quo*) that could be where that agent acted alone (singleton), or where the agent was part of a coalition that transformed to a different coalition. The three conditions include:

1. Individual rationality. Each player will accept a cooperative arrangement IF and only IF (IFF) they perceive it as better than the *status quo*.
2. Group rationality (in a multi-party case). The cooperative arrangement to any combination of players is preferred over any allocation in any sub-coalition they can establish.
3. Cooperative arrangement fulfills the efficiency condition. Full allocation of payoff (from cooperation) to Grand Coalition.

To demonstrate how the three conditions refer to the group of agents, we need to introduce a new concept—permutation.

To demonstrate the various options to reach a final agreement, assume three parties: A, B, C, that negotiate that agreement. A final agreement can indeed not be achieved, which means that each of the agents remains in the *status quo*

- A $\left.\right\}$
- B Individual, Status Quo, Singleton Coalitions
- C
- AB $\left.\right\}$
- BC Partial Coalitions
- AC
- ABC } Grand Coalition

Singleton/Individual coalition are the non-cooperation coalition, where each member (A, B, or C) continues as in the *status quo*. This is the benchmark by which all payoffs to the other coalitional arrangements are compared. The partial coalitions (AB, BC, and AC) are sub-coalitions among parts of the entire group members (A, B, and C). In some situations, when the entire group members are unable to reach an agreement, we can see that partial coalitions take place. The grand coalition is the desired setup for cooperation. It means, for example, that all countries in the world sign the global policy that is negotiated. But this may not always happen.

We can demonstrate the concept of permutation on a set of 4, or even larger number of, players, but the number of permutations will exceed exponentially without further adding to our understanding.

A more formal description of these relationships can be found in Annex A6.1. And more detailed discussion and examples can be found in Colman (1995), in Davis (1983) and in Dixit and Skeath (1999).

6.4 Allocation Rules

It can be assumed that negotiation leads to an agreement that allocates something among the parties that WANT to solve a conflict. (This can be either a situation where the players negotiate over net benefits or over net costs.) The negotiation process may lead to a formula to do it and, therefore, it is a cooperative approach.

We will introduce several popular solution concepts—The Core, Shapley Value, and the Nash–Harsanyi solution—and demonstrate their application to water-related conflicts.

6.4.1 *The core of an n-person cooperative game*

The core of an *n*-cooperative game in the characteristic function form is a set of game allocation gains that is not dominated by any other allocation set. The core provides a bound for the maximum (or minimum in terms of cost) allocation each player may request. In this respect, it is an overall solution for many allocation schemes that are contained within the core. The core fulfills requirements for individual and group rationality, and for joint efficiency (Shubik, 1982) that we discussed earlier. We have to make several additional clarifications to bring the GT concepts in line with the practical issues we are familiar with:

- GT assumes that players are economically rational. This means also that the decision of each player to join a given coalition is voluntary.
- GT assumes that sub-coalitions (s) speak in one voice.
- Ω_j is player j's core allocation of the coalition gains/savings. The core Eqs. (6.1)–(6.3) are (this specification is for a negotiation where the players have to share a joint cost). The equations for sharing joint benefits will be similar, but only the inequality signs will be reversed:

$$\Omega_j \leq v\{j\} \quad \forall j \in N. \tag{6.1}$$

This equation fulfills the conditions for individual rationality condition—that is the cooperative allocation for each player is preferred (cheaper) to the non-cooperation case.

$$\sum_{j \in s} \Omega_j \leq v(s) \quad \forall s \subseteq S. \tag{6.2}$$

This equation fulfills the group rationality condition—that the cooperative allocation to any combination of players is preferred (cheaper) to any allocation in any sub-coalition they can establish.

$$\sum_{j \in N} \Omega_j = v(N). \tag{6.3}$$

This equation fulfils the efficiency condition—that the value of the entire set of players will be fully allocated/paid for to/by the grand coalition participants.

The three conditions, individual rationality, group rationality, and efficiency, that were discussed earlier and are now defined in the three mathematical expressions above, are called THE CORE. The core is the locus of all cooperative arrangements that could be acceptable to the players. It provides a range of possible allocation solutions, some of which will be described later. As a matter of fact,

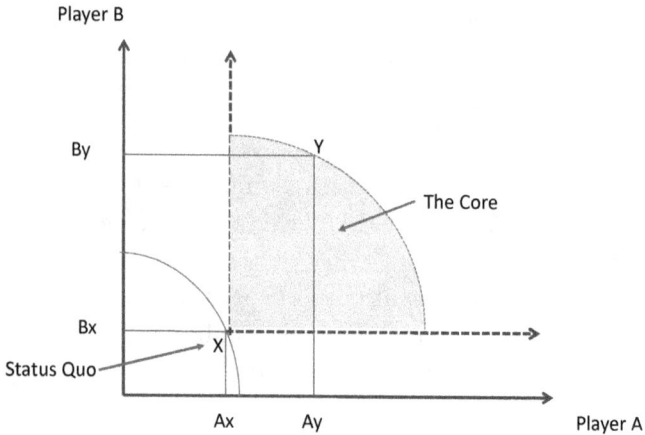

Figure 6.3. The core.

the core can also be empty—in which case there is no allocation solution that fulfills the set of conditions that defines the core. A graphic display of the core is presented in Figure 6.3.

The highlighted area in Figure 6.3 is the core of a game between Player A and Player B. The point X is the *status quo* where they do not cooperate and remain in their initial positions. The core is the P-ZOA between the two players. The point Y is one possible allocation solution where we can see clearly that Y is better than X (Ay > Ax and By > Bx). As mentioned earlier, the core can be empty, meaning that there is no P-ZOA among the players.

6.4.1.1 *Examples of use of core allocations*

In the following we will demonstrate the use of two very common allocation schemes in the classical case of a Dam that is shared by four countries. We will start by describing the situation, the cost function of the dam, and two water availability scenarios that affect the cost of the dam.

Assume a problem of using a river that flows through four countries.[1] Assume that there is in place a treaty that allocates the

---

[1]Based on data in Dinar and Howitt (1997).

Table 6.1. Annual water utilization for high and low water flow scenarios.

Country	Low flow	High flow
A	2,500	4,500
B	3,000	5,000
C	2,000	4,000
D	14,000	35,000
Total	21,500	48,500

water among the riparian counties, but the only way to realize the benefits of the water is by building dams, either by each country, or by groups of countries. Assume that all countries will use the same dam technology, so that the only important parameter is the size of the dam. Because the water in the river is allocated according to share of flow, consideration must be given to high and low flows in building the dam. Of course, the objective of the countries is to reduce their cost.

The dam cost function is: $C = e^{0.377} Q^{0.789}$ where the first component of the right-hand side of the equation is the fixed cost and the second is the annual capacity of the dam.

Assume two possible water flow scenarios—Low and High. In these cases, the use of water by each country is given in the Table 6.1.

Using the dam cost function and the possible coalition formation between the countries, a cost can be assigned to each coalition of countries (Table 6.2).

The equation system describing the core is (for the high flow):

$$\Omega_A \leq 1,112 \tag{6.4}$$

$$\Omega_B \leq 1,208 \tag{6.5}$$

$$\Omega_C \leq 1,013 \tag{6.6}$$

$$\Omega_D \leq 5,610 \tag{6.7}$$

$$\Omega_A + \Omega_B \leq 2,005 \tag{6.8}$$

$$\Omega_A + \Omega_C \leq 1,836 \tag{6.9}$$

Table 6.2. Dam cost for the High flow scenario.

Coalitions of countries	Water dammed	Dam cost
{A}	4,500	1,112
{B}	5,000	1,208
{C}	4,000	1,013
{D}	35,500	5,610
{AB}	9,500	2,005
{AC}	8,500	1,836
{AD}	39,500	6,172
{BC}	9,000	1,921
{BD}	40,000	6,233
{CD}	39,000	6,110
{ABC}	13,500	2,645
{ABD}	44,500	6,780
{ACD}	43,500	6,660
{BCD}	44,000	6,720
{ABCD}	48,500	7,257

$$\Omega_A + \Omega_D \leq 6{,}172 \qquad (6.10)$$

$$\Omega_B + \Omega_C \leq 1{,}921 \qquad (6.11)$$

$$\Omega_B + \Omega_D \leq 6{,}233 \qquad (6.12)$$

$$\Omega_C + \Omega_D \leq 6{,}110 \qquad (6.13)$$

$$\Omega_A + \Omega_B + \Omega_C \leq 2{,}645 \qquad (6.14)$$

$$\Omega_A + \Omega_B + \Omega_D \leq 6{,}780 \qquad (6.15)$$

$$\Omega_B + \Omega_C + \Omega_D \leq 6{,}720 \qquad (6.16)$$

$$\Omega_A + \Omega_C + \Omega_D \leq 6{,}660 \qquad (6.17)$$

$$\Omega_A + \Omega_B + \Omega_C + \Omega_D \leq 7{,}257 \qquad (6.18)$$

where Ω for $i = A, B, C, D$ is the final allocation, in the cooperative solution, to player i.

A method to calculate the possible extreme core allocations is based on incremental contributions of players joining existing

Table 6.3. Extreme points if the core for the case of high flows.

| Maximum incremental allocation | | | | Coalition formation |
A	B	C	D	sequence
1,112	893	640	4,612	ABCD
1,112	893	477	4,775	ABDC
1,112	809	724	4,612	ACBD
1,112	597	724	4,824	ACDB
1,112	608	477	5,060	ADBC
1,112	597	548	5,060	ADCB
797	1,208	640	4,612	BACD
797	1,208	477	4,775	BADC
721	1,208	713	4,612	BCAD
537	1,208	713	4,799	BCDA
547	1,208	477	5,025	BDAC
537	1,208	487	5,025	BDCA
823	809	1,013	4,612	CABD
823	597	1,013	4,824	CADB
724	908	1,013	4,612	CBAD
537	908	1,013	4,799	CBDA
550	597	1,013	5,097	CDAB
537	610	1,013	5,097	CDBA
562	608	477	5,610	DABC
562	482	603	5,610	DACB
547	623	417	5,610	DBAC
672	623	487	5,610	DBCA
550	597	500	5,610	DCAB
537	610	500	5,610	DCBA

coalitions (we will not discuss this technical approach here). However, the results are presented in Table 6.3.

The core provides a wide range of possible solutions that comply with the equation system (6.4)–(6.18) that was presented above. This system is solved with a mathematical programming procedure, which yields $\Omega = (797, 1{,}208, 477, 4{,}775)$. However, this is not the only solution, or even the best solution.

The extreme points of the core provide an ordering of the players' preferences. Player A is likely to prefer allocations closer to 537 than to 1,112. Player B will prefer allocations closer to 482 than to 1,208, Player C will prefer allocations closer to 477 than to 1,013, and player D will prefer allocations closer to 4,612 than to 5,610.

We introduce now two very common solution concepts, the Shapley Value and the Nash–Hansanyi (N–H) solution, and compare them.

6.4.1.2 *The Shapley Value*

The Shapley Value (Shapley, 1953) scheme allocates Φ_j to each player based on the weighted average of their contributions to <u>all</u> possible coalitions and sequences. In the calculation (Equation (6.19)), an equal probability is assigned for the formation of any coalition of the same size, assuming all possible sequences of formation.

The Shapley value is calculated as

$$\Phi_j = \sum_{\substack{s \subseteq S \\ j \in s}} \frac{(n - |s|)!(|s| - 1)!}{n!} [\nu(s) - \nu(s - \{j\})] \quad \forall j \in N \qquad (6.19)$$

where Φ_j is the Shapley cost allocation to Player j, n is the number of players in the game, and $|s|$ is the number of members in coalition s.

Using Equation (6.19) and the results shown in Table 6.3, the Shapley allocation of the regional game in the case of high flows is $= (745.7, 822.1, 627.7, 5, 061.5)$. The Shapley allocation satisfies the core requirements, and is fair and efficient. The Shapley value is a unique allocation, and it is in the core.

6.4.1.3 *The Nash–Harsanyi solution*

The N–H solution (Harsanyi, 1959) to an n-person bargaining game is a modification of the two-player Nash solution (Nash, 1953). This solution concept maximizes the product of the grand coalition members' additional utilities (income, or savings in this example) from cooperation, compared with the non-cooperative case, subject to core conditions, by equating the utility gains of all players. The N–H solution satisfies the Nash axioms (that were presented in the previous lecture) (Nash, 1953), it is unique, and it is contained in the core (if it exists). The solution might provide unfair allocations if there are big utility differences between the players (e.g., very rich player and very poor player).

$$\max \prod_{j \in N} (v\{j\} - \Lambda_j) \qquad (6.20)$$

subject to the core conditions, where Λ_j is the N–H allocation that satisfies efficiency and individual rationality conditions.

Maximizing Equation (6.20), subject to the relevant core conditions in Equations (6.1–6.3) and the data in Table 6.3, yields an optimization problem the solution to which is the cost allocation for the high flows, $h = (690.5, 786.5, 591.5, 5, 188.5)$.

6.5 Measures for Acceptability and Stability of the Solutions

The fulfillment of the core conditions for an allocation scheme is a necessary condition for its acceptability by the players. Thus, solutions not included in the core are also not stable. Although an allocation scheme may fulfill the core requirements, it still may not be accepted by some players that might view it as relatively unfair compared with another allocation. Allocations which are viewed as unfair by some players are less stable. Some players might threaten to leave the grand coalition and form a sub-coalition because of their critical position in the grand coalition. The stability of any solution is important given the existence of fixed investments some times, and a more stable solution might be preferred even if it is harder to implement.

A simple measure for stability of an allocation scheme is the number of players that prefer it over other schemes. In the cost allocation game, a player will prefer a scheme that assigns them the least cost and compare that assigned cost to their cost in the singleton coalition.

A Power Index (Loehman *et al.*, 1979) compares the gains in the grand coalition to a player with the gains to the coalition from that player joining the coalition.

The Propensity to Disrupt (Gately, 1974) the grand coalition is the ratio of how much the other players in the grand coalition would lose if player i refuses to cooperate to how much player i itself would lose if it refuses to cooperate.

We do not present here the calculations of these three measures of acceptability/stability of a cooperative solution in this example. Numerical results and explanations can be found in Dinar and Howitt (1997: Section 3.3).

6.6 Summary

The ability to meet existing or future environmental standards at an acceptable cost often requires regional approaches due to externalities or treatment economies of scale. Cooperative solutions to regional pollution problems have lower political and transaction costs than non-cooperative solutions. Several questions need to be addressed in the case of regional actions to meet environmental regulations. First, the technical feasibility of each cooperative arrangement; second, the economic feasibility compared to other alternatives; and, third, the regional setting in which this solution will operate. Assuming the existence of technical and economic feasibility, acceptability and stability of the cooperative solutions are the conditions for their success.

This chapter attempts to define acceptable and stable mechanisms of environmental control cost allocations among established resource management regions. Different schemes and states of nature that may affect the regional arrangements are tested, using a drainage problem in the San Joaquin Valley of California. In this chapter, we demonstrated, employing the best available data from that region, that, in order to solve a regional water quality problem, several necessary conditions for cooperation are met.

In our analysis we considered the variable nature of the drainage flows. For example, the continued drought and the reduction of surface irrigation water to the region diminished the amount of drainage water generated and disposed. In long-term planning of a treatment facility, the changes in water quantities for treatment need to be incorporated into the allocation scheme, or the solution will be unstable over time and cooperation is discouraged.

The analysis provides clear empirical evidence that the different allocation schemes have different outcomes in terms of their acceptability to the players, and the derived stability. The allocation schemes can be ranked by the players for their fairness in different ways. However, the N–H and proportional allocation are always ranked first and the marginal cost is always ranked last. The regional problem has also been analyzed for two representative state of nature drainage flow scenarios. Among the allocation schemes, N–H, proportional, Shapley, and SCRB were found.

Stability index for the low flow game.

Mechanisms for allocation of environmental control cost were more stable in both drainage scenarios ($S < 0.25$) while the nucleolus and the marginal cost allocations were less stable ($0.40 < S < 0.90$).

The stability of game theory allocations (Shapley, nucleolus) increases as drainage flows increase; however, the stability of the traditional cost allocation methods (SCRB, marginal cost) decreases as drainage flows increase. The proportional allocation method and the N–H solution have the same degree of stability in both drainage flow scenarios analyzed.

The propensity to disrupt index suggests that the players in the game do not consider defection from the grand coalition. Several players have higher levels of (negative) propensity to disrupt values than others, but in general it can be said that all six allocation schemes are stable.

Annex A6.1: Coalitions and Characteristic Functions

We start with several definitions:

- N is the set of all players in the negotiation game.
- S ($S \subseteq N$) is the set of all feasible coalitions in the game.
- s ($s \in S$) is a feasible coalition in the game.
- The non-cooperative coalitions, are $\{j\}, j = 1, 2, \ldots, N$.
- The grand coalition is $\{N\}$.

The number of possible coalitions between a group of n players is $2^n - 1$.

A corner stone of n-person CGT is the Characteristic Function (von Neumann and Morgenstern, 2004):

- A characteristic function (v) of a group (coalition) captures in a single numerical index the potential worth (value) of that group of players.
- $v\{j\}$ is the value of non-cooperative coalitions—what each player may obtain if she continues to be on her own (*status quo*).
- $v(s)$ is the value of partial coalitions—what sub-groups of players may obtain if they form these sub-groups.
- $v(N)$ is the value of the grand coalition of all players in the negotiation.
- Several requirements from the characteristic function:

    1. Superadditivity—the value of a coalition created from two sub-coalitions must be at least as the sum of values of the two sub-coalitions.

The characteristic function doesn't provide additional information on the power relations among the group members, or how the value of the coalition (the value created by the coalition) will be allocated among the members.

References

Axelrod, R., 1985. *The Evolution of Cooperation*. Cambridge, MA: Basic Books.

Colman, A. M., 1995. *Game Theory and its Applications in the Social and Biological Sciences*. Routledge: London.

Davis, M. D., 1983. *Game Theory—a Non-technical Introduction*. Monoela (NY): Dover Publications.

Dinar, A. and Howitt, R. E., 1997. Mechanisms for Allocation of Environmental Cost: Empirical Tests of Acceptability and Stability. *Journal of Environmental Management*, 49:183–203.

Dixit, A. K. and Skeath, S., 1999. *Games of Strategy*. New York: W. W. Norton & Co.

Gately, D., 1974. Sharing the Gains from Regional Cooperation: A Game Theoretic Application to Planning Investment in Electric Power. *International Economic Review*, 15:195–208.

Harsanyi, J. C., 1959. A Bargaining Model for the Cooperative n-Person Game. In: Tucker, A. W. and Luce, D. R. (Eds.), *Contributions to the Theory of Games*, vol. 4. Princeton, NJ: Princeton University Press, pp. 324–356.

Loehman, E., Orlando, J., Tschirhart, J., and Winstion, A., 1979. Cost Allocation for a Regional Wastewater Treatment System. *Water Resources Research*, 15:193–202.

Nash, J. F., 1953. Two Person Cooperative Game. *Econometrica*, 21:128–140.

Shapley, L. S., 1953. A Value for n-Person Games. *Annals of Mathematics Studies*, 28:307–318, and In: Kuhn, H. W. and Tucker, A. W. (Eds.), *Contributions to the Theory of Games*, vol. II. Princeton: Princeton University Press.

Shubik, M., 1982. *Game Theory in the Social Sciences*. Cambridge, MA: MIT Press.

von Neumann, J. and Morgenstern, O., 2004. *Theory of Games and Economic Behavior*, 60th-Anniversary edition. Princeton: Princeton University Press.

Chapter 7

Climate Change Policy*

Abstract

In this chapter, we review the history of developing the climate change policies and the different parties involved in that process starting from 1992 and ending in 2020. The chapter also demonstrates why climate change is defined as a global bad and how, even as a global bad, it affects different countries at different levels. Then, a milestone agreement, the Kyoto Protocol, is discussed with all mitigation and adaptation mechanisms that were built into it.

7.1 The History of Climate Change Talks/Negotiations

In 1992, the United Nations recognized, in the Rio Earth summit, that climate change is a serious matter, and it affects different countries in different ways. At that time, negotiations among countries started and have produced over the recent three decades notable accords, including the known Kyoto Protocol and Paris Agreement. But leaders have struggled to maintain momentum and failed to slow

---

*It is assumed that the reader is familiar with the physical background aspects associated with climate change. Therefore, some details are not addressed. Most of this chapter is dedicated to explaining the unequal distribution of climate change negative effects among developed and developing countries and how such disparity influences the negotiation for a global policy.

down the rise in global temperature. In this section, we review the milestones that such talks have gone through, while emphasizing the opposed interests of major players and especially the blocks of developing and developed (industrialized) countries.

7.1.1 *1992: Groundbreaking Rio Earth summit*

The summit results in some of the first international agreements on climate change, which become the foundation for future accords. Among them is the UN Framework Convention on Climate Change (UNFCCC), which aims to prevent 'dangerous' human interference in the climate system, acknowledges that human activities contribute to climate change, and recognizes climate change as an issue of global concern. The UNFCCC, which went into force in 1994, does not legally bind signatories to reduce greenhouse gas (GHGs) emissions and gives no targets or timetables for doing so. But it requires frequent meetings between the ratifying countries, known as the Conference of the Parties (COP). As of 2019, it has been ratified by 197 countries, including the United States.

7.1.2 *1995: First meeting of UNFCCC signatories*

UNFCCC signatories gather for the first COP, or COP1, in Berlin. The United States pushes back against legally binding targets and timetables, but it joins other parties in agreeing to negotiations to strengthen commitments on limiting GHGs. The concluding document, known as the Berlin Mandate, lays the groundwork for what becomes the Kyoto Protocol, but it is criticized by environmental activists as a political solution that does not prompt immediate action.

7.1.3 *1997: In Kyoto, first legally binding climate treaty*

At COP3 in Japan, the conference adopts the Kyoto Protocol UNFCCC (1997). The legally binding treaty requires developed countries to reduce emissions by an average of 5% below 1990 levels and establishes a system to monitor countries' progress. But the protocol does not compel developing countries, including high carbon emitters China and India, to take action. It also creates a carbon market for countries to trade emission units and encourage sustainable development, a system known as 'cap and trade.' Countries must now work out the details of implementing and ratifying the protocol.

7.1.4 *2001: Breakthrough in Bonn, but without the US*

The Kyoto Protocol is in jeopardy after talks collapse in November 2000 and the United States withdraws in March 2001, with Washington saying that the protocol is not in the country's 'economic best interest.' In July 2001, negotiators in Bonn, Germany, reach breakthroughs on green technology, agreements on emissions trading, and compromises on how to account for carbon sinks (natural reservoirs that take in more carbon than they release). In October, countries agree on the rules for meeting targets set by the Kyoto Protocol, paving the way for its entry into force.

7.1.5 *2005: Kyoto Protocol takes effect*

The Kyoto Protocol enters into force in February after it is ratified by enough countries to account for at least 55% of global emissions. Notably, it does not include the United States, the world's leading carbon emitter. Between 2008 and 2012, when the protocol is set to expire, countries are supposed to reduce emissions by their pledged amounts: the European Union commits to reduce emissions by 8% below 1990 levels, Japan commits to 5%, and Russia commits to keeping levels steady with 1990 levels.

7.1.6 *2007: Negotiations begin for Kyoto 2.0*

Before COP13 in Bali, Indonesia, the UN Intergovernmental Panel on Climate Change (IPCC) releases a new report with its strongest language yet confirming that global warming is 'most likely' caused by human activity. During the conference, discussions begin on a stronger successor to the Kyoto Protocol. But they come to a standstill after the United States objects to a widely backed proposal that calls for all industrialized nations to cut GHG emissions by specific targets. US officials argue that developing countries must also make commitments. A delegate from Papua New Guinea tells the United States to 'get out of the way' if it does not want to lead the international response to climate change. Washington eventually backs down, and the parties adopt the Bali Action Plan, which establishes the goal of drafting a new climate agreement by 2009.

7.1.7 *2009 (September): US joins bold statements at UN*

Three months ahead of the target date for a new agreement, several world leaders pledge actions during a UN summit on climate change hosted by Secretary-General Ban Ki-moon. Chinese President Hu Jintao announces a plan to cut emissions by a 'notable margin' by 2020, marking the first time Beijing commits to reducing its rate of GHG emissions. Japanese Prime Minister Yukio Hatoyama pledges to reduce emissions by 25%. US President Barack Obama, in his first UN address, says the United States is determined to act and lead, but he doesn't offer any new proposals. Ban expresses hope that leaders will reach a 'substantive deal' during the upcoming conference in Copenhagen.

7.1.8 *2009 (December): Disappointment in Copenhagen*

The successor to the Kyoto Protocol is supposed to be finalized at COP15 in Copenhagen, but the parties only come up with a nonbinding document that is 'taken note of,' not adopted. The Copenhagen Accord [PDF] acknowledges that global temperatures should not increase by 2°C above preindustrial levels, though representatives from developing countries sought a target of 1.5°C. (A 2009 report from the American Meteorological Society predicts a 3.5°C to 7.4°C increase in less than one hundred years.) After leading the negotiations, US President Barack Obama tells the conference that the accord is 'not enough.' Some countries later vow to follow the accord—though it remains nonbinding—and make their own pledges.

7.1.9 *2010: Temperature target set in Cancun*

There is increased pressure to reach a consensus in Mexico during COP16 after the failure in Copenhagen and NASA's announcement that 2000–2009 was the warmest decade ever recorded. Countries commit for the first time to keep global temperature increases below 2°C in the Cancun Agreements. Approximately 80 countries, including China, India, and the United States, as well as the European Union, submit emissions reduction targets and actions, and they agree on stronger mechanisms for monitoring progress. But analysts say it's not enough to stay below the 2° target. The Green Climate Fund, a $100 billion fund to assist developing countries in mitigating and adapting to climate change, is also established. As of 2019, only around $3 billion has been contributed.

7.1.10 *2011: New accord to apply to all countries*

The conference in Durban, South Africa, nearly collapses after the world's three biggest polluters—China, India, and the United States—reject an accord proposed by the European Union. But they eventually agree to work toward drafting a new, legally binding agreement in 2015 at the latest. The new agreement will differ from the Kyoto Protocol in that it will apply to both developed and developing countries. With the Kyoto Protocol set to expire in a few months, the parties agree to extend it until 2017.

7.1.11 *2012: No deal in Doha*

Negotiators in Doha for COP18 extend the Kyoto Protocol until 2020, but remaining participants account for just 15% of global GHG emissions. By this time, Canada has withdrawn from the treaty, and Japan and Russia say they will not accept new commitments. (The United States never signed on.) Environmental groups criticize countries for not reaching an effective agreement as Typhoon Bopha slams the Philippines, which they say exemplifies a rise in extreme weather caused by climate change. One of the conference's successes is the Doha Amendment, under which developed countries agree to assist developing countries mitigate and adapt to the effects of climate change. The agreement also sets delegates on the path toward a new treaty.

7.1.12 *2013: Walkout in Warsaw*

During the first week of COP19 in Poland, a grouping of developing countries, known as the Group of Seventy-Seven (G77), and China propose a new funding mechanism to help vulnerable countries deal with 'loss and damage' caused by climate change. Developed countries oppose the mechanism, so the G77's lead negotiators walk out of the conference. Talks eventually resume, and governments agree to a mechanism that falls short of what developing countries wanted. Countries also agree on how to implement an initiative to end deforestation known as REDD+, but the conference is described by analysts as the 'least consequential COP in several years'.

7.1.13 *2015: Landmark Paris Agreement reached*

196 countries agree to what experts call the most significant global climate agreement in history, known as the Paris Agreement. Unlike past accords, it requires nearly all countries—both developed and developing—to set emissions reduction goals. However, countries can choose their own targets and there are no enforcement mechanisms to ensure they meet them. Under the agreement, countries are supposed to submit targets known as nationally determined contributions. The mission of the Paris Agreement, which enters into force in November 2016, is to keep global temperature rise below 2°C and pursue efforts to keep it below 1.5°C. But analysts urge more action to achieve this goal. In 2017, President Donald J. Trump withdraws the United States from the agreement, saying that it imposes 'draconian financial and economic burdens' on the country.

7.1.14 *2018: Rules for Paris Agreement decided*

Just ahead of COP24 in Katowice, Poland, a new IPCC report warns of devastating consequences—including stronger storms and dangerous heat waves—if the average global temperature rises

1.5°C above preindustrial levels and projects that it could reach that level by 2030. Despite the report, countries do not agree to stronger targets. They do, however, largely settle on the rules for implementing the Paris accord, covering questions including how countries should report their emissions. They do not agree on rules for carbon trading, however, and push that discussion to 2019.

7.1.15 *2019 (September): UN Chief Plans Climate Action summit*

UN Secretary-General Antonio Guterres organizes the UN Climate Action Summit for world leaders in New York. Countries are mandated by the Paris Agreement to submit revised nationally determined contributions plans by the following year, so the meeting is a chance for leaders to share their ideas. But leaders of the world's top carbon-emitting countries, including the United States and China, do not attend. At the summit, Guterres asks countries to submit plans to cut GHG emissions by 45% by 2030 and reach carbon neutrality by 2050.

7.1.16 *2019 (December): Lost opportunity in Madrid*

COP25 is marked by a lack of progress on major climate issues despite a year of dire warnings from scientists, record heatwaves, and worldwide protests demanding action. Negotiators are unable to finalize rules for a global carbon market, and they disagree over whether to compensate developing countries devastated by effects of climate change including rising sea levels and extreme weather. The conference's final declaration does not explicitly call on countries to increase their climate pledges made under the Paris Agreement, and Secretary-General Guterres describes the talks as a lost opportunity.

7.1.17 *2020 (April): Talks postponed amid coronavirus pandemic*

The United Nations postpones COP26, originally scheduled for November 2020, until 2021 because of a pandemic of a new coronavirus disease, known as COVID-19. Countries were expected to strengthen their emissions reduction goals set under the Paris Agreement at the conference in Glasgow. Amid the pandemic, emissions fall worldwide as many countries implement nationwide shutdowns that drastically slow economic activity. But experts predict that the reductions won't last, with governments under pressure to boost output and disregard the environment to save their struggling economies.

7.2   Climate Change as a Global Bad

It is already known that climate change (or global warming) has been a man-made phenomenon resulting from economic development with high consumption of fossil fuels burned in the process to produce energy and releasing great volumes of GHGs represented well by carbon dioxide (CO_2). It is a global bad in the sense that one polluter in one part of the world contributes to the CO_2 pollution globally (Figure 7.1). Climate change is real and it poses a great threat to the planet and its inhabitants and ecosystems. But, it's not just CO_2 that is the problem. Additional gases include methane and nitrous oxide, also produced in large quantities through various sources including animal waste and fertilizer use.

A very simplified explanation goes like that: the sun sends heat radiation waves toward planet Earth (downward arrows in Figure 7.1). In addition, as a living organ, planet Earth produces heat from all economic and other activities in addition to the heat originated by the sun (upward arrows in Figure 7.1). However, due to the atmospheric cover (the black square structure surrounding planet Earth in Figure 7.1 that acts as a greenhouse) that acts as a trap, not all heat can be released and is trapped inside that greenhouse. The more pollution is produced on planet Earth, the thicker the impermeable layer surrounding planet Earth and the higher the inside temperature.

It is already agreed that the responsibility for global warming lays mainly on the shoulders of the developed (industrialized) countries, who have been developing faster and more energy-intensely and

No matter who pollutes and where, all are affected

Figure 7.1. Global warming scheme.
Note: Because planet Earth is covered/surrounded by the atmosphere that traps the pollution (GHGs), we experience a 'greenhouse effect' resulting in (global) warming.

producing most of the CO_2 emissions, since the industrial revolution. At the same time accumulated evidence suggests that the negative effects of climate change are realized in the developing world. A demonstration of the distribution of the negative climate change effects on the countries in the world can be seen in Figure 7.2.

Therefore, the world faces a serious equity issue with respect to the distribution of climate impacts across rich and poor countries. Developing countries were predicted to be more vulnerable to climate change than developed countries due to their location (see Figure 7.2), but also because so much of the developing country economies are in climate sensitive sectors such as agriculture. Low technology operations (such as agriculture) are expected to have less substitution and thus will affect the adaptation ability of the developing countries. In addition, human capital and governance are subject to major challenges in the developing world.

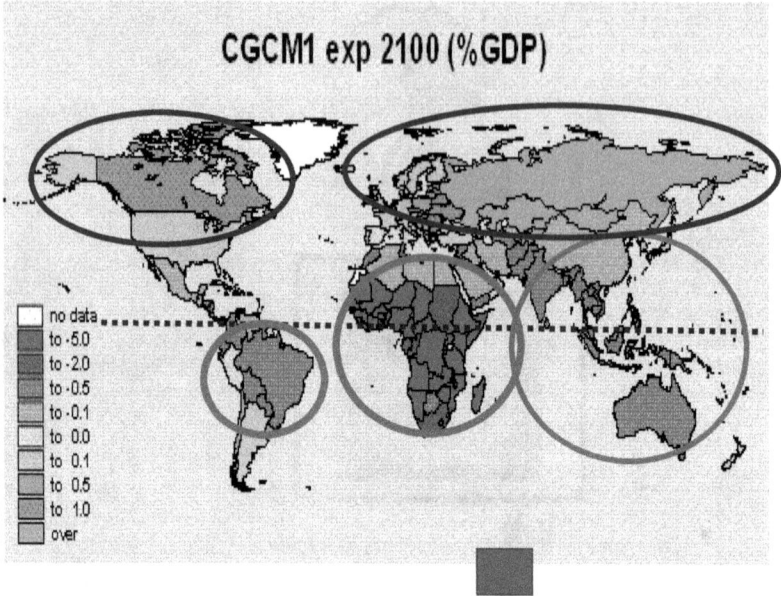

Figure 7.2.   Future impact on world economy (change in %GDP).
Source: Mendelsohn *et al.* (2005).

The world economy was simulated (in Figure 7.2) following a given scenario of climate change and a given Global Circulation Model (GCM) to predict the impact of global warming on the economy of all countries. This scenario and GCM model produced a range, between –5% and +5%, of change to GDP by 2100. As can be seen in Figure 7.2, some countries will realize an increase in GDP and some will realize a reduction in GDP. What is immediately seen is that the negative effects are concentrated around and south to the equator, or in other words, where all developing countries are located.

7.3 Dealing with Global Warming

Section 7.1 provides the history of the discourse around global warming and agreements' negotiations in the world. As is clearly seen from that brief history, there have been two suggested courses of action around which conflicts arose: mitigation and adaptation.

In this section, we briefly review the principles on the basis of suggested mitigation and adaptation policies (Schoeder, 2010).

The first serious agreed upon attempt to address global warming was the 1997 Kyoto protocol, which is a furtherance of the UNFCCC from 1992. What was also agreed is to meet frequently (annually) under the title Conference of the Parties (COP) to the UNFCCC. All is under the understanding of the needed reduction of emissions of GHGs into the atmosphere in order to reduce global warming. Main GHGs that were identified include: carbon dioxide (CO_2), methane (CH_4), NO_x, and ozone—depleting CFCs (chlorofluorocarbons).

So, how is that achieved? First, a global quantity to be reduced needs to be identified; second, allocation of that quantity, to each of the world countries has to be agreed on, and third, a timeline for reaching this target is also to be agreed upon. Admittedly, these three objectives are hard to manage and are subject to significant disagreements among the world countries, as well as being most likely subject to high costs of implementation in certain countries. Therefore, it could be anticipated that disagreements will prevail. But, some understanding/agreements were reached. First, it was understood and agreed that emission targets will be set only for each industrial country (developing countries were 'exempt'). Second, it was recognized that the cost of reaching such emission targets could be very high, suggesting a need for an adjustment period; an adjustment period of 10 years was set. Finally, countries agreed on a binding period by the end of which all signatories to the Kyoto Protocol have to abide by the agreement; a binding period for compliance was set for 2008–2012 (when the treaty expires).

7.3.1 *Handling country mitigation targets*

The UNFCCC divides countries in two main groups:

1. Annex I parties/countries that include the industrialized countries and countries with 'economies in transition'/EITs (the Russian Federation, the Baltic States, and several other Central and Eastern European countries).
2. All the others are called non-Annex I countries.

Table 7.1.   Agreed CO_2 target reductions in CO_2 (millions of CO_2 ton-equivalent) in Annex B countries (industrialized and emerging economies).

Country	Base year CO_2 emission (1990)	Kyoto target in 2012 (90% of 1990 with adjustments)	Actual CO_2 emissions in 2005
Australia	423	457	525
Canada	599	563	747
Germany	1,226	1,128	1,001
Japan	1,272	1,196	1,360
Netherlands	213	196	212
Russian Federation	2,990	2,990	2,133
UK	776	714	657
USA	6,103	5,676	7,241
Total (including all countries)	18,266.3	17,304.3	17,609.4

Source: UNFCCC (1997: Annex B).

The Kyoto Protocol commits Annex I Parties/countries to individual, legally binding targets that limit or reduce their GHG emissions to X% of 1990 level (see sample country reductions in Table 7.1). The individual targets for Annex I countries are listed in the Kyoto Protocol's Annex B (= Annex I to the UNFCCC).[1]

Table 7.1 suggests that some of the Annex I (B) countries will face a hard time to reach the targets set up for them while some of the countries already reached these targets. But Table 7.1 doesn't tell the whole story. There were major negotiation efforts by some countries to get even lower targets than what they were assigned. For example, in the case of Australia and the Russian Federation, the Kyoto Target reflects a 'discount' they were able to get.

Recognizing the high adjustment mitigation costs for many countries, the Kyoto Protocol introduced for the Annex I countries

---

[1]From here on we use Annex B and Annex I interchangeably.

alternative options by which they can meet their CO_2 targets. Countries can:

1. Reduce CO_2 emission;
2. Cooperate with another Annex I country (or countries) to reduce their CO_2 emissions; there are more options for this type of cooperation and they will be discussed in what follows; and
3. Invest in Clean Development Mechanism (CDM) projects to be hosted by non-Annex I countries. This option will be discussed in Chapter 8.

Options 2 and 3 are called 'Flexibility Mechanisms of the Kyoto Protocol'.

7.3.2 *How to achieve the CO_2 reduction standards?*

Due to special circumstances, countries face different cost of reducing (mitigating) their CO_2 emissions. In economic terms, this is reflected in different Marginal Abatement cost functions (different slopes). Therefore, during the negotiations on mitigation targets for different countries, the point of fairness and justice has always come up. The question of whether or not it is fair to impose similar CO_2 reduction standards (targets) on all countries, or to differentiate among countries, based on certain criteria.

Indeed, negotiations over country level CO_2 reduction target took place in various occasions over the years, leading to changes and adjustments in country-levels of reductions, and especially in the negotiations leading to the Kyoto Protocol (see Table 7.1). But these differential standards were not sufficient and left several countries with a very high mitigation cost of their CO_2 reduction targets.

To address such inequalities and dis-incentives, the concept of Flexibility Mechanisms (to help polluter countries meet their targets) was introduced: the idea is that Countries invest (abate) in reducing emissions not necessarily on their own land but anywhere, mainly because climate change negative effects are global (see Figure 7.1). The following mechanisms were introduced.

7.3.2.1 *International emission trading*

An Annex B country can cut emissions by more than its reduction target (commitment) and sell 'permits'—Certificates of Emission Reductions (CERs) (for profit) to another country that cuts by less than its commitment.

7.3.2.2 *Joint implementation*

Two Annex B countries may undertake joint projects to reduce emissions and agree on how to divide the reduction target emissions against their quota.

7.3.2.3 *The Clean Development Mechanism*

The CDM is a special flexibility option that was designed to allow developed countries to invest in projects in developing countries to reduce CO_2 emissions. We designated Chapter 8 to the CDM and thus will not discuss it now.

7.4 Kyoto's Flexible Mechanisms (Summary)

Designed for helping Annex 1 (=B) countries reduce the cost of meeting their emission reduction targets in 2008–2012. International Emission Trading permits countries to transfer parts of their 'allowed emissions' ('assigned amount units', AAUs).

Joint Implementation (JI) allows countries to claim credit for emission reductions that arise from investment in other industrialized countries, which result in a transfer of equivalent 'emission reduction units' (ERUs) between the countries.

The CDM allows emission-reduction projects that assist in creating sustainable development in developing countries to generate CERs for use by the investor country.

Activities Implemented Jointly (AIJ) PILOTS between 1990 and 2002 to test novel aspects of the project-related provisions to benefit in the post treaty activities.

Public and private sector companies were authorized to participate in the flexible mechanisms.

References

Mendelsohn, R., Dinar, A., and Williams, L., 2005. The Distributional Impact of Climate Change on Rich and Poor Countries. *Environment and Development Economics*, 11(2):159–178.

Schoeder, H., 2010. The History of International Climate Change Politics: Three Decades of Progress, Process and Procrastination. In: Max Boykoff (Ed.), *The Politics of Climate Change: A Survey*. London: Routledge.

UNFCCC, 1997. Kyoto Protocol to the United Nations Framework Convention on Climate Change.

Chapter 8

The CDM: A Cooperation Mechanism?*

Abstract

Following the 1992 Earth Summit in Rio de Janeiro, Brazil, countries took up the complicated task of finding a common approach that would slow down the accumulation of greenhouse gas (GHG) emissions in the atmosphere and delay changes to the planet's climate. A widespread concern among many of the participants in the newly formed United Nations Framework Convention on Climate Change (UNFCCC) was that the emission reductions needed to significantly affect climate change would cost so much that it could jeopardize the chances of a coordinated international solution. To address this concern, several flexible mechanisms were designed, including the Clean Development Mechanism (CDM). While many · had high hopes from the CDM, others were concerned with its performance and achievements, and whether or not it will be continued beyond 2012. Critics argue that it has not delivered on the sustainable development objective for which it was established, and that projects are unevenly distributed, both geographically and sectorally.

8.1 Introduction

The Kyoto Protocol, which is the umbrella global policy under which the Clean Development Mechanism (CDM) operated, has not been in effect for long time. However, it was so fundamental

---

*This chapter is based to some extent on Dinar *et al.* (2011).

133

and path-breaking that it should be studied. The CDM is one of the flexibility mechanisms that were introduced into the Kyoto Protocol. It allows Annex B (developed) countries to finance emission reduction projects in non-Annex B (developing) countries in such a way that they could contribute to two objectives: (1) reduction in greenhouse gases (GHGs); and (2) investment in development projects in the project host (developing) countries, which could help increase economic growth. In that sense, CDM had dual goals, and thus, has been watched very closely by both climate change and development advocacy groups. In this chapter, we will look at another aspect of CDM—the likelihood of bringing developing and developed countries into cooperation ventures and what promotes or inhibits such cooperation.

8.1.1 *Purpose and advantage of CDM*

Start by describing the purpose and likely advantages of the CDM, keeping in mind the dual objectives of that mechanism.

CDM encourages efforts aimed at reducing emissions in two ways: (1) through implementation of efficient activities, technologies, and techniques in developing countries; and (2) through the possibility for entities subjected to GHG emission targets to make additional emission reductions at lesser economic costs. This second purpose is the main attraction imbedded in CDM—the incremental reduction in GHGs leading to economic savings due to lowering average abatement costs.

Several advantages to CDM activities can be listed: (1) environmental advantages (both locally and globally) that are realized via reductions in GHG emissions and other environmental performances that help achieve sustainability of the ecosystem; (2) development advantages (economic and social for the host developing country) in the form of skills enhancement, job creation, improved governance, technological improvements; (3) economic advantages (for host and investor countries) in the form of direct advances from cooperation; and (4) also via a global market for exchanging carbon certificates that can best minimize the cost of achieving abatement of GHGs.

8.1.2 The opportunity and the dilemma with CDM

The CDM introduced both opportunities and dilemmas, which have to be seriously considered by policymakers.

8.1.2.1 The opportunity with CDM

An intrinsic comparative advantage of developing countries presented a remarkable opportunity for international trade in emission reductions with developed countries. All was about developed countries that faced carbon emissions reduction costs ranging from $25 to well over $50 per ton of CO_2 abated, while many developing countries could do the same at costs below $5 per ton of CO_2 abated. The difference between the abatement cost of $25–$50 per ton of CO_2 abated by the developed countries and the $5 per ton of CO_2 abated by the developing countries is the basis for a market for abatement permits.

Such trade could result, over the longer term, in considerable new and additional sources of finance in developing countries for low carbon energy and infrastructure development and improved land management.

8.1.2.2 The dilemmas with CDM

Several dilemmas arose, which created major obstacles for measuring and comparing performance of different CDM projects. These include:

1. How to define and measure carbon emission reductions within the framework of the Kyoto Protocol?
2. How to strengthen institutions in the host (developing) countries to better accommodate investment by the developed countries?
3. How to design a technically-strong market regulation structure for the trade between the investor countries who gained credit for their projects?

With this background (opportunities and dilemmas), let us move on to understand the cooperative nature of CDM.

8.2 CDM Objectives and Country Interests

The CDM[1] has come a long way since its launch in Marrakech in 2001. As of December 31, 2009, 5,687 CDM projects have been submitted to the CDM Board for validation (UNFCCC, 2010). It was expected that by 2012, the transition year when the Kyoto Protocol terminates and a new protocol is expected to be in place, the CDM Board would issue Certified Emission Reductions (CERs) equivalent to 800–1,150 million tons of Carbon dioxide (CO_2), approximately 42% of which would be abated through the CDM projects with partnerships between developed and developing countries (UNDP 2006, 11).[2]

The main objective of CDM is the GHG emission reductions that can be credited to the developed/investor country from projects implemented locally that support sustainable development in the developing-host country. Thus, CDM projects provide *a-priori* incentives for cooperation between host and investor countries. What are the attributes that make the CDM attractive to both host and investor countries? From the perspective of the host countries, investment in CDM projects can be seen as a means of development assistance, with all derived benefits to them. Thus, certain development attributes may play important roles in explaining levels of investment in CDM projects (Michaelowa and Michaelowa, 2007).

With a development objective, CDM trends can be explained, using several supply-side variables such as export promotion, political hegemony, donor budget allocations, and donor internal politics, which are mainly political economy variables. But, CDM trends can also be explained using demand-side considerations, where the developing countries formulate policies for investor country investments in CDM projects (Brechet and Lussis, 2006).

---

[1]The Kyoto Protocol, where more explanation on the CDM is provided, can be accessed at: http://unfccc.int/resource/docs/convkp/kpeng.html.

[2]The remaining projects is presented to the Board 'unilaterally' by the host country and do not necessarily involve foreign investors.

CDM is one of the various flexibility mechanisms such as Activities Implemented Jointly (AIJ), Joint Implementation (JI), and the CDM. For more information on AIJ, see Larson and Breustedt (2009). While the AIJ mechanism was in effect for a limited period and was not much attractive, it was used as a laboratory for the transition to the CDM.

8.2.1 *Kyoto's flexible mechanisms (Summary)*

Flexible mechanisms were designed to help Annex 1 (=B) countries reduce the cost of meeting their emission reduction targets by the end of the Kyoto agreement (2008–2012). To start with, CO_2 emissions, abatements, and/or trade are measured by 'assigned amount units' (AAUs), which are the allowable amounts of CO_2 assigned to each country.

For example, International Emission Trading permits countries to transfer parts of their 'allowed emissions' (AAUs) to other countries.

The JI mechanism allows countries to claim credit for emission reductions that arise from investment in other industrialized countries, which result in a transfer of equivalent 'emission reduction units' (ERUs) between the countries.

The CDM allows emission-reduction projects that assist in creating sustainable development in developing countries to generate 'CERs' for use by the investor country.

AIJ was another mechanism that was piloted between 1990 and 2002 with the objective to test novel aspects of the project-related provisions and to benefit in the post-treaty activities.

It should be emphasized that public and private sector companies were authorized to participate in any of the activities associated with either JI, AIJ, and CDM.

In this chapter, we identify factors that affect cooperation in carbon abatement projects between the governments of investor countries and host countries. We examine bilateral and multilateral CDM projects that were submitted to the UNFCCC between 2003 and 2009 in order to provide useful assessment of policy interventions for possible enhancement and extension of the CDM mechanism beyond 2012.

In particular, we are interested in understanding the grouping of countries in the CDM market, namely what explains cooperation in CDM between certain dyads of countries and non-cooperation between other dyads, and why certain countries are heavily involved while others are not. Let us use different measures to explain cooperation levels, including the number of joint CDM projects, the amount of CO_2 abated through CDM projects[3], and the level of investments in CDM projects. Examine characteristics of potential and actual investor-host country dyads, building on previous economic, political, and institutional work.

8.3   A Conceptual Framework

Let us look at CDM joint investment projects between two countries as a cooperative investment decision that is affected by both domestic factors and by economic and political interactions between these countries (refer also to Chapter 5). For this reason, variables related to mitigation opportunities and business environments are likely to affect investment decisions. At the same time, CDM projects require the issuance of an approval letter by the host country, which implies an additional level of cooperation. Consequently, let us utilize theories on international cooperation from international relations and international economics literature to explain this additional aspect of CDM cooperation.

In general, the determinants of cooperation relate to the bilateral characteristics of the pairing—for example trade, or unilateral characteristics of the investor and the host—for example, characteristics of their respective energy sectors. With this is mind, cooperation between a given dyad of countries i and h can be written as

$$C_{ih} = C(D_{ih}, \underline{I}_i, \underline{H}_h, \underline{I}_i \times \underline{H}_h). \tag{8.1}$$

---

[3]Investor countries' ultimate interest is in project CER credits, while host countries' interest is in the project investment funds in their countries and the likely multiplier effect.

where C is the level of cooperation, D represents the bilateral characteristics of a given host–investor pair, and $\underline{I}$ and $\underline{H}$ are vectors of variables strictly attributable to investor and host country i and h, respectively. Some interaction effects are between the investor (i) and the host (h) countries because certain variables in host countries are linked to considerations by investor countries.

CDM is expected to evolve into a form similar to Foreign Direct Investment (FDI) with opportunities for collaboration for project developers in investor countries to interact with host country investors (UNEP/GRID-Arendal, 2000). Therefore, let us apply the theory used for explaining FDI flows and stocks (Dunning, 1993, 1996; Nonnemberg *et al.*, 2004; Nunnenkamp, 2002; Siegel *et al.*, 2010). For a full list and explanation of the variables included in the analysis (and not discussed in this chapter), see Dinar *et al.* (2011).

The interest of firms in investor countries to consider foreign investments is affected by tax policy in the investor country (Dunning, 1996); transaction costs in the investor and host countries[4]; and the size and status of the market for the particular product/technology.[5] In the case of the CDM market, one should also consider the opportunity cost of meeting the Kyoto CO_2 reduction quota in the investor country. This depends on the country's economy structure and growth trajectory, the energy dependency of the economy, the level of CO_2 emission of the economy, and the clean energy resources it possesses (Velasco, 2007).

Vulnerability to climate change and natural disasters as an incentive for needed related actions has been well documented in the literature (Tsur and Zemel, 2008). Countries that face harsher environmental conditions would be early adopters of technologies, implement policies, and look for partners to sign treaties to ease their scarcity situation (Dinar, 2009).

But cooperation in the CDM market does not only depend on country-specific variables. Higher levels of joint investment indicate

---

[4]The ease of doing business variable aggregates all of these considerations.
[5]For discussion on additional variables, see Michaelowa and Michaelowa (2007).

higher degrees of cooperation, and no investment suggests no cooperation. Therefore, it is conceivable that international relations theories are likely to play some role alongside the profit maximization motives of the parties as in any international cooperation such as trade and FDI. Let us consider the literature on trade and FDI in the international conflict and cooperation in what follows (Polacheck *et al.*, 2007).

Like other forms of FDI, many CDM projects are irreversible with an economic value that depends upon a stream of future benefits. CDM investors are motivated by opportunities to meet emission reduction goals at lower cost. In a similar way, for CDM projects, there is an expectation that the projects will contribute to the host country's development objective and promote technology transfer, leading to multiplier effects from clean energy technologies.

Of special interest for our chapter is a subset of the studies by economists and political scientists that emphasizes how the strength of bilateral relationships affects FDI. Strong relationships are expected to lower transaction costs related to asymmetric information, search costs, and also to reduce many types of risks, especially political risks. Culture is often seen as an underlying determinant of strong bilateral ties. However, trade or security agreements between countries can also be seen as political institutions that reduce risks and transaction costs in a more formal way (Busse and Hefeker, 2007).

In a similar vein, aid donor–recipient relationships are affected also by the set of incentives facing the countries and existing governance (e.g., rent-seeking and corruption) structures (Paul, 2006). However, while democracy is significant, a greater importance is attributed by the donor countries to prior aid commitment, prior colonial ties, peace/war relationship in the recipient country, and its economic performance.

Several empirical studies argue that the extent of trade between countries provides an appropriate measure of their overall relations. Trade is a measure of both openness of a country to the global economy and the interaction between countries. The fear of losing the gains from trade deters conflict. Along the same lines, it has been argued that nations with cooperative political relations will engage in more trade, while conflictive nations are expected to trade less (Pollins, 1989). On the other hand, there has been the conjecture that high international trade, interdependence, and conflict are positively related (Waltz, 1979). Intensive interactions increase frictions among the countries, and therefore may lead to conflict.

International trade also acts as a contract enforcing mechanism. Stein argues that trade increases the likelihood of certain disputes between countries, but provides the parties with an opportunity to resolve them at a lower level of international conflict (Stein, 2003).

The above examination of the literature leads us to suppose that the level of relations among countries, measured by the extent of trade among them, is an appropriate measure for assessing the likelihood of cooperation (Neumayer, 2002). It is suggested therefore that the likelihood of a CDM project is relatively higher in the case of better or stronger relations among countries.

Such relations include also a history of colonial ties and membership in organizations that allow the states to achieve common objectives, such as International Governmental Organizations (IGOs). Colonial ties may be important in explaining CDM partnerships because many former colonies still maintain strong ties with their former colonizers (Dolšak and Dunn, 2006). IGOs may reduce the transaction cost of establishing and executing a CDM project (Mitchell and Hensel, 2007).

A final set of variables that enters the analytical framework includes those that provide an enabling environment for CDM cooperation in the host country. These include: governance, regulations, and business climate. When considering international cooperation, in general, and international investment in projects, in particular, domestic institutions may play a major role in either facilitating or inhibiting success of the cooperation-project in question (Dinar *et al.*, 2011). It reflects not only the state's interest in the project but also its ability to enter into, and honor, an investment agreement, which may require financial investments (Congleton, 1992: 412–413). The political stability and enabling institutions of a given state are, therefore, a principal mode to judge the viability of its domestic institutions, its general inclination to negotiate a project agreement, and its capacity to support the project.

Politically unstable countries have inferior institutional capacity to carry out a project, and more politically stable countries may, in turn, have little interest in cooperative ventures with those. Being part of an agreement requires both competence (also in terms of appropriate investment climate and supporting regulation) and stability inherent in a particular polity, which will in turn be able to honor the signed project agreement (Young, 1989: 365).

8.3.1   *What to expect?*

From the above discussion and based on previous work on FDI and AIJ determinants that resemble behavioral patterns similar to those of CDM, it is reasonable to hypothesize that, while all other variables are held constant, CDM level of cooperation between host and investor countries will increase (decrease) with higher (lower) levels of energy use (or economic development), and thus emission intensities, of its economy. Let us hypothesize that for an investor country the level of cooperation will decrease (increase) and for host country it will increase (decrease) with more renewable energy resources available in that country; and the more (less) vulnerable to climate change the economies are, the higher (lower) will the cooperation be.

Additional variables included in the empirical models are trade, business environment, political constraints, contiguity relationships, IGO membership, and governance. Based on our conceptual framework it can be expected that CDM level of cooperation between host and investor countries will increase (decrease) as trade widens (shrinks); will decrease (increase) as transaction cost of doing business (notice that the higher the value of *Ease of Doing Business* (EDB), the higher the transaction cost) increase (decrease); will decrease (increase) as level of political constraints increases (decreases); will increase (decrease) as length of the contiguity relationship grows (reduces); will increase (decrease) as the number of joint IGO membership increases (decreases); will increase (decrease) as governance level in the country increases (decreases); will increase (decrease) as climate change vulnerability level in the country increases (decreases).

8.4 Data Used and Some Empirical Specification

Data used in this study are derived from several different sources. A dataset consisting of all CDM projects that have been sent to the UNFCCC CDM Board for validation up until 31 December 2009 is obtained from the CDM/JI Pipeline Analysis and Database of the United Nations Environment Programme (UNEP) (Risoe Center, 2007. During that period, 5,687 CDM projects were sent to UNFCCC for validation. Table 8.1 displays projects that were submitted for approval even until 2010.

Table 8.1. Major types of CDM projects by December 2010.

Project type	Number of projects		Annual abatement		Abatement by 2012	
	Number	% total	$KtCO_2e$	% total	$KtCO_2e$	% total
Renewable resource-based	4,181	62.40	380,795	43.65	1,321,041	37.67
Methane, coal mine, etc.	1,142	17.04	159,812	18.32	700,088	19.96
Supply-side energy eff.	689	10.28	120,065	13.76	391,855	11.17
Demand-side energy eff.	301	4.49	11,976	1.37	46,327	1.32
Fossil fuel switch	170	2.54	52,637	6.03	223,290	6.37
HFCs, PFCs, & N_2O	116	1.73	138,099	15.83	792,811	22.61
Forest	66	0.99	5,547	0.64	21,051	0.60
Transport	35	0.52	3,543	0.41	10,467	0.30
Total number of projects	6,700	100.00	872,473	100.00	3,506,930	100.00

Note: $KtCO_2e$ stands for million tons of CO_2 equivalent.
Source: Rahman *et al.* (2012).

The dataset provides detailed information about each individual CDM project. That information includes project name, type, and current status, host country, expected emission reduction (ktCO$_2$ per year and total CO$_2$ reduction up until 2012 and 2030), credit buyers, potential energy outputs, etc.

Cooperation level was measured, using three variables, namely, *Number of Projects*, *Total CO$_2$ Abatement* in million tons of CERs of CO$_2$ equivalent (KtCO$_2$e), and *Volume of Investment* in million constant US dollars. When direct information on project costs is missing (only 2,804 projects have direct capital investment cost data), projects were categorized by type (nine types: subsectors) and size (two sizes: small and large) and calculated an average investment cost value for each type-size. Average investment cost was used to extrapolate to projects for which investment cost data were missing.

Eighteen projects that entered the CDM project cycle but were subsequently withdrawn were dropped from the dataset. Unilateral projects do not entail cooperation as such, and accordingly are not included in the analysis. However, they do represent an alternative to cooperative investment and likely affect bilateral investment outcomes. Consequently, the analysis takes into account the capacity to arrange domestic project financing and is included in the empirical models. For the multilateral projects (more than two countries), project activities are equally divided and attributed to all plausible dyads. For example, for a CDM project with $N > 2$ investor countries, N separate dyads are formed with the same host. Amount of carbon abatement and capital costs are then equally divided and attributed to n investor countries in the dyads. For the project count variable, there is no distinction between bilateral and multilateral cooperation. Projects that were subsequently rejected by the CDM board were still kept in the dataset because they indicate propensity to cooperate, which is the subject of this chapter.

As discussed in the context of Equation (8.1), both pair-wise and country-level characteristics are used as determinants in the statistical models. The following variables are used for the pair-wise measures: the level of bilateral trade among the countries

(*Trade*); a measure of the colonial ties between the countries (*Contiguity Length*); and a measure of the number of IGOs that both countries are members of (*Number of Joint IGO Membership*). Several additional country characteristics are also used for both the host and investor countries: the economic development of the countries measured in terms of energy use (*Average Annual Energy Use*), the energy sources' status (*Renewable Energy Stock*), climate vulnerabilities of the countries (*Impact Vulnerability*), governance level of the countries (*Governance*), and EDB in the countries.

Data for major development indicators such as annual gross domestic product (GDP), energy use, and the volume of CO_2 emissions for all countries of the world during 1960–2003 are obtained from the World Development Indicators (World Bank, 2007). In addition, country-level estimates of total energy available from nonrenewable sources (e.g., coal, oil, gas, oil shale, and bitumen) and annual energy available from renewable (e.g., solar, onshore and offshore wind, hydro, geothermal, and biofuels) sources are obtained from Buys *et al.* (2007). Two separate variables are constructed to reflect intensity of energy use in each country: *Average Annual Energy Use* and *Annual per Capita Energy Use*.

Measures for countries' vulnerability to climate change and emissions reduction mandates are important variables based on Buys *et al.* (2007), differentiating between sources of and impact of vulnerability. Impact vulnerability refers to the country's ability to sustain climate change impacts such as weather damage and sea-level rise. The quantitative score (scale of 1 to 100) of the *Impact Vulnerability* is determined for the host and investor countries of the CDM.

Estimates of six dimensions of governance (Voice and Accountability, Political Stability and Absence of Violence, Government Effectiveness, Regulatory Quality, Rule of Law, and Control of Corruption) of the host and investor countries are obtained from Kaufmann *et al.* (2007) to construct a *Governance* variable (using a Principal Component Analysis (PCA) that reflects overall governance level of the host and investor countries for each of the CDM projects.

The EDB indicators are used as a proxy for the transaction costs associated with the CDM projects implementation. EDB indicators, comparing business regulations and protection of property rights across 178 countries and over time, are obtained from World Bank (2007). The EDB index ranks economies from 1 to 178 by measuring regulations affecting 10 stages of a business's life (see Dinar *et al.*, 2011 for details). The rankings remain almost the same over the years, so a simple average of the rankings over the years is used to calculate the overall *EDB* in each country.

The political feasibility for government policy change is based on the political constraints index for each individual country constructed by Henisz (2002). The political constraint index (III) ranges from 0 to 1, with a larger value indicating that the political environment of a country is less favorable for government policy change. Thus, a country with a higher political constraints index faces a higher level of difficulty in CDM cooperation.

Three different measures are used to represent the strength of bilateral ties within each country dyad: colonial/dependency contiguity relationship, joint membership in IGOs, and bilateral trade. The length of colonial/dependency contiguity data are obtained from Correlates of War 2 Project.[6] Version 3.0 of the Correlates of War Colonial/Dependency Contiguity data identifies all contiguity relationships between states in the international system from 1816 through 2002 through their colonies or dependencies. That is, if two dependencies of two states are contiguous, or if one state is contiguous to a dependency of another, the dataset reports a contiguity relationship between the two main states. For the purpose of this study, the longest contiguity length (in years) for each dyad is used. The longer the length of the contiguity relationship, the higher is the likelihood for the extent of CDM cooperation.

The number of IGOs that the countries in each dyad are members of are obtained from the IGO dataset constructed by Pevehouse *et al.* (2004). The IGO datasets contain information

---

[6] Online: http://correlatesofwar.org.

about intergovernmental organizations (international organizations that have at least three nation-states as their members) identifying all state members of the IGO in years during 1815–2000.[7] A larger number of joint IGO membership for a dyad indicates a higher possibility of CDM cooperation.

Data on annual bilateral trade between all countries in the world are obtained from International Monetary Fund (IMF, 2007), for the period of 1960–2003. Using the sum of the volumes of bilateral trade and *GDP* (in current US$) of the host and investor countries, the trade variable, *Trade*, is constructed following Dinar *et al.* (2011) expressing import and export measures between the dyad countries.

Table 8.2 presents the variables that participated in the statistical analysis and their measurements and units. This chapter does report general results without focusing on the statistical aspects of the results. More information and details can be found in Dinar *et al.* (2011).

8.5 Results

Results will be presented first to describe the size of the cooperating interactions between host and investor countries. Then, qualitative results of the estimated statistical relationship will be presented. Readers interested in more technical discussion can read it in Dinar *et al.* (2011, 2013).

8.5.1 *The investor–host results*

There are 34 investor countries (excluding Australia and the USA) and 175 host countries in the dataset, so, there are 5,950 possible host–investor dyads.[8] But only 305 of the host–investor dyads

---

[7] See Chapter 9 for the role of NGOs and IGOs in setting global policies.

[8] Australia and the USA are excluded from the dataset because Australia did not ratify Kyoto until 2005 and the USA is yet to ratify Kyoto (as of 2009). Few host countries are also omitted from the dataset because they are very small and country-level data are not available for those.

Table 8.2.   Definition of variables used in the statistical analysis.

Variable	Description	Unit of measurement
Ease of Doing Business	Ease of doing business, a relative ranking of the countries reflecting the state of business regulation	Smaller value indicates less favorable business environment
CDM Incidence	A dichotomous variable with 0 if there are no, and 1 if there are any, number of CDM dyad projects	0 or 1
Average Annual Energy Use	Average annual energy use over the period 1960–2003	Thousand trillion tons of oil equivalent
Governance	Indicator reflecting the overall governance level, a principal component product of 6 governance indicators	Smaller value indicates poorer level of governance
Impact Vulnerability	Impact vulnerability index (reflecting country vulnerability in terms of various impacts of climate change)	Scale of 1 to 100 (1 = lowest, 100 = highest)
Number of Projects	Number of CDM projects	
Renewable Energy	Renewable energy resources (annual) available per capita	Thousand trillion tons of oil equivalent
Total CO_2 Abatement	Total amount of CO_2 abatement (CERs) until 2012	Kiloton of oil equivalent
Annual CO_2 Abatement	Annual amount of CO_2 abatement (CERs) until 2012	Kiloton of oil equivalent

Table 8.2. (*Continued*)

Variable	Description	Unit of measurement
Trade	Total trade (the sum of the volume of bilateral imports and exports) between the host and investor countries as a fraction of the sum of the countries' GDPs	Share
Volume of Investment	Volume of investment in CDM projects: _*TOT* reflecting total investment and _*YR* reflecting annual investment	Thousand US $ (constant 2000)
*hst_**	Variable related to the host country	*represents the variables described above
*inv_**	Variable related to the investor country	*represents the variables described above
*hst_inv_**	An interaction term	*represents the variables described above

Source: Dinar *et al.* (2013).

have CDM project activity, while 57 host countries have unilateral projects. Dyads without any CDM projects ae regarded as the non-cooperation dyads. Due to the use of three different left-hand side variables, a missing values problem results in different sample sizes for each dependent variable, making it harder to compare the results. Therefore, only 2,771 dyad-level observations with full set of variables are used (full descriptive statistics table can be found in Dinar *et al.*, 2013).

But still, several results are of interest. First, there are main differences in the various variables between host and investor countries in the dyads. Investor countries have higher *Average Annual Energy Use*, better ranking of *EDB*, better *Governance*, higher *Political Constraints*, and lower *Impact Vulnerability*. However, host countries have higher endowments of *Renewable Energy Stock* than do investor countries. These differences are expected to attract investor countries to host countries, leading to cooperation.

8.5.2 *Selected results for the cooperation estimates*

Level of cooperation is measured by three variables: *Number of CDM Projects, Total CO$_2$ Abatement, and Volume of Investment.* In each of the cooperation models, positive coefficients of the right-hand side of the equation represent a positive impact of the estimated variable on cooperation and vice versa. For the purpose of our discussion, we will refer to qualitative results across all three models, which can be found in Table 8.3.

All three models in Table 8.3 present similar trends (signs) and importance (significant levels) for all explanatory variables for all measures of cooperation. Higher economic development levels measured as *Average Annual Energy Use* by both host and investor countries are significant and positive; *EDB* shows a negative and significant sign assigned to the host country and an insignificant coefficient assigned to the investor country. *Governance* of the host country is not significant and that of the investor country are positive and significant. The *Renewable Energy Stock* of the host country has a positive and significant coefficient and that of the investor country are negative and significant in two of the three models. *Impact Vulnerability* is positive and significant for both host and investor country. The *Trade* variable has a positive and significant coefficient in two models. *Political Constraints* of the investor country are negative and significant, but insignificant for the host country. Coefficient estimates of *Contiguity Length* and *Number of Joint IGO Membership* are positive and significant. Most interaction terms are insignificant except for the *Impact Vulnerability*, which is negative and significant.

8.6 Conclusion and Policy Implications

The analysis of CDM cooperation used three types of variables that indicate the extent of joint involvement between host and investor countries in carbon abatement projects. Following the two objectives

Table 8.3.   Qualitative results for three measures of cooperation.

Variables	Coefficient estimates		
	Dependent variable 1[a]	Dependent variable 2[b]	Dependent variable 3[c]
Intercept	$-$***	$-$***	$-$***
Hst_Avg. Annual Energy Use	$+$***	$+$***	$+$***
Inv_Avg. Annual Energy Use	$+$***	$+$***	$+$***
Hst_Inv_Avg. Annual Energy Use	$+$	$+$***	$+$***
Hst_Ease of Doing Business	$-$***	$-$**	$-$**
Inv_Ease of Doing Business	$+$	$-$	$+$
Hst_Inv_Ease of Doing Business	$+$	$+$	$+$
Hst_Governance	$+$	$-$	$-$
Inv_Governance	$+$***	$+$***	$+$***
Hst_Inv_Governance	$-$	$+$	$+$
Hst_Renewable Energy Stock	$+$**	$+$***	$+$***
Inv_Renewable Energy Stock	$-$**	$-$	$-$*
Hst_Inv_Renewable Energy Stock	$-$	$-$***	$-$***
Hst_Impact Vulnerability	$+$***	$+$**	$+$**
Inv_Impact Vulnerability	$+$***	$+$**	$+$**
Hst_Inv_Impact Vulnerability	$-$**	$-$	$-$
Trade	$+$***	$+$*	$+$
Hst_Political Constraints	$+$	$+$	$+$
Inv_Political Constraints	$-$***	$-$	$-$
Contiguity Length	$+$***	$+$**	$+$**
Number of Joint IGO Mem.	$+$*	$+$	$+$

Note: ***, **, and * indicate 1%, 5%, and 10% significance levels, respectively. [a]No. of CDM projects per host-investor dyad; [b]CER generation per host-investor dyad; [c]Capital investments per host-investor dyad.

of the CDM mechanism, the dependent variables that measure CER generation and volume of capital investment suggest that indeed, the two objectives are comparable and explain a great deal of host–investor cooperation. GHG emission reductions that can be credited to the investor country (measured by the CER generation by the CDM projects) and the investment in CDM projects that support sustainable development in the host country, both provide *a-priori* incentives for cooperation between host and investor countries.

It was found that countries with strong trade relations, implying also other types of international relation ties, are more likely to cooperate in CDM activities. Therefore, the general conclusion is that any type of active relations among the countries in host–investor dyads would lead to higher likelihood of cooperation in CDM projects. Similarly, colonial ties and previous contiguity length are a major factor explaining CDM cooperation. While it is quite reasonable to accept such results, conclusions could be far-reaching. Colonial ties may not only refer to dependency, but also to better cultural exchanges that allow countries to feel more comfortable working together. It also could be that infrastructure and existing institutions are more familiar and make cooperation more comfortable. In turn, this is expected to reduce transaction costs among countries with shared cultural heritages.

The level of development of the country, measured as average annual energy use, is an important factor in promoting cooperation. Despite differences in size of coefficients of the investor country compared to those of the host country, still coefficients of both host and investor are highly significant.

As suggested in many other international cooperation studies, governance matters and institutional strength is a prerequisite for better performance, both domestic and international. A similar interpretation can be attributed to the variable measuring the EDB. The results suggest that the situation in the investor country doesn't matter. What matters is the level of EDB in the host country, which attracts domestic and international investors.

All other variables measure natural endowment of a country, and thus, may be less affected by policy interventions. The policy discussion would, therefore, be focused only on the suggestion that international development institutions focus mainly on the strengthening of multilateral interactions between countries and on domestic structural changes and reforms of economies, so that they are better prepared not only to adapt to climate change but also to cooperate in the CDM market and take advantage of the CDM dividend—development—that results from CDM joint investment.

This study shows that, three factors, namely better business environment, higher level of governance, and stronger international trade relations have positive impacts, increasing future viability of the CDM. Thus, there are scopes for both state-level and international-level policy interventions addressing these three factors, which governments and international development institutions have already identified as important directions for their future commitment.

References

Brechet, T. and Lussis, B., 2006. The Contribution of the Clean Development Mechanism to National Climate Policies. *Journal of Policy Modeling*, 28:981–994.

Busse, M. and Hefeker, C., 2007. Political Risk, Institutions and Foreign Direct Investment. *European Journal of Political Economy*, 23(2): 397–415.

Buys, P., Uwe, D., Craig, M., ThaoTon, T., and David, W., 2007. *Country Stakes in Climate Change Negotiations: Two Dimensions of Vulnerability*. World Bank Policy Research Working Paper No. 4300, Washington, D.C.

Congleton, R., 1992. Political Institutions and Pollution Control. *Review of Economics and Statistics*, 74:412–421.

Correlates of War 2 Project. *Colonial/Dependency Contiguity Data, 1816–2002*. Version 3.0.

Available at http://correlatesofwar.org. Accessed on October 6, 2010.

Dinar, S., 2009. Scarcity and Cooperation along International Rivers. *Global Environmental Politics*, 9(1):109–135.

Dinar, S., Dinar, A., and Pradeep, K., 2011. Scarcity and Cooperation Along International Rivers: An Empirical Assessment of Bilateral Treaties. *International Studies Quarterly* (accepted for Publication May 26, 2010).

Dinar, A., Larson, D. F., and Rahman, S. M., 2013. *The Clean Development Mechanism (CDM): An Early History of Unanticipated Outcomes*. Chapter 7. Singapore: World Scientific Publishing.

Dolšak, N. and Dunn, M., 2006. Investments in Global Warming Mitigation: The Case of Activities Implemented Jointly. *Policy Sciences*, 39:233–248.

Dunning, J. H., 1993. *Multinational Enterprise and the Global Economy*. Wokinghan: Addison-Wesley.

Dunning, J. H., 1996. The Role of FDI in a Globalizing Economy. In: Green, C. J. and Brewer, T. L. (Eds.), *Investment Issues in Asia and the Pacific Rim*. New York, NY: Oceania, pp. 43–64.

Henisz, W. J., 2002. The Institutional Environment for Infrastructure Investment. *Industrial and Corporate Change*, 11(2):355–389.

International Monetary Fund. 2007. Direction of Trade data. Available at http://www.imfstatistics.org/dot/. Accessed on June 21, 2021.

Kaufmann, D., Aart, K., and Massimo M., 2007. *Governance Matters VI: Aggregate and Individual Governance Indicators 1996–2006*. Policy Research Working Paper 4280, Development Economics Group, World Bank.

Larson, D. F. and Breusted, G., 2009. Will Markets Direct Investments under the Kyoto Protocol? Lessons from the Activities Implemented Jointly Pilots. *Environmental and Resource Economics*, 43(3):433–456.

Michaelowa, A. and Michaelowa, K., 2007. Climate or Development: Is ODA Diverted from its Original Purpose? *Climatic Change*, 84:5–21.

Mitchell, S. M. and Hensel, P. R., 2007. International Institutions and Compliance with Agreements. *American Journal of Political Science*, 51(4):721–737.

Neumayer, E., 2002. Does Trade Openness Promote Multilateral Environmental Cooperation? *World Economy*, 25:815–832.

Nonnemberg, M., Bragaand, M., and de Mendonça, J. C., 2004. The Determinants of Foreign Direct Investment in Developing Countries. *Estudos Econômicos, São Paulo*, 35(4):631–655.

Nunnenkamp, P., 2002. *Determinants of FDI in Developing Countries: Has Globalization Changed the Rules of the Game?* Kiel Working Paper 1122, Kiel Institute for World Economics, Kiel.

Paul, E., 2006. A Survey of the Theoretical Economic Literature on Foreign Aid. *Asian-Pacific Economic Literature*, 20(1):1–17.

Pevehouse, J. C., Timothy, N., and Kevin W., 2004. The COW-2 International Organizations Dataset Version 2.0. *Conflict Management and Peace Science*, 21(2):101–119.

Polacheck, S. W., Carlos, S., and Jun, X., 2007. *Globalization and International Conflict: Can FDI Decrease Conflict?* Unpublished paper presented at the Allied Social Science Association Winter Meeting, Chicago, IL.

Pollins, B., 1989. Conflict, Cooperation, and Commerce: The Effect of International Political Interactions on Bilateral Trade Flows. *American Journal of Political Science*, 33:737–761.

Rahman, S. M., Larson, D. F., and Dinar, A., 2012. *The Cost Structure of the Clean Development Mechanism*. World Bank Policy Research Working Paper 6262, November 2012.

Siegel, J. I., Licht, A. N., and Schwartz, S. H., 2010. *Egalitarianism, Cultural Distance, and FDI: A New Approach*. Available at http://papers.ssrn.com/sol3/papers.cfm?abstract_id=957306. Accessed on October 20, 2010.

Tsur, Y. and Zemel, A., 2008. Regulating Environmental Threats. *Environmental and Resource Economics*, 39:297–310.

UNDP United Nations Development Program, 2006. *An Assessment of Progress with Establishing the Clean Development Mechanism*. New York, NY: UNDP.

UNFCCC, 2010. *Clean Development Mechanism (CDM)*. Available at http://cdm.unfccc.int/index.html. Accessed on March 3, 2010.

United Nations Environmental Programme (UNEP) Risoe Center, 2007. *CDM/JI Pipeline Analysis and Database.* Available at http://cdmpipeline. org. Accessed on November 6, 2008.

United Nations Environmental Program UNEP/GRID-Arendal, 2000. *Methodological and Technological Issues in Technology Transfer.* Available at http://www.grida.no/climate/ipcc/tectran/index.htm. Accessed on July 29, 2007.

Velasco, A. P., 2007. Variables Underpinning Technology Transfers Through the CDM. *Joint Implementation Quarterly,* 13(3):5–6.

Waltz, K., 1979. *Theory of International Politics.* New York, NY: McGraw-Hill.

WDI (World Development Indicators), The World Bank, 2007. Available at http://publications.worldbank.org/WDI. Accessed on October 6, 2010.

Young, O., 1989. The Politics of International Regime Formation: Managing Natural Resources and the Environment. *International Organization,* 43(3):349–375.

Chapter 9

Shaping Global Policies by International Organizations and NGOs

Abstract

We will focus on the role of international organizations (IOs) in shaping global policies. As we have already become aware of, several IOs such as the World Bank, the OECD, the World Health Organization, the World Trade Organization (WTO), the United Nations Development Program, to name a few, have played major roles in initiating and framing several global policies. We will explore the motivation of, and the strategies used by, IOs to develop and implement global policies, their own interests, and the conflicts created with states that were part of the development of those policies. We will also discuss the interactions between IOs and NGOs, both local and international.

Additional sources to this chapter:

https://escholarship.org/content/qt88m371wz/qt88m371wz.pdf

https://books.google.com/books?id=4tjmDICqUOYC&printsec=frontcover#v=onepage&q&f=false

9.1 Background

The theory of global policy development suggests that many organizations, states, and even influential individuals are involved in various stages of policymaking. In this chapter, we refer to a subset of organizations that have been identified in previous studies to have both interactions among themselves and at the same time to have the ability to affect the content of the global policies in question. Figure 9.1 describes those players involved in the global policymaking, and their effects on each other. We generalized the figure to include International Non-Governmental Organizations (INGOs), such as Greenpeace International, International Union for Conservation of Nature (IUCN), World Wide Fund for Nature (WWF), Human Rights Watch, Amnesty International; International Organizations (IOs), such as the World Bank, The Organization for Economic Co-operation and Development (OECD), and the International Monetary Fund (IMF); domestic Non-Governmental Organizations (NGOs) in the different countries; and each of the 196 states in the world.

While the process of determining the design and approval of a global policy is complicated, lengthy, and specific to the topic of each global policy and the various organizations (IOs, NGOs, and INGOs)

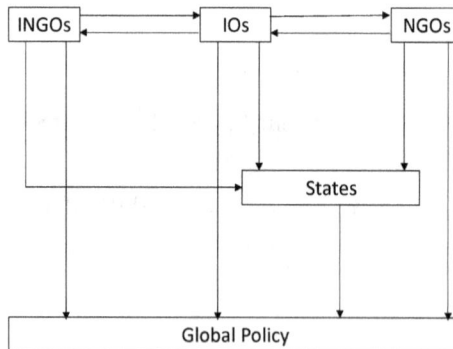

Figure 9.1. The interaction among all stakeholders involved in the global policymaking.

involved, still, there are some common patterns that will be discussed in Section 9.2. Then several examples, using the involvement of certain IOs, such as the World Bank, and certain INGOs and NGOs, will be discussed in Sections 9.3 and 9.4.

9.2 How do International and National Organizations Behave During the Process of Global Policy Design and Approval?

Before identifying the principles by which IOs are motivated and act upon, we must define IOs and the resources they can mobilize into the process of influencing global policies. It is well known and recognized that IOs are involved in shaping global policies for quite some time. Why do IOs get into such an activity? What makes such IOs so successful (or less successful) in the process of influencing the making of global policies? In this chapter, we rely on Dolowitz *et al.* (2020).

IOs are international organizations with mandates to develop nations or regions, using infrastructure investments and/or policy programs at the local, national, and regional levels. Using their financial and economic leverage, IOs such as the World Bank, IMF, World Trade Organization (WTO), OECD, and others use their resources to promote different agendas, believed to support progress and welfare-promoting policies around the world. In that sense, they act in a semi-autonomous manner to set policy agendas at a global scale. For example, the World Bank mandate at its establishment in 1945 was to reconstruct Europe after World War II. This has translated into loans for infrastructure. In the 1960s, the World Bank mandate was expanded to address poverty around the world, by engaging in development projects of irrigation, hydropower, transportation, education, and other domains. But in recent years, starting in the 1980s, the World Bank has expanded its activity by adding institutional and knowledge components to the 'traditional' loans focused solely on infrastructure.

Dolowitz *et al.* (2020: 3) developed the analysis in their work by building upon and inferring a set of four hypotheses:

1. IOs are semi-autonomous organizations with motivation that depends also on external private and public actors with multi-diverse objectives;
2. The influence of an IO depends on its ability to make policy issues understandable and controllable;
3. The boundaries and contents of IOs' expertise is subject to the nexus over which it is produced and disseminated; and
4. The legitimacy of the IOs' new (knowledge) activities takes the form of economic interpretation of the problems and solutions of the issues they address.

In the following, we will demonstrate these hypotheses, using examples of certain IOs' involvement in global policies.

9.2.1 *Migrant care workers policies*

The global policy in question addresses transnational care chains where demand for healthcare workers (mainly women) from certain countries to provide care services in host countries may create negative economic, social, and political externalities both in the caregiver exporting and the care-consuming countries.

Following Mahone (2020), this section will demonstrate, based on hypotheses (b), that the IOs in question (in this case the World Bank and the OECD) develop internal division of labor to enable them to identify and focus on sets of manageable problems. As is argued by Mahone (2020: 79), such division of expertise may address individual parts of the global care-chain system, but neither of these organizations showed the ability to address the whole problem.

Looking at the 1990 UN 'International Convention on the Protection of the Rights of All Migrant Workers and Members of Their Families' (https://www.ohchr.org/en/professionalinterest/pages/cmw.aspx), it would be interesting to compare the aspects present in the OECD and World Bank documents and to what extent they were able to modify the principles on the basis of the UN treaty.

It would also make sense to look at the UN Convention on the Elimination of all Forms of Discrimination Against Women (https:// www.un.org/womenwatch/daw/cedaw/cedaw.htm) and see how and to what extent the OECD and World Bank observations and concerns regarding care workers meet the language in this treaty.

9.2.1.1 *The OECD*

Established in 1961, the OECD included originally western European countries, Canada, and the USA and was mandated to promote economic growth within its member states while promoting development in the Global South. Several years later, OECD grew to include also several eastern European countries and several non-European developing and developed countries.

Given the welfare disparity among its European member states, intra-European migration has been an issue of concern to the OECD from early stages of its creation, but in the 1990s it was apparent that the main flows of migrant care workers were from the South. OECD units started to invest in studies to identify the extent of high-skilled and low-skilled migrant care workers from withing Europe and from the South into OECD member countries with all related interruptions of the economic and social order. To increase its capacity, OECD conducted several studies on the subject with the Asian Development Bank (ADB), as many migrant caregivers arrived in Europe from countries the ADB is serving.

Several of the knowledge and fact-finding reports by the OECD criticized the OECD member countries for silence on the issue and lack of protection of migrant care workers in the host countries. The accumulated amount of knowledge in such reports has been highly criticized for being partial in identifying the global care chain issues rather than the entire parts of the chain and the interactions between them. OECD is criticized for viewing only the North–South relations of the global care chain and the domestic effects on OECD members only (Razavi, 2014: 144).

To sum up, the OECD's main concern is its member states and the common internal problems they face. The various policy units within OECD recognized that certain member states rely on migrant care workers to meet the demand for such services. At the same time, it was also recognized that low pay and poor working conditions will make it harder to recruit quality services for the aging groups in Europe. The OECD has recognized the important role the remittance payments play in the welfare economics of the supply side countries. OECD has paid little attention to the gender aspects of care supply and the consequences on both home and host countries.

9.2.1.2 *The World Bank*

Similarly to the OECD, the World Bank departed in the mid 1990s from its original mission to focus on financing of development projects to re-invent itself as a knowledge bank, with focus on development. Gender has become an major aspect in the Bank's development agenda. Different units in the World Bank took charge of 'gender migration and development,' but the South–South and South–North migration of women, mostly from poorer to wealthier countries, was not brought into play in gender migration and development.

In early 2000s, the World Bank established a program on international migration and development, but again the overall focus was on migration-remittance contribution to development. Only several years later was gender added to the equation, as it was recognized that women account for half of the international migrants.

World Bank work on gender migration and development took an important step forward by issuing two new reports by highly recognized outside experts that were hired to produce the work. Some of the findings and recommendations (which are quite new compared to previous work) suggest innovative activities both in home and host countries, such as: (1) promoting increased public awareness of migrants' contributions to their families, communities, and societies, by both home and host governments; (2) securing resources to support the families left behind in the home countries; and (3) regulation and monitoring of the recruitment agencies. In terms of the host countries, World Bank called for regulation of work hours, health, and other social protection of the migrant workers, and for elimination of immigration laws that discriminate against women.

To sum up, the World Bank concern was the promotion of the concept of remittance payments as a development mechanism in the home countries and the different roles male and female migrant workers can play in determining the remittance flow and its use. The policies recommended by the World Bank did not address well the question of migration, including encouragement of the home states to support the migrants and their families that were left behind.

9.3 IOs are not Working in a Vacuum—Role of INGOs and NGOs

We already know that IOs are not the only organizations active in global policy development. As suggested in Figure 9.1, interactions between domestic NGOs and INGOs, states, and IOs affect the direction and nature of global policies. Domestic NGOs usually are involved in local policies, but this must not be the rule. We have seen heavy involvement of NGOs also in the establishment of global policies such as climate change agreements, or various other global environmental policies such as the Montreal Protocol on Substances that Deplete the Ozone Layer (Annex A4) or the Convention to Combat Desertification (Annex A6). We will start with the role of INGOs and then continue with NGOs. While our examples include INGOs and NGOs that are involved in environmental global policies, the mechanisms we identified hold for other global policies as well. As a general rule, both NGOs and INGOs rise in their involvement when governments and international bodies fail to address negative externalities associated with policymaking.

9.3.1 *INGOs involvement in global policy outcomes*

INGOs are powerful organizations with a focused objective in a social or environmental sphere. Generally, INGOs have a headquarter in one country and branches in several/many other countries around the world. Their offices can be in developing or in developed countries, but what connects them is the objective and the similar rules of operation. INGOs may have powerful impacts on governments and IOs, they have a significant operational budget, and they are involved in the policymaking as equal participants, such as the case of IUCN in the climate change negotiations.

INGOs have the capacity and influence that have fewer and different constraints compared with those faced by states, where the power to influence the political inclinations of their voting publics around the world becomes a power to influence the local policy approaches of not just one but many governments. Particularly with the existence of international bodies such as the World Bank, the IMF, the United Nations agencies, the OECD, and other global non-government actors, there is a recognition that there are many important international actors who interact frequently and at many levels of importance. These interactions determine the outcome of policies with global attention (Stilwell and Ozodike, 2006).[1]

Why do governments and global non-governmental institutions (IOs) pay attention to INGOs? All is about their fear of losing favorite public opinion, which is the glue to connecting governments, global IOs, and NGOs and INGOs. Several examples are provided as follows. James Wolfensohn, the president of the World Bank during massive NGO campaigns to modify World Bank environmental and natural resources policies, has credited NGO pressure with 'spurring needed changes in the way that the World Bank does business' (Hurrell and Kingsbury, 1992: 313). Indeed, INGOs in collaboration with NGOs were able to pressure the World Bank to modify its water resources development policy (World Bank, 1993) and revisit its dam investment portfolio plans (World Bank, 1996a,b, 1997, 1998, 1999, 2001a,b to name a few). In some cases, INGOs (such as IUCN, WWF) became partners and co-authors with the World Bank on several global policies.

---

[1] As opposed to this thesis, Arts and Verschuren (1999) suggest, based on an empirical investigation of eight NGO groups, that NGO groups are rarely effective in achieving their goals.

Another important aspect of the increase in INGOs' (and of NGOs') involvement and success to mobilize global policies in a direction that takes into account social views is globalization and accessibility to information in real time. Evidence suggests that progress in technological advancements in media and communication networks facilitate flow of information across the globe, it becomes easier for the NGOs and INGOS to develop a more politically effective involvement. However, such an evolving political engagement and influence is negatively affected by rhetoric, fake information, and manipulation of statistics to achieve subjective interests of certain groups, either domestic or global. With increased awareness among the world citizens of issues beyond their immediate reach, political spaces are opened and governments need to begin catering for the diversification of their constituencies' political interests. This is why we see more interaction between NGOs, INGOs, IOs, and not always for the better.

9.3.2 *NGOs involvement in global policy outcomes*[2]

NGOs activities have evolved from influencing the articulation of environmental and human rights-related standards of conduct, to the initiation and implementation of policies both in individual nation-states and through influencing IOs' policies, through moral and scientific basis, to the exercise of power. NGOs at present have the capacity to influence multinational organization policy and to intervene directly in choices traditionally in the domain of sovereign states.

In most cases, the growth in influence and involvement of NGOs has been a positive aspect in the development of international environmental protection policies. International environmental policies are an interesting example of the influence of intense preference groups in the establishment of environmental priorities overcoming the inability of formal governmental institutions to respond to scientific information. These groups have great success in shaping

---

[2]Based to a large extent on ideas in Tarlock (1992).

the environmental agenda of individual states, convention and treaty processes, and the work of the United Nations. Environmental NGOs can be traced back to the formation of the International Union for the Conservation of Nature in 1948, but the first United Nations conference on the environment gave their current status. Since the 1972 Stockholm conference, NGOs have played an increasingly important role in the development of global environmental standards and institutions as well as in the implementation of policies in individual countries (Tarlock, 1992).

NGO performance success can be attributed to advantages that they show over action by states. Several examples hold: (1) in the formulation of standards of performance, they can articulate powerful universal, single-purpose standards. They need not trade-off environmental to other objectives because they have a single purpose, so they are not bound by the needs of elected political officials to avoid offending powerful constituencies; (2) for the same reason, there is little incentive to subordinate science to other considerations, so their priorities are not subject to compromises; and (3) INGOs often work with lower-level, local environmental NGO groups, who lack both resources and political legitimacy, to support environmental initiatives. This is how local NGOs become more effective. For example, Greenpeace's work with local NGOs in Central America on international environmental policies is an interesting example of the influence of intense preference groups in the establishment of environmental priorities due to the inability of state governmental agencies to respond to and incorporate scientific information.

NGOs lack legal status in classic international law and in the system of IOs, but their lack of formal status has not hindered their growing influence in foreign countries and IOs. NGOs thrived in the United States and in Europe because they had a legal status which served as the basis of a broader political role. In contrast, INGOs lack an international legal status, but they have been able to build on the legitimacy of domestic NGOs to project themselves into the international arena. NGO participation in the establishment and enforcement of global environmental policies, such as climate change and human rights policies is quite impressive. Domestic

NGOs and INGOs pursue to exercise the same kind of legal and political influence, but the legal position of NGOs in the international community is different. In the United States, NGOs have a tenuous constitutional status and thus are subject to the discipline of the legal as well as the political process. International and many foreign NGOs generally lack any legal status and sometimes operate on the margins of established political processes. This extra-legal character of NGOs has both positive and negative consequences: NGOs are at the mercy of IO and foreign domestic rules on access and participation; however, their lack of legal status allows them to define their role unconstrained by the law. This allows them to develop more creative and effective approaches to environmental protection than those offered through litigation, especially before international tribunals.

NGO success and involvement in both IOs and individual nations has generally been hailed as a positive development because they fill such a large void in both domestic and international environmental competencies. This is a powerful justification for their role. Adequate responses to environmental problems require large allocations of scarce resources. NGOs help allocate scarce resources to environmental issues in advance of the nation-centered international community. They watch IOs and provide valuable information and other assistance to developing nations. 'To date, NGOs have been a positive force in bringing environmental issues onto domestic and international political agendas since so much in current economic and political organizations is hostile to effective environmentalism' (Tarlock, 1992: 64–65).

References

Arts, B. and Verschuren, P., 1999. Assessing Political Influence in Complex Decisionmaking: An Instrument Based on Triangulation. *International Political Science Review*, 28:411–424.

Dolowitz, D., Magdalena, H., and Romuald N., 2020. Introduction. In: Dolowitz, David, Magdalena Hadjiisky, and Romuald Normand (Eds.), *Shaping Policy Agendas, the Micro Politics of Economic International Organizations*. Cheltenham, UK: Edward Elgar.

Hurrell, A. and Kingsbury, B., 1992. *The International Politics of the Environment*. Oxford: Oxford University Press.

Mahon, R., 2020. Transnational Care Chains as Seen by the OECD, the World Bank, and the IOM. In: Dolowitz, David, Magdalena Hadjiisky, and Romuald Normand (Eds.), *Shaping Policy Agendas, The Micro Politics of Economic International Organizations*. Cheltenham, UK: Edward Elgar.

Razavi, S., 2014. The OECD Closing the Gender Gap: Act Now 2012. *Global Social Policy*, 14(1):141–144.

Stilwell, J. and Ozodick, N. O., 2006. Global Policy Outcomes: The Role of NGOs. *Graduate Journal of Political Science*, 3(1):27–48.

Tarlock, D. A., 1992. The Role of Non-Governmental Organizations in the Development of International Environmental Law. *Chicago-Kent Law Review*, 61:68. Available at: https://scholarship.kentlaw.iit.edu/cklawreview/vol68/iss1/8.

World Bank, 1993. *Water Resources Management: A World Bank Policy Paper*. Washington, D.C.: World Bank Group. http://documents.worldbank.org/curated/en/940261468325788815/Water-resources-management.

World Bank, 1996a. *Analysis of Alternatives in Environmental Assessment*. Environmental Assessment Sourcebook Update No. 17. Washington, D.C.

World Bank, 1996b. *World Bank Lending for Large Dams: A Preliminary Review of Impacts*. OED Précis No. 125. Operations Evaluation Department, Washington, D.C.

World Bank, 1997. *Hydropower Dams and Social Impacts: A Sociological Perspective*. Environment Department Paper No. 44. Environment Department, Social Policy and Resettlement Division, Washington, D.C.

World Bank, 1998. Environmental Assessment Operational Policy 4.01. Includes BP 4.01, Annex B: Application of Environmental Assessment to Dam and Reservoir Projects. Washington, D.C.

World Bank, 1999 Operational Policy Note No. 11.03: Management of Cultural Property in Bank-Financed Projects. Washington, D.C.

World Bank, 2001a. Operational Policy 4.04: Natural Habitats. Includes Bank Procedures 4.04 and Good Practices 4.04. Washington, D.C.

World Bank, 2001b. Operational Policy 4.12: Involuntary Resettlement. Washington, D.C.

Annex

A1. Purpose of the Annex

This annex includes a sample of five cases of the analysis of global–local policy interactions. Each case follows a similar format:

1. The motivation for establishing the policy (including previous versions of the policy);
2. The objectives of the *present version* of the global policy analyzed;
3. The politics and history involved in the process of reaching the policy;
4. The structure of the policy and the institutions established to monitor and enforce it: the policy regulatory mechanisms;
5. The problems associated with the policy implementation (both technical and political);
6. The role of the local (state) interests in shaping the global policy;
7. Stability of the policy;
8. Analysis of the effectiveness of the policy (including use of suggested indexes that measure effectiveness); and
9. How the policy could benefit from features and experiences of other global policies (that have been discussed in the class, and others researched by the student).

A2.　Convention on the Suppression of Financing of Terrorism[1]

The convention on the suppression of terror financing is one of the recent global efforts to curtail a global negative externality that affects many countries. But, as we will learn in this annex, there are indirect interests of some countries that have affected the way the Convention was designed.

A2.1　*The motivation for establishing the policy (including previous versions of the policy)*

Terrorism is a global threat that inflicts negative externalities on countries around the world. It has been a prominent issue in modern times and the onset of globalization has served to increase the reach and scale of attacks. Furthermore, it has been acknowledged by the international community that merely reacting to attacks as they occur is not sufficient. To disable global terror networks, the financing that fuels their operations must be halted. Prior to the 1999 Convention, there was no treaty focusing specifically on financing terrorism. Combating international terrorism in those times revolved around a network of about a dozen multilateral treaties that mostly sought to deprive terrorists of sanctuaries and ensure cooperation in bringing them to justice (Lavalle, 2000: 491). These treaties mostly focused on specific acts and include conventions such as the Suppression of Terrorist Bombings (1997), Safety of Civil Aviation (1971), and Seizure of Aircraft (1970). The reason for this was mostly the lack of consensus on a precise definition of terrorism (Schaak and Maxwell, 2017).

While these treaties were useful, none of them were capable of targeting the ability of terrorists to carry out such acts. Also, many of the mechanisms used by states at that time for carrying out policies against the financing of terrorists were outdated. For instance, the United States was using the 1977 International Emergency Economic Powers Act (IEEPA), originally designed to be used against other

---

[1]Modified from Adam Jantz and Edgar Castelan, Final Paper submitted for the course PPBL224, June 14, 2018. Authors' consent was obtained.

states, to target the foreign assets of non-state individuals well into the 1990s (Clunan, 2006: 586). Regarding criminal financing, most policies were focused only on money laundering. This changed after the 1996 UN Ad-hoc Committee on Terrorism was formed. The committee found noticeable gaps in international law regarding terrorist financing and sought to draft a new treaty to fix these holes.

The International Convention for the Suppression of the Financing of Terrorism (ICSFT) broke away from the previous conventions by focusing on the cessation of the phenomenon as a whole and by depriving terrorism of what can be considered its 'lifeblood' (Lavalle, 2000: 492). This makes the treaty unique in its preventative nature and allows suspects to be prosecuted for financing terrorism without the occurrence of an actual attack.

A2.2 *The objectives of the present version of the policy*

In 1996, the UN General Assembly established an ad-hoc Terrorism Committee to develop a package of terrorism-related treaties. One of the leading UN members in the Committee was France. In a 1998 meeting, France argued that a 'terrorist group's ability to strike, acquire a powerful arsenal, make itself known, and recruit and train its members depends on its sources of funding, ...' (France, 1999). However, at the time there was no UN policy aimed specifically at terrorist financing/funding, which many found to be a lamentable gap in international law. Therefore, with France in the lead, the UN drafted a terrorist financing treaty with several objectives in mind. The main objective was to create an international treaty that specifically criminalized the fundraising and financing of specific terrorist groups and acts. The treaty did not set out to define terrorism specifically. Instead, it identifies the purpose of such acts, as being '...to intimidate a population, or compel a government...' and criminalizes the funding of them along with the acts specified in nine other annexed treaties (UN Treaty Text Art. 2 Par. 1&2).

The second major objective was to deprive terrorists and their financiers of their sanctuaries. They did this by establishing a broad basis for jurisdiction where countries can claim jurisdiction if the offense of financing occurred in their territory, by one of their

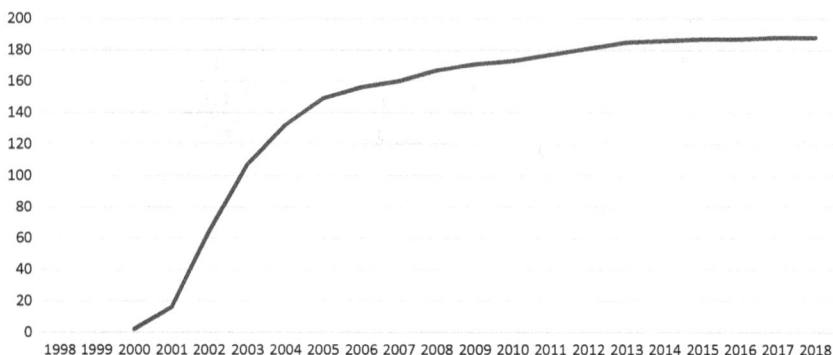

Figure A2.1. Ratification history of the convention on the suppression of financing of terrorism.

nationals, on a vessel registered by their state, or was directed toward carrying out an act in their state. Other objectives of the treaty were to help establish frameworks for the identification and confiscation of funds relating to terrorism, as well as allow for the circumvention of banking secrecy. They also wanted a way to ensure mutual legal assistance revolving in cases related to terrorist funding, which means extradition and asset freezing. The treaty was negotiated and finalized in 1999 and was adopted by the UN on December 9, 1999, under Resolution 54/109 (UN Treaty Collection Penal Matters, 2018). As can be seen in Figure A2.1, after 18 years since its adoption, only eight countries have not yet ratified the convention (Burundi, Chad, Eritrea, Iran, Lebanon, Somalia, South Sudan, and Tuvalu).

A2.3 *The politics and history involved in the process of reaching the policy*

One of the first areas of negotiation was the establishment of the Financing Convention as a separate instrument. The convention was initially supposed to be a step in a series of anti-terrorism treaties being implemented by the UN General Assembly's Ad-Hoc Committee on terrorism (Diaz-Paniagua, 2008: 436). The plan was to first negotiate the Terrorist Bombings Convention, then the Nuclear Convention, and finally a comprehensive anti-terrorism treaty. However, there was a difference in goals between the wealthy developed countries such as Japan, USA, France, and the developing countries of the Non-Aligned Movement. Wealthier countries tend to have more resources and leverage when dealing with other countries, which makes them better equipped to deal with terrorism. They merely wanted to fill in the gaps in international law, and therefore favored a step-based approach with multiple terrorism treaties, rather than a far-reaching comprehensive treaty. Conversely, developing countries have less infrastructure and governance to deal with terrorism and also suffer the most attacks (Dudley, 2016). They also have less influence to evoke cooperation from economically powerful countries.

Most of the developing countries are part of the Non-Aligned Movement, which consists of 120 members from South America, the Middle East, Southeast Asia, and Africa. Their side was led by India, and they preferred a comprehensive terrorism treaty that addresses all acts of terrorism and establishes clear definitions. Both sides held their positions for a while, but after weighing their options, India and the Non-Aligned Movement nations conceded. Figure A2.2

		Non-Aligned Movement nations	
		Financing Only/Step Based	Comprehensive
Advanced Nations	Financing Only/Step Based	At least some treaties are passed	Advanced countries stall and nothing is passed or it takes a long period to pass and ends up with step-based approach anyway
	Comprehensive	Negotiations are stalled and little is accomplished	Obtain comprehensive treaty

Figure A2.2. A matrix game of negotiating incremental vs. comprehensive anti-terrorism treaty.

presents the game matrix of the negotiation between the Non-Aligned Movement group and its 'rival', the Advanced Nations. The negotiation game yields the BATNA (Best Alternative to a Negotiated Agreement) as the *status quo* for both blocks of countries. This means that the passing of any treaty regarding terrorism would be a better outcome than nothing, thus the conceding agreement for the Non-Aligned Movement. The final agreement between the groups was to accept France's draft for a Financing-only convention. The Non-Aligned Movement conceded on the condition that a Comprehensive-terrorism treaty with hard deadlines is drafted immediately following the Financing treaty (Diaz-Paniagua, 2008: 438). In summary, the Non-Aligned Movement nations gave up the priority of their draft so that at least one terrorism treaty could pass and received a promise that their draft would get consideration afterward. In the end, the wealthy nations were able to submit their draft on the Financing convention, but the comprehensive terrorism treaty has not yet come to fruition.

A2.4 *Structure of the policy including monitoring and enforcement*

While combating terrorist financing may seem straightforward at first, the implementation of the treaty involves many levels and networks. Implementation starts with local and national financial institutions, with the objective to facilitate international cooperation while preserving the sovereignty of domestic institutions. As per Article 18 of the Convention, financial institutions are supposed to report transactions suspected of stemming from criminal activity, cease the opening of accounts with unidentifiable beneficiaries, verify the structure of legal entities, and maintain appropriate records for all transactions (IMF, 2013: 63–64). The reporting of suspicious transactions is usually done by a designated Financial Intelligence Unit (FIU). FIUs are mostly central/national institutions within individual countries that process and analyze information before passing it on to the requisite authorities. However, they are not law enforcement institutions, and therefore any legal action is carried out by designated domestic enforcement agencies.

FIUs are also participants in the Egmont network (IMF, 2013: 62). The Egmont network is an informal network of FIUs, currently consisting of 156 members throughout the world that collects and shares information regarding money laundering and terrorist financing. If an FIU receives information pertaining to crimes in a different country, the information is passed on through FIUs in the network to a representative in the designated country, who can then refer it to the public prosecution agencies. In the United States, the FIU is known as Financial Crimes Enforcement Network (FinCen) and operates under the Department of the Treasury.

The specific technical standards and protocols for meeting the requirements of the convention are developed by the Financial Action Task Force (FATF). The FATF is an intergovernmental task force that was formed in 1989 to combat money laundering. In 2001, the FATF added terrorist financing to its targeted activities and developed a set of recommendations for countries, called the Combating Financing of Terrorism (CFT) standards. The group convenes on a regular basis to add and revise protocols. If a country has domestic institutions with adequate provisions for following the Convention, they can keep those or only adopt certain policies. The International Monetary Fund (IMF) and World Bank help in an advisory capacity by providing technical assistance and capacity-building (Clunan, 2006: 579). Adherence to counter-terrorism protocols is supposed to be monitored by the UN Counter-Terrorism Committee (CTC), which was formed on September 28, 2001, under UN Resolution 1373 (UN SCCTC, 2018).

On a wider regional level, there are external groups that work with the parties to implement the convention's protocols. The Caribbean Financial Task Force and the 2005 *Council of Europe Convention on Laundering, Search, Seizure, and Confiscation of the Proceeds from Crime* are two such groups that focus on regional implementation (Klein, 2009: 5).

The highest level of dispute resolution under the Convention refers to the International Court of Justice (COJ), which is part of the United Nations (UN). Article 24 of the Convention says that any dispute regarding the Convention that cannot be resolved in

Table A2.1.   The Russia Ukraine dispute—implementation difficulties.

Level	Functions
Local Groups: Local Financial Institutions	Report suspected criminal activity to law enforcement or FIU
National Level: FIUs	Process and analyze information; provide reports; respond to requests from other FIUs and countries
Enforcement	Domestic law enforcement
Regional: Local Coalitions/ Groups	Regional groups provide another layer of cooperation; such as the *Council of Europe Convention on Laundering, Search, Seizure and Confiscation of the Proceeds from Crime* and on the financing of terrorism, Caribbean FATF
International Level: FATF	Develops standards and protocols
IMF World Bank	Provides technical assistance and capacity-building
UN Security Council Counter-Terrorism Committee	Monitors compliance with counter-terrorism provisions in treaties
Egmont Network	Shares information between FIUs
International Court of Justice	Arbitrates and settles disputes between parties

a reasonable period of time can be referred for arbitration at the request of one party (UN Treaty Text, 1999, Art 24). If the dispute is not resolved in six months, the case can be submitted to the International Court, which can order provisional measures. One such dispute has arisen, between the members Ukraine and Russia. This case will be discussed in another section. Table A2.1 summarizes this structure and highlights how complex the treaty implementation is.

Enforcement against those suspected of financing terrorism is always carried out by domestic law agencies. Enforcement against other parties over adherence to the protocol falls to the UN and International Criminal Court of Justice and the UN Security Council on Terrorism. The FATF also drafts protocols and monitors the effectiveness and compliance of countries regarding anti-terrorist financing laws (FATF Gafi Mutual, 2018). As with most global treaties, there is an issue linkage with state sovereignty. Therefore, it is stressed in most Articles of the Convention that the implementation of protocols is subject to the domestic principles of each member country.

A2.5 *Policy regulatory mechanisms*

Although there is some element of peer pressure brought on countries through the FATF and various UN groups to comply, the main policy regulatory mechanism is in Article 24, which has the clause on the dispute resolution between parties (United Nations, 1999). Under Article 24, disputes between states over the application or interpretation of the treaty are subject to arbitration by the UN if no resolution can be negotiated between the states themselves (UN Treaty Text, 1999). If the rules of arbitration cannot be agreed upon within six months, either party is then able to refer the case to the International COJ for a ruling. Parties are able to press for provisional measures in the Court and have a public hearing. The 2017 Ukraine vs. Russia case was one example of how this mechanism performed in action.

After the rebel conflict in Eastern Ukraine broke out, Ukraine spent years of attempting to cease Russian involvement in the conflict, but Russia was uncooperative. Russia either ignored Ukraine or took ridiculously long to respond to requests. After 6 months, no agreement could be reached. As per Article 24 of the Convention, the case was then referred to the International COJ. Therefore, on April 21, 2016, Ukraine pressed to send the case to arbitration by the UN (International COJ January, 2017: 5). Ukraine accused Russia of providing weapons and financing to separatists with the knowledge that they will use terrorist tactics and target civilians. They accused Russia of failing to honor their commitments to the Convention in regard to preventing and investigating the financing of terrorism. Ukraine sought provisional measures from the court that would order Russia to cease supporting the separatists and to secure their borders to stem the flow of weapons to the separatists. They also simultaneously filed suit against Russia under the Convention on the Elimination of All Forms of Racial Discrimination (CERD) under accusations of attempting cultural erasure and discrimination against the Tatars.

The Court ruled on April 19, 2017 (International COJ March, 2017) that there was no sufficient basis to warrant instituting any provisional measures against Russia. The judges' reasoning was that Ukraine had not provided enough evidence that Russia had the intent and knowledge that their support would go toward terrorist acts. Conversely, they did find Russia in violation of CERD and ordered that the Crimean Tatars must be allowed to keep their representative institutions and ensure the availability of Ukrainian language education.

A2.6 *Problems with implementation*

While it may seem like combating terror financing would be straightforward, it actually represents a classic collective action problem (Clunan, 2006: 572). All states benefit from limiting the infiltration of terrorist groups into their financial systems and bolstering investor confidence. However, there is also an incentive to pass on the costs of implementation to other parties. Convincing states to expend the effort to comply with a myriad of financial monitoring measures is difficult. One way is through peer pressure and shaming. Some of the organizations, such as the FATF, maintain lists of high-risk and non-cooperative countries in order to impose peer pressure and name/shame them (FATF Gafi High-Risk, 2018). Another method for sustaining compliance would be reciprocity, but that only works if terrorism is an important issue for the other parties. Most countries will only superficially comply unless they are very motivated.

Another problem with implementation is the siphoning of funds from charitable organizations to terrorist organizations. Many charities operating in tumultuous regions inadvertently supply funds to terrorist groups, some are even aware of it. Disabling humanitarian NGOs could negatively impact those who are reliant on them. The general assumption is that most charities and those who donate have no intent to support terrorism and so the treaty is somewhat lenient with enforcement on them. A third issue with implementation is that terrorism is composed of many acts which by themselves are not illegal. There is no efficient way to deal with these last two implementation problems except for having as much information as possible and evaluating on a case-by-case basis.

A2.7 *Role of local (state) interests in shaping policy*

This Convention is a clear case of several competing interests vying to have their input considered. Therefore, shaping the language and nomenclature of the treaty is an indicator of how different countries view the issues. It also illustrates how different regional blocks and issue coalitions come together in the process to advocate for their specified stance. Initially, there was no sufficient consensus on the definition of terrorism to move forward with the convention. A monolithic block of parties that included Cuba, Syria, Libya, and Pakistan pressed for a definition of terrorism that addressed state-sponsored actions and excluded resistance and liberation movements from being included as terrorist acts. There was an attempt at linking the issue to the Israel/Palestine conflict as many Islamic Middle Eastern countries did not want any definition that allowed Palestinian actions against Israelis to be considered terrorism. When the draft convention was being considered in the Sixth Committee, these states insisted on a differentiation between acts of terrorism committed by 'individuals, groups, or states, and the legitimate acts of resistance undertaken by peoples subjected to colonial rule, oppression, and foreign occupation with a view to regaining their legitimate rights' (Aust, 2018: 292). The G8 feared that this step would complicate the process of moving forward with the treaty and possibly prevent it from being adopted at all.

Figure A2.3 visually shows the negotiation between the blocks. Each group's BATNA was the *status quo*, seen at the back square's intersection. As such, any negotiated agreement, to get something, would be better. The UK suggested that instead of defining terrorism and addressing state-sponsored terrorism, they instead just specify acts that are criminalized. Thus, they found an agreement in the middle of the potential zone of agreement and continued to negotiate

Group A Countries:
Germany, USA, Ireland,
Australia, Sri Lanka,
Algeria, France

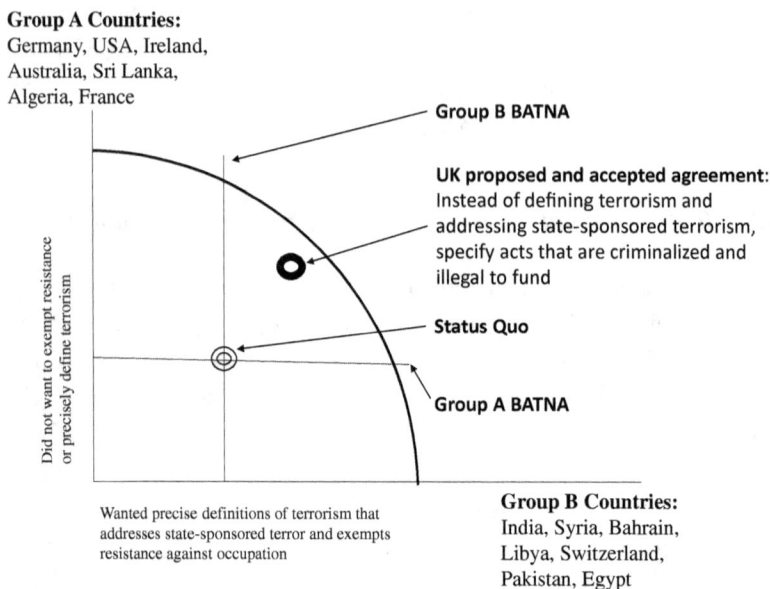

Group B Countries:
India, Syria, Bahrain,
Libya, Switzerland,
Pakistan, Egypt

Figure A2.3. The policy negotiation game space with the BATNA and the actual achievements.

specific aspects of the treaty. We summarize some of the other key issues of negotiation in Table A2.2. It shows some of the parties and the positions taken as well as the final outcomes for the key issues of Financial Reporting, Mutual Legal Assistance, Freezing/Seizing of Funds, and use of Confiscated Assets. Table A2.3 further shows the overall Gains/Losses to parties over certain issues.

A2.8 *Stability of the policy*

While the convention was initially successful, as the memory of the 9/11 attack faded, countries' zealousness has waned. Banks have reported a feeling of 'blocking fatigue' from freezing assets (Clunan, 2006: 595). A rift has also started to form between the United States and other countries. The US is seen as being too focused on Islamic terrorism and only using the international networks when it wants leverage over other countries (Clunan, 2006: 582). There is also a growing disillusionment with the UN and other Global bureaucracies

Table A2.2. Dynamics of parties/blocks' positions during the negotiation of the policy.

Topic	Position A	Position B	Final position
Financial Reporting	Wanted all large and unusual transactions reported (India, USA, Sweden, Australia)	Only wanted to pay attention to suspicious accounts—not necessarily reported (Switzerland, Luxembourg)	Swiss & India merged requests: Pay special attention to unusual transactions and report only if they are suspected of stemming from criminal activity
Mutual Legal Assistance & Extradition	Wanted it to be impossible to deny assistance on grounds of banking secrecy (France, G8)	Cannot deny assistance based 'solely' on the grounds of banking secrecy (Belgium, Austria)	State parties may not refuse a request for mutual legal assistance on the grounds of banking secrecy
Freezing of Funds	Freezing Optional (France)	Freezing mandatory (Sudan, South Africa, Iran, Australia, Neth.)	Made parties 'obliged' to freeze funds
Use of Confiscated Funds/ Property	Go to 'root' causes of terrorism (Lebanon)	Compensate victims (Ecuador, France, USA, UK, Africa)	Distribute funds to compensate victims of terrorism

which is exemplified by the recent rise of populist movements. The COJ's recent failure to do anything about Russia in Ukraine is also contributing to this view. This is creating a divide between the US and its other Western counterparts who prefer to focus more on the root causes of terrorism.

Table A2.3. Gains and losses of parties/blocks over various topics in the negotiated policy.

Topic	Gains	Losses
Banking Secrecy	Possible reporting of suspicious transactions. Less anonymity for account holders (India, USA, Sweden, Australia)	Loss of some degree of banking privacy; by requiring only suspected criminal transactions worthy of reporting some guilty accounts may go unreported (Switzerland, Luxembourg—wanted less stringent requirements)
Extradition	Smaller countries outside of the G8 have more legislative power to request extradition	Might have problems with multiple parties fighting over jurisdiction
Seizure of Funds/ Property	Seizing of funds used for terrorism; help prevent new acts; distribute funds to victims (countries that are victims of terrorism gain) (Ecuador, Ireland, USA, and Belgium)	Those who want the root causes of terrorism addressed (Lebanon)
FIU Access	Member countries have access and power to request transactional information from other member countries with a guarantee of confidentiality	Potential risk of information being misappropriated to the wrong party, posing a national security concern

Additionally, the policy has failed to consider factors such as technological advancement which has increased the effectiveness of funneling money to terrorist groups.

Current anti-money laundering tools have been largely ineffective as technology outpaces regulations. As standing notes 'There has been a great deal of banking legislation and the establishment of thousands of Financial Investigation Units, but the overall impact in terms of making it harder for criminals to launder money has been minimal' (Standing, 2010: 4). The internet and now cryptocurrencies are further increasing the time and costs associated with detecting illicit financing. In terms of stability, we will not see countries withdraw from the treaty. There is no reason to go through the effort to withdraw and it would also look very bad. Instead, we will likely see less compliance with international protocols and increased regional cooperation between more motivated parties, such as the Caribbean FATF or the 2005 Council of Europe Convention on Laundering. A new treaty will likely replace it in time.

A2.9 *Analysis of effectiveness of the policy*

Looking at the ratification timeline for the CSFT, it can be seen that the treaty was not very popular initially. However, after the 9/11 attack occurred, the UN temporarily became a monolithic party in terms of prioritizing terrorism. Ratifications increased dramatically in 2002 and 2003. Countries raced to expand their financial regulatory frameworks to incorporate anti-terrorism measures. In the aftermath of 9/11, 188 countries passed domestic legislation allowing them to freeze Taliban assets, and 170 passed laws to freeze assets of terrorist groups more broadly (Clunan, 2006: 579). Over $147 million in Al Qaeda and Taliban assets were frozen. The Egmont network of FIUs grew by 40 countries in 5 years. The Convention was effective in establishing terrorist financing as its own criminal act and incorporating it into existing regulatory frameworks.

While the policy was initially effective, subsequent years have seen interest and compliance diminish. It is difficult to quantify the effectiveness of the treaty in terms of stopping terrorism. However, the FATF does conduct evaluations of compliance for combating financial crimes. Currently, most countries comply only moderately. For example, a 2014 statement by the FATF President noted that only 88 of 192 (45%) countries complied with Targeted Financial Sanctions (aka Asset-Freezing) (Wilkins, 2014). The FATF put out a worldwide Terrorist Financing report intended for the G20 that looked at 194 countries. The report found that while almost all jurisdictions had criminalized terrorist financing, only 17% of jurisdictions had ever achieved convictions for such acts (FATF, 2015: 2). Oddly, the country with the highest number of terrorist financing convictions since 2010 is Saudi Arabia at 863, with the USA at second place with around 100 (FATF, 2015: 4). Israel had around 25. This seems to indicate that while the convention helped integrate terrorism financing into domestic law enforcement networks and spurred the creation of domestic regulatory mechanisms, the compliance of most states has been largely superficial.

A2.10 *Benefits from features and experiences of other global policies*

An important issue highlighted in this treaty is the importance of definitions. The UN Convention against Transnational Organized Crime is a timely and closely related policy that can be learned from. It breaks apart the issue of Transnational crime into three protocols, known as the Palermo Protocols. One is a Trafficking Protocol, designed to target the trafficking of human beings, specifically women and children. It precisely defines trafficking situations as meeting three conditions—Act (i.e., recruitment), means (use of force), and purpose (forced labor). The other two protocols address migrant smuggling and firearm trafficking (UN Office of Drugs & Crime, 2000). The treaty has 189 parties, so it is a very successful treaty in terms of ratifications. The lesson gleaned from the protocols is the importance of definitions. The Financing treaty could benefit from incorporating a set of conditions that can be used to define terrorism, rather than hinging a definition on rigid wording.

The failed Comprehensive Terrorism Treaty also highlights the importance of definitions, although in a different manner. Following the Terrorist Financing Convention, the UN set about drafting Comprehensive Treaty, as per the agreement with India. Unlike the Finance convention, this treaty could not sidestep defining terrorism. However, no consensus could be reached, as Islamic countries would not accept a definition that did not exempt acts of self-determination (Diaz-Paniagua, 2008: 515). This tells us that while it is important to have clear definitions, one must also be flexible and know how to pick battles, otherwise, it could end with a treaty that remains in deadlock for almost 20 years.

References

Aust, A., 2001. *Counter-Terrorism—a New Approach*. Retrieved from http://www.mpil.de/files/pdf1/mpunyb_aust_5.pd

Clunan, A., 2006. The Fight Against Terrorist Financing. NPS Archive: Calhoun. *Political Science Quarterly*, 121(4).

Diaz-Paniagua, C., 2008. Negotiating Terrorism: The Negotiation Dynamics of Four Un Counter-Terrorism Treaties, 1997–2005. Vol. 1. Dissertation. City University of New York. Retrieved from https://papers.ssrn.com/sol3/papers.cfm?abstract_id=1968150.

Dudley, D., November 16, 2016. *The Ten Countries Most Affected by Terrorism*. Forbes Business. Retrieved from https://www.forbes.com/sites/dominic dudley/2016/11/18/countries-most-affected-by-terrorism/#3084cd3130d9.

FATF, November 16, 2015, Terrorist Financing—FATF Report to the G20 Leaders. Retrieved from http://www.fatf-gafi.org/media/fatf/documents/reports/Terrorist-financing-actions-taken-by-FATF.pdf.

FATF Gafi High-Risk, 2018. High Risk and Other Monitored Jurisdictions. Retrieved from http://www.fatf-gafi.org/publications/high-riskandnon-cooperativejurisdictions/?hf=10&b=0&s=desc(fatf_releasedate).

France, March 11, 1999.—Working Document: Why an International Convention against the Financing Of Terrorism? Para 1, later reproduced as: U.N. Doc. A/AC.252/L.7/Add.1.

International Court of Justice, January 17, 2017. Application Instituting Proceedings. Ukraine vs Russian Federation. Retrieved from http://www.icj-cij.org/files/case-related/166/19314.pdf.

International Court of Justice, March 9, 2017. Press Release No 2117/11. The Hague. Retrieved from http://www.icj-cij.org/en/case/166.

IMF, 2003. International Monetary Fund. Legal Department. Suppressing the Financing of Terrorism. A Handbook for Legislative Drafting. Retrieved from https://www.imf.org/external/pubs/nft/2003/SFTH/pdf/SFTH.pdf.

Klein, P., 2009. International Convention for the Suppression of the Financing of Terrorism. United Nations Audiovisual Library of International Law.

Lavalle, R., 2000. *The International Convention for the Suppression of the Financing of Terrorism*. Max-Planck Institute. Retrieved from http://www.zaoerv.de/60_2000/60_2000_1_b_491_510.pdf.

Schaak, B. and Maxwell, I., October 11, 2017. *Terrorist Financing: A Backgrounder*. Retrieved from https://www.justsecurity.org/45810/terrorist-financing-backgrounder/.

Standing, A., December, 2010. *Transnational Organized Crime and the Palermo Convention: A Reality Check.* Retrieved from https://www.ipinst.org/wp-content/uploads/publications/e_pub_palermo_convention.pdf.

UN Office of Drugs & Crime, November 15, 2000. *United Nations.* United Nations Convention against Transnational Organized Crime and the Protocols Thereto. Retrieved from http://www.unodc.org/unodc/en/organized-crime/intro/UNTOC.html.

UN SCCTC, 2018. *United Nations Security Council Counter-Terrorism Committee.* Retrieved from https://www.un.org/sc/ctc/.

United Nations Treaty Text, December 9, 1999. *International Convention on the Suppression of Financing of Terrorism.* Text. Retrieved from http://www.un.org/law/cod/finterr.htm.

United Nations Treaty Collection, April 16, 2018. *International Convention on the Suppression of Financing of Terrorism.* Chapter XVIII Penal Matters. Retrieved from https://treaties.un.org/Pages/ViewDetails.aspx?src=IND&mtdsg_no=XVIII-11&chapter=18&lang=en.

United Nations, March 16, 1999. Press Release L/2916. AD HOC COMMITTEE BEGINS FIRST READING OF DRAFT CONVENTION ON SUPPRESSION OF TERRORISM FINANCING. Retrieved from https://www.un.org/press/en/1999/19990316.l2916.html.

Wilkins, R., December 14, 2014. Many countries are still not able to freeze terrorists' assets effectively, says FATF President Roger Wilkins, AO. FATF. Retrieved from http://www.fatf-gafi.org/publications/fatfrecommendations/documents/many-countries-still-not-able-to-freeze-terrorist-assets-effectively.html.

A3. Framework Convention on Tobacco Control (WHO FCTC)[2]

The WHO Framework Convention on Tobacco Control is the first global public health treaty to emerge under the auspices of the World Health Organization. What makes the WHO FCTC truly revolutionary is that the framework focuses not on an individual disease or illness. The WTO FCTC focuses on one of the causes associated with many of the globe's preventable diseases. Specifically, the WTO FCTC aims '...to protect present and future generations from the devastating health, social, environmental and economic consequences of tobacco consumption and exposure to tobacco smoke...'

---

[2]Modified from Jorge Gavino and Jacquelyn González, Final Paper to the course PPBL224, June 14, 2018. Authors' consent was obtained.

(WHOFCTC, 2008). The WHO FCTC requires an extensive commitment and effort by many nations which brings with it many positives and many hurdles.

A3.1 *Objectives and motivations*

The WHO FCTC emerged via an international consensus, understanding, and as a response to the global spread out of the tobacco epidemic (WHOFCTC Overview, 2015). This framework requires complex cooperation and understanding by neighboring nations and cross-border negotiation to further allow nations to foster their right to protect public health (WHOFCTC, 2008).

The rise of globalization had allowed the tobacco industry to gain a large foothold in many nations. Production and consumption of tobacco had become deeply rooted in many developed and developing nations. This was recognized as a concern of the international community regarding the devastating global health, social, economic, and environmental consequences of tobacco consumption and exposure to tobacco smoke (WHOFCTC, 2008). The unified concern of the international community was the drive behind the creation of the convention on tobacco control.

A3.2 *Political history*

The impetus for the WHO FCTC began in the late 1900s when, 'the global increase in tobacco-related diseases had become a public health challenge that called for radical and creative measures, triggering the first use of WHO's constitutional treaty-making power.' (Nikogosian, 2010).

At present, illnesses related to the consumption of tobacco are the leading causes of preventable death around the globe. For the remainder of the 20th century, the beginnings of the framework continued to be conceptualized and a need for it was identified. Negotiations began in the early 2000s with the World Health Assembly adopting the WHO FCTC in 2003. By February of 2005, the WHO FCTC officially entered into force. Since then the WHO FCTC has become one of the most widely and rapidly ratified conventions among the

United Nations' treaties (Nikogosian, 2010). The WHO FCTC has enjoyed 168 parties signing on to it and is legally binding in 181 countries.

A3.3 *Structure of the policy and regulatory mechanisms*

The WHO FCTC created rules and regulations that govern the production, sale, distribution, advertisement, and taxation of tobacco. While the WHO FCTC creates a minimum requirement, many nations are encouraged and do have stricter regulations. The following 12 topics and measures are outlined and regulated by the WHO FCTC: Lobbying, Demand Reduction, Passive Smoking, Regulation, Packaging and Labeling, Awareness, Tobacco Advertising, Addiction, Smuggling, Minors, Environment, and Research. Description of these measures can be found in Table A3.1.

Most importantly, the WHO FCTC identifies the immediate need to reduce the supply and demand of Tobacco. As outlined in Article 6, the framework highlights that taxation is an important part of reducing demand. Article 6 encourages taxation and prohibits duty-free tobacco products. While Article 7 focuses on non-price measures that will lead to the legislation, regulation, and policies that will aid in lowering demand in nations.

As for the supply of tobacco, it is important to note that the WHO FCTC recognizes the monetary value that the growth and sale of tobacco can have on countries' economies. This dependence on a tobacco source of revenue can make it difficult to maintain compliance. Article 15 also highlights the importance of eliminating illicit trade of tobacco and tobacco products. In this instance, cross-border negotiation and cooperation are vital to the success of the FCTC and nations' efforts.

A3.4 *Role of local (state) interests*

Interests, investments, and extent of implementation vary among blocks of states. For the purposes of this brief, the roles of tobacco growing regions (developed and developing) as well as developed regions will be examined. It is important to note that at the time

Table A3.1. Measures and mechanisms in the treaty to implement tobacco control policies.

Measure	Mechanism	Article(s)
To limit the power of tobacco industry and influence on lawmakers	Lobbying	5
To lower the demand for tobacco and tobacco products via the taxation of such products	Reduction of Demand	6 & 7
To reduce people's exposure to secondhand smoke in both public areas and work spaces	Passive Smoking	8
To regulate the contents and emissions of tobacco products. Disclosure of the ingredients of tobacco products	Regulation	10
Must include health warnings on packaging that take up at least 30% of packaging. Deceptive labels are prohibited	Packaging and Labeling	9 & 11
Increase public awareness on the dangers and consequences of tobacco and its various forms	Awareness	12
Ban all forms of tobacco advertising, specifically those aimed at children. *may conflict with countries' freedom of speech laws	Tobacco Advertising	13
Encourage and create programs to help individuals quit smoking/using tobacco products	Addiction	14
Eliminate the illicit trade of tobacco products (cross-border cooperation necessary)	Reductions to the Supply of Tobacco and Illicit Trade	15
Ban/restrict the sale to minors	Minors	16
Protection of the environment	Address concerns regarding the serious risk posed by tobacco farming	18
Encourage, support, and freely share tobacco-related research and information	Research	20, 21, 22

of the initial implementation of the WHO FCTC, an $8 million budget was proposed for the first two years of implementation of the treaty (WHO FCTC, 2018). Of the 113 parties present at the treaty conference, funding for the $8 million was to be made through voluntary assessed contributions.

In addition, it was proposed that the treaty would also explore 'economically viable alternatives to tobacco growing and production' as a way to diversify economies, particularly in countries that were reliant on the tobacco-agriculture industry (WHO FCTC, 2008). Therefore, the cooperative arrangements made among each WHO region, or blocks of states, established them as economically rational players given that each block of countries pledged or did not pledge payment toward the $8 million budget unless they saw a potential maximized profit. In general, the role of states varied in the cooperation and negotiation process of participating in the treaty implementation, with an additional policy actor in the midst of it all: the tobacco industry.

A3.5 *Tobacco growing regions*

According to WHO's Tobacco Atlas (2012), tobacco is grown in over 125 countries, on nearly four million hectares. Therefore, it is critical to examine the role of states' interest within tobacco growing regions, including both developing and developed Parties. Among those growing regions some states (the block) depend on tobacco cultivation and industry for economic development purposes. Within this block of states are the following WHO Regions: Southeast Asia, Africa, the Eastern Mediterranean, the Americas, and China, from the Western Pacific region, standing alone within the block.

This block of countries advocated examining economically viable alternatives for workers, growers, and individual sellers of the tobacco industry (WHOFCTC, 2008). In addition, it was proposed to establish an ad-hoc study group of experts to study these alternatives to tobacco growing and production as a means to support growers and workers in developing countries. All WHO Regions committed payments for the initial implementation of WHO FCTC with the exception of the Eastern Mediterranean, which pledged that their Parties would make every effort to honor budget commitments.

A3.6 *Developed regions*

In contrast, the second block of states among the developed regions had somewhat an opposite role to that of the tobacco growing regions. Both the WHO Region of Europe as well as Japan from the WHO Region of the Western Pacific did not pledge payments. The European Community was not in full agreement given that crop-specific rural development policies were rare and because they needed more information on the financial implications in order to satisfy the total budget (WHO FCTC, 2018). It should be noted, however, that these countries also have high rates of illicit trade, which makes tobacco products more affordable and accessible to low-income groups and to children (WHO, 2015).

A3.7 *Cooperation and negotiation*

Among the blocks of countries who gained the most in their role were the WHO Regions of Southeast Asia, Africa, and the Eastern Mediterranean region. Each of these blocks of states are among those whose economies depend heavily on the production of tobacco. In particular, the WHO African Region noted that 'tobacco growing was a form of subsistence agriculture, and the growers must be helped to combat poverty which blocked all other opportunities.' Therefore, their economically rational decision to participate was particularly based on that the treaty would financially support these regions to explore economically viable alternatives to tobacco growing, which in turn could assist in further developing these regions' economies. Furthermore, their assessed contributions to fully participate in the treaty was relatively low, ranging from 0.001% to 0.45%, so their participation cost was significantly lower than other regions, therefore, maximizing their long-term profit. Although the cost was high for Member States such as Mexico, China, Canada, and Brazil, who voluntarily pledged payment toward the budget, their gains were in terms of the future economic benefit toward the investigation in economic alternatives to tobacco as it would also diversify their own economies.

Given that there were fewer Parties for the Convention (113), as previously mentioned, the assessed contribution scale was increased proportionately to meet the $8 million budgeted for the initial implementation of the treaty. Therefore, some Parties had higher assessed contributions than others, not surprisingly, those Parties were hesitant to pledge payment and implementation of the treaty as decided by the Conference. Japan, for example, had an assessed contribution of 22%, the highest of all Parties; therefore, it was appropriate that it advocated a ceiling cap of 22% so that they would not increase further. Other Parties who were hesitant to pledge payment because they would lose more financially were the Member States of the European region such as Germany, France, Netherlands, Spain, the United Kingdom, etc.

A3.7.1 *Tobacco industry as policy actor*

Among the cooperative arrangements and negotiation process of the treaty, the tobacco industry's role and interests cannot be ignored. Given that the industry 'relies on the use of the evolving strategies [of the WHO FCTC] to further their interests and undermine implementation,' (ITC Project, 2015). For example, according to Pangestu (2018), approximately 10% of the world's smokers reside in Southeast Asia. Moreover, countries such as India, Indonesia, Bangladesh, and Thailand are within the top 20 tobacco producing nations (WHO Tobacco Free Initiative, 2013). Although a region like Southeast Asia is actively participating in the treaty, there still appears to be some industry influence on the region, circumventing and evolving with some of the strategies within the WHO FCTC.

A3.8 *Stability of the policy*

Since the WHO FCTC came into force, there have been some significant improvements in tobacco control around the world. In 2016, WHO FCTC became one of the most widely adopted UN treaties consisting of 180 Parties to date (Society for the Study of Addiction,

2017). According to a study of the treaty by the International Tobacco Control (ITC) Project (2015), it has been an important driving force for tobacco regulation legislation across nations. Countries such as Canada, Iceland, Mexico, and Norway have reduced smoking by more than half for both men and women since 1980 (Murray *et al.*, 2012). Parties have been intentional and active in implementing strategies such as restricting sales of tobacco to minors; protection from tobacco exposure in spaces such as restaurants, schools, workplaces, etc.; education communication, training, and public awareness; and packaging labeling of tobacco products.

However, while significant progress has been made, there continues to be tobacco industry interference. As demonstrated in the above statistics, the tobacco industry has continued presence and provides economic strength in Southeast Asia, with more than 80% of the world's one billion smokers living in low and middle income countries (ITC Project, 2015). In addition, lack of financial support by some countries, lack of accountability, and lack of enforcement of global tobacco regulatory policies have also been challenges to the implementation of the treaty. We will discuss these regulatory policies and actions in the subsequent section.

A3.9 *Analysis of effectiveness*

As previously alluded to, WHO FCTC has had a positive impact on pushing tobacco control legislation across the country through various mechanisms. For the purposes of this brief, we will analyze the effectiveness of the implementation of some of these policies. In particular, we will be examining the implementation of policies such as price and tax measures, preventing tobacco industry interference, protections from tobacco exposure, and public disclosure of information on tobacco products (Chung-Hall *et al.*, 2016).

A3.9.1 *Price and tax measures*

Among one of the tobacco control legislative policies, Article 6 of the WHO FCTC obligates Parties to adopt pricing and taxation measures in order to reduce tobacco consumption, and is considered

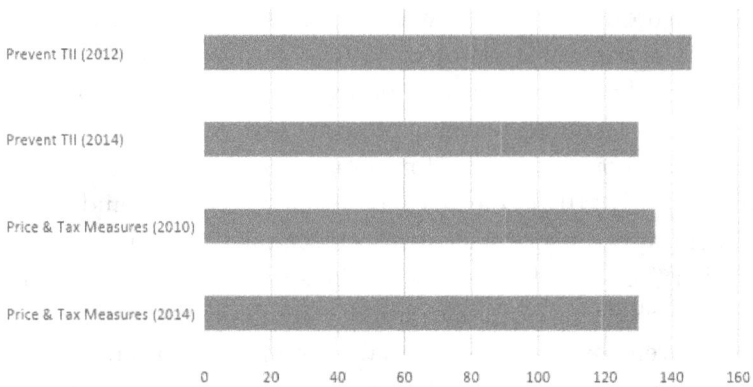

Figure A3.1.   Implementation of tobacco control policies (I).

to be the most effective population-based strategy to reduce tobacco consumption and encourage cessation (ITC Project, 2015). This has certainly been demonstrated between the years of 2010 and 2014. In the year 2010, 67%, or 90 out of 135, reported instituting tax increases on tobacco products (Figure A3.1). Then, approximately four years later (2014), that number jumped up to 92% of reporting states that issued tax increases (119 out of 130). Countries such as Pakistan, the Philippines, Chile, and Costa Rica are some of the states that instituted much more robust tax systems on tobacco products.

A3.9.2   *Preventing tobacco industry interference*

Another component within Article 5.3 of the treaty requires states to take appropriate steps and measures to prevent tobacco industry interference in tobacco control efforts. Again, the role of the tobacco industry in the evolution of tobacco cultivation and consumption over the years is apparent. However, gradually more Parties are implementing actions to prevent industry influence. For example, in 2012, 55% of reporting Parties, or 80 of 146, indicated executing and enforcing these preventative measures (Figure A3.1). This number grew to 68% of the reporting Parties. Therefore, progress was made in the span of two years, but there is still more work to be done.

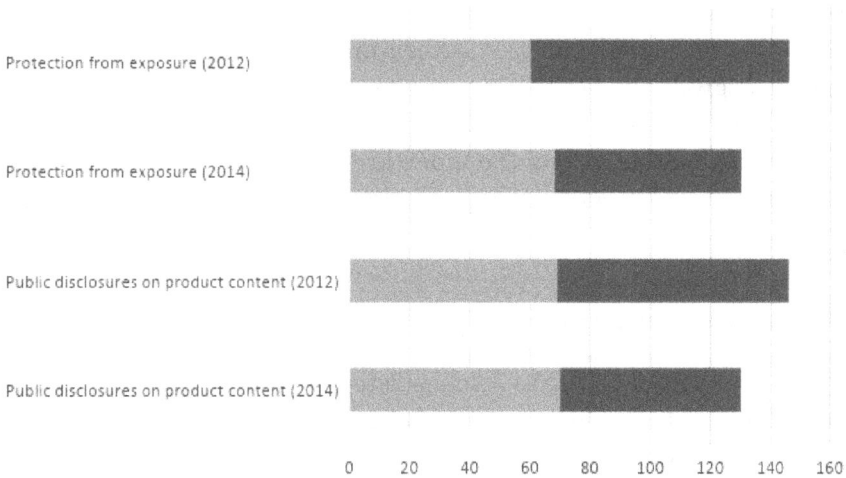

Figure A3.2. Implementation of tobacco control policies (II).

A3.9.3 *Protection from tobacco exposure*

The treaty calls for Parties to enforce legislation and policies that protect individuals from exposure to tobacco smoke. This is emphasized, particularly, in public places such as schools, workplaces, public transportation, and other indoor spaces. As a result, far-reaching smoke-free regulations have been one of the key legislative outlets in executing the enforcement of protection from tobacco exposure. In general, the progress has been gradual and steady. For example, in 2012, 41% of states implemented some form of a smoking ban, increasing to 52% in 2014 (Figure A3.2). For example, Ireland was among one of the first nations to implement smoke-free laws in public spaces.

A3.10 *Public disclosures on product content*

Lastly, a key measure in tobacco control legislation has been that of disclosures of contents and emissions of tobacco products. Canada, for example, was among one of the first Parties to implement pictorial health warnings on their products. Nevertheless, according to the ITC Project (2015), the tobacco industry, as a whole, has a long history of using various strategies that block regulatory agencies from disclosing the ingredients used in their products. This is perhaps most apparent given the very slow progress in implementing such public disclosure policies. In 2012, public disclosure of contents on products was approximately 47% of the reporting Parties, while in 2014 it was 54% (Figure A3.2). Overall, the progress of this policy was slow and gradual.

A3.11   *Conclusion and relevance to other global policies*

While the WHO FCTC has demonstrated progress in certain areas in regulating and reinforcing tobacco control legislation, there are still some accountability challenges in its implementation. Therefore, it is critical to learn from other global policies that have been successful and perhaps not as successful. In regards to WHO FCTC limitations, some of the key challenges are similar to that of the Kyoto Protocol. Among one of the principle problems with the Kyoto Protocol was that of the 'absence of any specific expectations from developing to curb (greenhouse gas) emissions' (Soroos, 2005). This perhaps holds a similar truth to that of the WHO FCTC as in developing countries, particularly those in tobacco growing regions, are not enforcing tobacco control legislative measure as robustly as they could. This is apparent in the rates of implementation of specific measures discussed in the previous section as well as how more developed states such as Canada and Ireland are among the pioneers for robust tobacco control.

Furthermore, we must also examine other effective global policies such as one of the most successful treaties, the Vienna Convention for the Protection of the Ozone Layer. According to Soroos (2005), one of the reasons the Vienna Convention was able to be successful was the utilization of science as leverage to inform policymaking. As such, there is a need for more critical research on the effectiveness of tobacco control legislation. Moreover, another strength WHO FCTC can consider is implementation of economic incentives for developing countries while not curbing accountability.

References

Chung-Hall, J., Craig, L., Gravely S., Sansone, N., and Fong, G. T., June 2016. *Impact of the WHO Framework Convention on Tobacco Control on the Implementation and Effectiveness of Tobacco Control Measures: A Global Evidence Review.* ITC Project. University of Waterloo, Waterloo, Ontario, Canada.

Nikogosian, H., 2010. *WHO Framework Convention on Tobacco Control: A Key Milestone.* Retrieved from https://www.ncbi.nlm.nih.gov/pmc/articles/PMC2814489/.

Pangestu, T., March 2018. *Tobacco Companies Making a Fortune in Southeast Asia.* The News Lens. Retrieved from https://international.thenewslens.com/article/90722.

Society for the Study of Addiction, 2017. *Recommendations for the Implementation of WHO Framework Convention on Tobacco Control Article 14 on Tobacco Cessation Support.* Retrieved from https://onlinelibrary.wiley.com/doi/pdf/10.1111/add.13893.

Soroos, M. S., 2005. Gurret Hardin and Tragedies of Global Commons. In: Dauvergne, Peter (Ed.), *Handbook of Global Environmental Politics.* Cheltenham: Edward Elgar.

World Health Organization, February 2008. *Conference of the Parties to the WHO Framework Convention on Tobacco Control.* Summary Records of Committees, Geneva.

World Health Organization, 2012. *Growing Tobacco.* Retrieved from http://www.who.int/tobacco/cn/atlas16.pdf.

World Health Organization Regional Office for Europe. 2015. *Implementation of the WHOFCTC.* Retrieved from http://www.euro.who.int/en/health-topics/disease-prevention/tobacco/publications/key-policy-documents/who-framework-convention.

A4. Montreal Protocol on Substances that Deplete the Ozone Layer[3]

The Montreal Protocol on Substances that Deplete the Ozone Layer (Montreal Protocol) is an international protocol whose main objective is to protect human health and the environment through the reduction and prevention of identified substances known to deplete the Earth's ozone layer (United Nations Environment Programme

---

[3]Modified from Fortino Morales and Michael Parmer, Final Paper to the course PPBL224, June 14, 2018. Authors' consent was obtained.

& Ozone Secretariat, 2003: 3). The protocol mandates participating parties to take measures to reduce and phase-out ozone-depleting chemicals. Through a special provision, the Montreal Protocol enables participating countries to respond rapidly to new, emerging scientific information regarding harmful ozone-depleting chemicals (United Nations Environment Programme & Ozone Secretariat, 2003: 4).

A4.1 *Objectives of the Montreal Protocol*

The Montreal Protocol obligates parties to take appropriate measures to: research and exchange information that results in deepening a global understanding of the ozone layer, its depletion, and the effects on human health and the environment (Aucamp *et al.*, 2011); adopt legislative and administrative measures and policies within their respective jurisdictions and control to prevent the depletion and modification of the ozone layer; collaborate to adopt and implement appropriate protocols, measures, annexes within Montreal Protocol; collaborate with international agencies and organizations to implement this protocol and other protocols; and base the implementation of protocols, measures, annexes within Montreal Protocol on scientific and technical information (United Nations Environment Programme & Ozone Secretariat, 2003: 4).

A4.2 *Motivation for establishing the Montreal Protocol*

The Montreal Protocol was appealing to countries for a number of reasons, but particularly because the lack of action of countries to phase-out ozone-depleting chemicals would result in the catastrophic collapse of the ozone layer by 2050 (About Montreal Protocol (n.d)). This dire warning from the scientific community, while not the single biggest reason, was an important motivation for countries to sign on and ratify the protocol as ozone depletion was 'associated with more-certain and more-costly consequences than problems like global warming' (Murdoch and Sandler, 1997: 347).

The global public was also instrumental in providing support for countries to adopt and ratify the protocol as they too were concerned about the consequences of not taking any action. This resulted in the global public maintaining political interest in the depletion of the ozone and in the search for a solution(s) (Morrisette, 1989: 814).

Another motivation for establishing the Montreal Protocol was that the debate about chlorofluorocarbons (CFCs) shifting from determining whether regulation was necessary, to when and how to regulate (Morrisette, 1989: 816). This was driven by both economic and regulatory incentives and mechanisms as industry leaders (such as DuPont and Imperial Chemical Industries) were developing CFC substitutes and looking to bring these alternatives to the market (Morrisette, 1989: 815–816; Skjærseth, 1992: 297–298).

Lastly, both industrial (Non-Article 5) and developing (Article 5)[4] countries were motivated to establish the Montreal Protocol due to nested negotiations which assisted in allowing for their two interests to be separated, providing for more politically salient and agreeable solutions that addressed the unique needs of both developing and industrial countries and increased both parties' ability to see past the 'veil of uncertainty' (Skjærseth, 1992, 1992: 299) For Article 5 countries, provisions in the protocol that were brought by the nested negotiations provided delays of up to 10 years to decrease emissions, while providing monetary resources, technical assistance, and technology. Industrialized countries stood to benefit too as joining the protocol meant increased opportunities to trade as trade was banned among non-participating countries.

A4.3 *Politics and history of the process*

The negotiation process of the Montreal Protocol is very unique compared to other international protocols and treaties. This was due, in part, to the sense of urgency and awareness of ozone depletion as

---

[4]List of article 5 (developing) and Non-article 5 (developed) countries is provided in the treaty.

well as the universal nature of depletion as depletion would affect the global population (Green, 2009: 259–260). Furthermore, this protocol was also the first global environmental treaty to address a theoretical problem as ozone depletion had not yet been observed when the protocol process first started (DeSombre, 2000: 49–50).

The parties participating in the negotiations were primarily monolithic. Each party, according to Rules of Procedure for Meetings of the Parties to the Montreal Protocol (Rule 16—Representation and credentials), consisted of a small delegation of accredited representatives and a designated head (Ozone Secretariat, 2018). However, the negotiating parties were not necessarily internally monolithic. An example of this is the United States as there were a number of disagreements in the United States's goals and priorities. In fact, President Reagan 'overruled dissenting Cabinet members to approve the US goals for the treaty' (Wampler, 2015).

'The Montreal Protocol utilized and provided a successful (and in some ways revolutionary) approach to the principle of common concern, the precautionary principle, state sovereignty, and the breakthrough principle of common but differentiated responsibilities' (Green, 2009: 259). These approaches were instrumental in creating unity, common ground, and cooperation with the negotiating parties as the urgency of inaction and global impact were of great concern. One approach to negotiations of the Montreal Protocol were nested negotiations. These nested negotiations resulted in the separation of industrialized and developing countries' interests to allow for negotiations that were more politically salient, gave greater allowances for the separate parties, and were more agreeable (Parson and Zeckhauser, 1993: 29–30). To date, over 720 decisions have been made and adopted by the parties to the Montreal Protocol (The Montreal Protocol on Substances that Deplete the Ozone Layer, n.d).

A rare issue linkage occurs in the Montreal Protocol between trade and environmental policies. The Montreal Protocol has trade restrictions between parties (countries who signed onto the protocol) and non-parties (countries who elected to not sign), which actually serve as an incentive to join the protocol as competitive advantage falls to the participating parties. 'Importation by parties from non-parties had to be gradually ceased, and exportation to non-parties by parties was banned entirely' (Green, 2009: 264).

In studying the signatories of the Montreal Protocol, there is a linear relationship found between the amount of emissions cutbacks and national income (Murdoch and Sandler, 1997). This speaks to the way in which developing nations were incentivized to join the protocol allowing them 10 years to decrease their emissions, while providing resources for technical assistance. Murdoch and Sandler (1997) also find that the Montreal Protocol may not have been as effective citing the nations prior initiatives to reduce CFC emissions, '61 nations in our sample set reduced CFC emissions by 41.6% from 1986 to 1989, which is well in excess of the 20% cutback mandated by the Protocol from the year commencing on July 1, 1993' (Murdoch and Sandler, 1997: 17). The concept of the BATNA seems to be the premise of Murdoch's assumption, that the Parties would have reached the BATNA even without the agreement.

By the final stages of the Montreal Protocol, all UN state actors had ratified the agreement, making it one of the first examples of the use of 'precautionary principle' for global environmental issues with such a consensus. Furthermore, 'the Montreal Protocol did not present a prisoner's dilemma because key nations, including the United States, would gain from unilateral action; and in fact, many nations engaged in such action' (Sunstein, 2006: 6).

A4.4 *Structure of the Montreal Protocol*

The structure of the Montreal Protocol consists of measures to reduce, and eventually eliminate, global emissions of various ozone-depleting substances through the gradual phase-out of their consumption and production. (Ozone Secretariat, 2017: 6) There are two parties of the protocol; Industrial (Non-Article 5) countries and Developing (Article 5) countries. Article 5 of the Montreal Protocol gave special situations for developing countries 'whose annual calculated level of consumption of the controlled substances is less than 0.3 kilograms per capita on the date of the entry into force of the Protocol for it, or any time thereafter until January 1, 1999'. To date, there are 147 Article 5 countries and 50 Non-Article 5 countries (including the United States of America) who ratified the treaty (Ozone Secretariat, n.d.).

Both groups of countries have equal but differentiated responsibilities with binding, time-targeted, and measurable commitments (UNEP, n.d.). Over time, the measures of the protocol have become progressively more comprehensive, effective, and ambitious (Ozone Secretariat, 2017: 6). Developing countries were granted a 10-year delay before phasing-down of the production and consumption of various identified ozone-depleting substances. Further, a Multilateral Fund (MLF) was developed to support Article 5 countries by providing monetary resources, technical assistance, and technology transfers. Non-Article 5 countries provide funding for the MLF. Trade is prohibited between signed parties and non-signed parties.

To date, there have been five amendments to the protocol: London Amendment (1990), Copenhagen Amendment (1992), Montreal Amendment (1997), Beijing Amendment (1999), and the Kigali Amendment (2016). The protocol also provides adjustments to be made which allows parties to accelerate reduction schedules and do not require ratification. Adjustments have been made in 1990, 1992, 1995, 1997, 1999, and 2000.

The Montreal Protocol requires participating countries to meet regularly, with the main meeting taking place on an annual basis (Article 11). Additionally, an annual Open-ended Working Group (OEWG) is held to address specific issues and recommend actions to the OEWG. Three assessment panels (the Technology and Economic Assessment Panel (TEAP), the Scientific Assessment Panel (SAP), and the Environmental Effects Assessment Panel (EEAP)) meet every four years to review data, compile respective reports with their findings and analysis, and assist nations to strengthen public–private partnerships to heal the ozone. Last, an Implementation Committee (ImpCom) guides non-compliance procedures and findings. Meetings are arranged and organized through the Ozone Secretariat at the United Nations Environment Programme in Nairobi.

A4.5 *Policy regulatory mechanisms*

A4.5.1 *Trade restrictions*

One of the regulatory mechanisms that was implemented with the Montreal Protocol was the creation of trade restrictions between participating countries and non-participating countries. These were some of the main mechanisms for reducing ODS levels, as it was through reducing the supply of the ODS that their reduction could be measured vs. trying to track emitters of ODS.

A4.5.2 *Multilateral fund*

Another regulatory mechanism was the creation of the MLF, which maintained that Article 5 countries had to contribute to the fund while the non-Article 5 countries could draw from the fund to support reduction efforts and technology transfers. This mechanism is also what enables funding of the other portions of the Montreal Protocol.

A4.6 *Assessment Panels*

As part of the agreement three panels were set up to ensure the integrity of the policy regularity mechanisms. The TEAP was created to ensure that the technology and economic transfers were taking place with the best available science and through the appropriate economic means. This is an integral part of the agreement as it is an incentive for non-Article 5 countries to participate so that they are able to accelerate their advancements in ODS reduction efforts.

Another panel that was created was the SAP, this panel gathers the latest research to ensure that the targets and goals set by the Montreal Protocol are the most up-to-date information. This again is an integral part of the of Montreal Protocol in that it ensures that their policy is being led by the latest science. The last panel that was created was the EEAP, this panel focuses on the ODS measurement aspect to ensure that the Montreal Protocol is successful in its goal of reducing ODS and increasing the Ozone levels in the atmosphere.

It also ensures that the technology transfers that are being deployed are effective in their approaches.

A4.7 Committees

There are two committees which oversee management issues, the Implementation Committee deals with non-compliance issues and the Executive Committee of the MLF ensures that the overall direction and vision are being followed, made up of the World Bank, UNEP, UNDP, and UNIDO.

A4.8 *Problems associated with the Montreal Protocol*

A4.8.1 *Technical issues*

Despite efforts to phase-down the production and consumption of ozone-depleting chemicals, there remain challenges. First, hydrochlorofluorocarbons (HCFCs) have shown modest increases, suggesting non-compliance in Article 5 countries have offset compliance efforts of non-Article 5 countries (Simmonds *et al.*, 2017: 4651). Additional reasons for this increase could also be, in part, the black market demand in both the United States and the European Union leading to smuggling operations for CFCs and other ozone-depleting chemicals (Jones, 1996: 830–834, 842).

A4.8.2 *Political issues*

During negotiations, side payment demands of China and India resulted in developed countries agreeing to the establishment of the MLF, prompting China to sign the protocol and the London Amendment in 1990 and India signing the following day (Pfluger, 2010: 98). However, the MLF still faces long-term uncertainty. Trump originally threatened to dramatically cut the US' contribution to the fund (May 24 and Doniger, n.d.).

In addition, President Trump quietly accepted the Kigali Amendment to the Montreal Protocol, though has yet to ratify it (Scientific American, 2017). Even then there are conflicting reports about whether or not the US will pull out from it or not (Cama, 2018).

Given the current volatility of the political climate and discourse, and the fact that the US only recently pulled out of the Paris Accord (another climate change treaty, though broader), the future remains uncertain for the United States's support of the protocol.

A4.9 *Role of the local interest in shaping global policy*

To illustrate local interest in shaping global policy, we look at the US's interest in participating in the Montreal Protocol, which was driven by the predicted increases in rates of cancers attributable to CFC emissions and their subsequent negative effects on the ozone. This is the basic premise of the Stag-Hunt Game where there are two hunters that go out to hunt in the same field. They can hunt hare individually successfully, but a hare provides minimal gains for the hunter. They are also able to hunt a stag which provides multiple times more benefits, but neither can do so individually. They must cooperate for the hunt of a stag to be a success.

The US was making provisions as an individual country to reduce the amount of CFCs, which in this case would be the gains the hunter would receive if they hunted the hare individually. With the possibility of the Montreal Protocol, the effectiveness could be raised by up to three times the amount of CFC emissions reduced, increasing the individual benefits for the US that would otherwise not be realized (Sunstein, 2006).

A4.10 *Article 5 and non-Article 5 countries:*
Non-cooperative Nash equilibrium

Game theory is one tool that can be used to understand how local interest can shape global policy. In climate change negotiations, such as the Montreal Protocol, it can be designed and evaluated through the prisoner's dilemma. Simplified, the prisoner's dilemma is a scenario that looks at the costs, benefits, and risks (also referred to as the gains and losses) associated with a country's decision on whether to participate in the Montreal Protocol.

The Nash equilibrium states that the maximum payoff of each involved party depends on the other party's strategies. That is, every player selects the best decision for herself, based on what she thinks others will do. And no-one can do better by changing strategy: every member of the group is doing as well as they possibly can.

For the following scenario, there are essentially four outcomes that could occur for a single country in the negotiations. This includes:

1. A country signing the protocol and joining other countries in reducing ozone-depleting chemicals. In this scenario, all signing parties share the costs and benefits from reduced risk of ozone-depletion.
2. A country decides to sign; however, the signing countries exploit the protocol. The country that signed is burdened with the cost while realizing their efforts likely will not make a significant difference. The other countries benefit from exploitation and create a competitive advantage among themselves.
3. All countries could choose to exploit the phase-down of ozone-depleting chemicals. This could create economic benefits in the near-term, however, the consequences of exploitation would have severe damaging effects on the future.
4. All countries could sign on to the protocol and absorb the costs from the single country should it exploit the protocol. While there is a reduced risk of ozone depletion, this scenario creates a competitive advantage as well as limits to costs.

Regarding the Montreal Protocol, the scenario is complicated. While the analysis of coordination games lends insights as to some of the factors behind ratification of the Montreal Protocol, it does not identify whether full cooperative gains have been achieved. When continuous choices are allowed, coordination games have multiple matching-behavior equilibria. Otherwise, Murdoch and Sandler (1997) demonstrate that the initial requirements of the protocol as well as the actions taken by countries to curb CFC emissions in 1989 are in keeping with a non-cooperative Nash equilibrium. This points to the fact that they would have come to these solutions without the Montreal Protocol, yet they still decided to join due to the other benefits involved.

A4.11 *Stability of the Montreal Protocol*

The stability of the Montreal Protocol is internationally recognized in that there are not many that are as stable and as successful and it has recently achieved its 30th anniversary. The Montreal Protocol was signed by all 197 local actors in September 16, 1987 and was entered into force on January 1, 1989. It was ultimately ratified on September 16, 2009. Every amendment since has also been signed by all 197 local actors; London (1990), Copenhagen (1992), Montreal (1997), and Beijing (1999) (Ozone Secretariat, 2017). The most recent Kigali amendment has reached the number of signatories for it to enter into force on January 1, 2019.

There has been wide spread consensus on the scientific findings about the ODS and their effects on the Ozone layer. This, coupled with participation among Article 5 countries and non-Article 5 countries, has been an integral part of the agreement. This relationship allows for mutual benefits, the Article 5 countries are able to achieve reductions in global ODSs through funding the MLF and the non-Article 5 countries receive funds and technical support in order to achieve the necessary ODS reductions. The target goals of ODS levels are set based on scientific evidence and not political maneuvering, and so the solutions also follow that logic through the MLF funding streams and projects. There is also flexibility built into the agreement that allows the ODS targets to be changed according to new scientific discoveries without having to pass an amendment. Ultimately, the effectiveness of the Montreal Protocol and its reliance on scientific evidence has created an agreement that is trusted and benefits all the participating states.

A4.12 *Analysis of the effectiveness*

There are two general categories in which to examine the effectiveness of the Montreal Protocol, one is on the effectiveness of the ability to reach an agreement among the local states and the other is on the effectiveness in reaching the goals of the Montreal Protocol, namely measurable ODS reductions.

A4.12.1 *Reaching agreement*

In the first instance, the Montreal Protocol receives high marks in any measurable sense and has become the case study of how to effectively reach international agreements among local state actors. All 197 local actors have signed on and ratified the agreement and all subsequent amendments, except for the current open amendment which has already reached the necessary number of signatories for it to enter into force January 1, 2019.

A4.12.2 *Measurable reductions in ODS levels*

The ultimate goal of the Montreal Protocol is to reduce the levels of ODS, and in this case the agreement has also been largely successful, lowering levels in all ODSs with the exception of HCFCs and HFCs. According to the latest report of the Scientific Assessment of Ozone Depletion (2014), there have been reductions in the levels of all categories of ODSs as illustrated in Appendix: ODS Levels. Table A4.1 shows areas of measurement that are to be used in measuring success of the Montreal Protocol.

Thus far according to the Minister of Environment and Climate Change of Canada, Catherine McKenna, since 1987, the Montreal Protocol has resulted in the 'elimination of more than 135 billion tons of carbon dioxide equivalent and the phase-out of close to 100 ozone-depleting substances (11th meeting of the Conference of the Parties).

Table A4.1.   Measuring success of the Montreal Protocol.

Scientific measurable index	
ODS levels	Reductions in CFC, CH_3CCl_3, CCl_4, halon-1211, HCFC, halon, CH_3Br
Status of global ozone	Increases in middle and upper stratospheric ozone column
Status of polar ozone	Recovery of ozone levels of Artic (2025–2035) & Antarctic (2045–2060)

Note: Adapted from the: Scientific Assessment of Ozone Depletion (2014).

A4.13 *Lessons from other global policies*

The Montreal Protocol is one of the international treaties that is commonly used as a reference for a policy that reached unanimous agreement using scientific knowledge as the driving force in the formation of the regulatory conditions. In this way, many global policies draw lessons from the Montreal Protocol.

The global policy that the Montreal Protocol draws upon the most is the Vienna Convention for the Protection of the Ozone Layer proposed in 1985 and entered into force in 1988. This agreement was to recognize the need to protect the Ozone layer and won widespread adoption with 197 countries signing it. It unfortunately did not have the regulatory teeth to enforce those goals, and this is where the Montreal Protocol builds on the Vienna Convention (United Nations, 1985). The lesson being that scientific knowledge can be a good basis for regulatory frameworks and still gain unanimous support and compliance.

References

About Montreal Protocol|OzonAction. (n.d.). Retrieved June 10, 2018, from http://web.unep.org/ozonaction/who-we-are/about-montreal-protocol.

Aucamp, P., Olof Björn, L., and Lucas, R., 2011. Questions and Answers About the Environmental Effects of Ozone Depletion and its Interactions with Climate Change: 2010 assessment. *Photochemical & Photobiological Sciences*, 10(2):173. https://doi.org/10.1039/c0pp90040k.

Cama, T., February 5, 2018. Trump undecided on supporting Obama pollution treaty, adviser says [Text]. Retrieved June 14, 2018, from http://thehill.com/policy/energy-environment/372357-trump-still-undecided -on-supporting-obama-pollution-treaty-adviser.

Jones, T. T., 1996. Implementation of the Montreal Protocol: Barriers, Constraints and Opportunities. *Environmental Lawyer*, 3:813–858.

Morrisette, P. M., 1989. The Evolution of Policy Responses to Stratospheric Ozone Depletion, 29.

Murdoch, J. C. and Sandler, T., 1997. The Voluntary Provision of a Pure Public good: The case of Reduced CFC Emissions and the Montreal Protocol. *Journal of Public Economics*, 63(3):331–349.

Ozone Secretariat, May, 2017. Meetings of the Parties Primer: An Introduction to the Meetings of the Vienna Convention and the Montreal Protocol. United Nations Environment Programme.

Pfluger, A., 2010. Why the Montreal Protocol is not a Template for Multilateral Environmental Agreements: An Examination of Why China and India Ratified, 8.

Simmonds, P. G., Rigby, M., McCulloch, A., O'Doherty, S., Young, D., Mühle, J.,... Prinn, R. G., 2017. Changing Trends and Emissions of Hydrochlorofluorocarbons (HCFCs) and Their Hydrofluorocarbon (HFCs) Replacements. *Atmospheric Chemistry and Physics*, 17(7):4641–4655. https://doi.org/10.5194/acp-17-4641-2017.

Skjærseth, J. B., 1992. The 'Successful' Ozone-Layer Negotiations: Are There any Lessons to be Learned? *Global Environmental Change*, 2(4):292–300. https://doi.org/10.1016/0959-3780(92)90046-A.

Sunstein, C. R., 2006. Montreal versus Kyoto: A Tale of Two Protocols, University of Chicago, John M. Olin Program in Law and Economics, Working Paper No. 302.

The Montreal Protocol on Substances that Deplete the Ozone Layer |Article 5: Special situation of developing countries|OZONE SECRE-TARIAT. (n.d.). Retrieved June 10, 2018, from http://ozone.unep.org/en/handbook-montreal-protocol-substances-deplete-ozone-layer/22.

United Nations Environment Programme & Ozone Secretariat. 2003. *Handbook for the International Treaties for the Protection of the Ozone Layer: the Vienna Convention (1985), the Montreal Protocol (1987)*. Nairobi, Kenya: Ozone Secretariat, United Nations Environment Programme.

United Nations, March 22, 1985. Vienna Convention for the Protection of the Ozone Layer. United Nations.

A5. Convention on the Prohibition of Use, Stockpiling, Production, and Transfer of Anti-Personnel Mines and on Their Destruction (Mine-ban Treaty)[5]

The Mine-ban Treaty, otherwise known as 1996 Oslo Convention on the Prohibition of Use, Stockpiling, Production, and Transfer of Anti-Personnel Mines and on Their Destruction, and correspondingly the Ottawa Treaty of 1997, was designed to achieve the prohibition on the use, production, stockpiling, and transfer of anti-personnel mines on a worldwide scale. This policy is unique among other arms

---

[5]Modified from Yang Li, Final Paper in the course PPBL224, June 13, 2020. Author's consent was obtained.

control agreements as it was conceived without the backing of major international powers (Bower, 2012). Prominent global powers such as the United States, China, Russia, and India as well as regional powers such as Israel, Saudi Arabia, Vietnam, or Pakistan have not lent their support to this treaty and have thus not signed it as of today (The Human Rights Watch, 2003). This annex will seek to answer several questions: the motivation of the treaty, the negotiation process, implementation effects, as well as future prospects of this treaty.

A5.1 *Background*

The primary motivation of the Mine-ban Treaty stemmed from the negative externalities generated by the proliferation of anti-personnel land (APL) mines around the world. First hailed into widespread use in the 19th century, the modern APL is a static area denial weapon that is usually deployed underground in large numbers and is aimed to produce either blast or fragmentation injuries upon people who came in contact with the mines' detonation mechanisms. While the blasts and fragmentations from the detonation of APL may be fatal to its victims, the small explosive charge contained in the modern APL may only be sufficient to cause a permanently disabling wound to a victim's lower extremities. Additionally, APL are fitted with much more sensitive fuse compared to their anti-vehicular counterparts in order to guarantee the detonation upon contact.

These features of APL mines have created significant negative externalities that affect not just the combatants but also the civilians both within and outside of the areas of conflict. First, the APL (and mines in general) is an indiscriminate weapon that will injure or kill anyone that encounters it. This could be anyone from an enemy combatant, a friend, or a civilian who inadvertently ventures onto the site where the mine is buried. Second, the APL is a permanent threat until it has been properly detected, removed, and disposed of. This means that APLs will have a lasting socioeconomic effect in places where they are deployed by rendering the areas with all attached infrastructures unusable. The combined effects of these two externalities of APL meant that areas where such weapons have been deployed in conflict will continue to incur costs upon their inhabitants or visitors in the form of mine clearance, damage repairs, health costs, and losses in productivity (Giannou, 1997; Walsh, 2009). The efforts to correct the negative externalities caused by APLs are further complicated by political-geographical boundaries, lack of proper documentation for minefields, ground movements causing the shift of mine burial sites, the technical difficulties in mine detection, as well as the decreased stability of old mines that have passed their shelf-life (JMU Scholarly Commons, 2009). Thus, many states would have significant incentives to limit the further proliferation of APL and seek measures to curb existing externalities.

A5.2 *Negotiation*

The first feature of the Mine-ban Treaty is the predominance of the Non-Government Organizations (NGOs) in the creation and negotiation process of the treaty. Inspired by the passing of the Convention on Certain Conventional Weapons (CCW) as well as the negative externalities of the APL in the form of human and economic costs, the initiative was first spearheaded by a consortium of NGOs including the Human Rights Watch, Medico International, Mines Advisory Group, Physicians for Human Rights, and the Vietnam Veterans of America Foundations (Cottrell, 2009). This group of NGOs have operated as a monolithic party by jointly publishing the Manifesto against Anti-Personnel Land Mine Use, Production, Stockpiling and Transportation in October 1992. The initial stage of the negotiation process for the Mine-ban Treaty have also demonstrated the feature of issue linkage as proponents of this treaty seek to connect the it to the existing control treaty on conventional weapons.

The initial block of proponents for the Mine-ban Treaty was expanded over the years as sovereign state and Security Council member (France) submitted a request to review the existing CCW treaty to include the section on land mines. This support was echoed by the rest of the European Union in 1995. The unanimous support of European Union members along with a growing number of NGOs have formed a larger, monolithic group with a unified intent which resulted in the First Austrian Draft that formed the basis of the Oslo Accord and eventually the Ottawa Treaty. This treaty is multilateral in nature and encompasses all major areas that would contribute to the use of APLs (production, stockpiling, transfer, and use).

States such as Austria have made additional efforts in support of the Mine-ban Treaty by outlawing all APLs in their territories in 1997. On the other hand, major international powers such as the United States, China, and Russia, along with other influential states such as India, Pakistan, Israel, and the Koreas have all refused to participate in the creation process of this treaty as APLs formed an important part of their military strategy or because they are actively involved in armed conflicts. Additionally, because many of the non-supportive states had active stakes in the international arms market and/or have actively maintained a large arsenal of APLs, they were also reluctant to participate due to the potential economic costs. Therefore, the opponents of the Mine-ban Treaty did not appear as a monolithic party as each state has its own agenda and set of reasons for its opposition to the treaty (Casey-Maslen, n.d).

During the negotiation process, Canada proposed an alternative approach to this issue by suggesting to split the original treaty's comprehensive ban on the production, transfer, stockpiling, and use of APLs into four separate treaties for each of the actions. This would allow states to participate in individual treaties as they see fit but at the cost of disconnecting the singular issue of comprehensive ban on APLs into separate actions, thus unintentionally breaking the monolithic nature of the pro-ban camp. This proposal of breaking the Mine-ban Treaty into a series of sub-treaties was ultimately rejected by other members during the negotiation process. The United States sought to participate in the discussion on the treaty in Oslo under several conditions. These conditions included the exception for APL use in South Korea, the re-definition of APLs under mixed-use munition systems, the inclusion of transitional and deferral periods, strengthening of the verification regime, and the clause permitting a party to withdraw subject to national interests. Other members of the conference did not support this proposal, and the United States withdrew from the Oslo conference (The Human Rights Watch, 2019).

The Mine-ban Treaty was adopted in September 1997 and was opened for signing in December during the Ottawa Conference. The treaty was signed by 166 members during the conference in Ottawa and the ratification and additional signing process continued until 2017, with Sri Lanka being the latest signatory state. The treaty requires the signatory states to provide a working plan on eliminating the presence of land mines in their territories and to provide annual reports on the progress. Most of the original opponents of the treaty did not sign the treaty, thus limited the effects of this treaty in practice (ICBL, 2013).

Due to the multilateral nature and the multitude of motivations of each state in rejecting this treaty, it is difficult to analyze the result of this treaty through a singular matrix. While the participation rate of this treaty still leaves some room for improvement and APLs are still exacting human and economic tolls in areas of active military conflicts, the use of APLs, along with their production, stockpiling, and transfers, have been heavily diminished in other parts of the world. This is partially because technological progression has rendered traditional APLs obsolete. Additionally, the non-signatory states also seek to mitigate the reputational damage stemming from their refusal to participate and hence publicly complying even without signing could be a way to mitigate. For the signatory states, some still maintained a stock of APLs for demining research and training purposes while others have claimed for exemption in certain areas. Hence, it is fair to say that the two blocks (signatory and non-signatory states) have arrived at a point of limited mutual cooperation in most cases, with the exception of those that are still in active conflicts or ineffective governance and thus cannot comply (Wexler, 2003; Maslen, 2005).

However, even with the clearly outlined harms of APL, not all states would completely agree with the terms of Mine-ban Treaty. The first of the conflicts is the individual state's strategic needs.

Even Japan, which was one of the founding members of the Mine-ban Treaty, has expressed its view on the importance of APL as a part of its national defense strategy due to the effective deterrence effects of mines against the possibility of armed invasions (Adachi, 2005). Other countries have expressed similar sentiments as they believe APL's military utility as a peacetime border deterrence as well as a wartime device to delay the advancing enemy have far outweighed the negative externalities associated with such a weapon. This was the opinion of almost all non-signatory states. Hence, states that are facing on-going or potential military conflicts are reluctant to remove this tool from their disposal, even when the experiences from past conflicts have shown little effectiveness of APLs in providing deterrence (Good, 2010).

The reluctance by non-signatory states to abandon their arsenal of APLs have led to an outcome of egotism with dead loss to all parties. APL minefields are still being deployed and maintained in areas of conflict and potential conflicts as deterrence and delay measures and would still generate the negative externalities in the form of 6,897 documented mine casualties from around the world in 2018. Additionally, because of the examples set by major and intermediary powers, the Mine-ban Treaty has still not attained the status of an international law of war. This means that land mines are still being actively used by non-signatory parties without impunity in the ongoing conflicts in Afghanistan, Syria, and Yemen with significant human and economic costs (The Human Rights Watch *et al.*, 2019).

Secondly, states may choose to disagree with the Mine-ban Treaty as it impacts their economic interests in the international arms market. China and Russia, for example, have traditionally been the largest exporters of mines and associated equipment in the post-war period. However, even as these states have refused to sign the Mine-ban Treaty, they have made significant efforts to cooperate by curtailing the production of APLs and to comply with arms control requirements in their arms dealings (Landmine and Cluster Munition Monitor, 2019). The reason for the cooperative measures is two-fold. First of which is the natural progression of weapon and munition technology that has effectively rendered certain types of APLs obsolete and hence no longer suitable for deployment and export. Secondly, the non-signature states seek to remedy the reputational repercussions through the dismantling of outdated mine stockpiles and production capabilities as a measure of good faith that is also mutually beneficial. While such measures were far from ideal, the conflicting parties have nonetheless chosen a path where all parties would suffer minimal losses through a partial adaptation of the disarmament process.

Therefore, the supporters of the Mine-ban Treaty were motivated by the desire to eliminate the negative externalities of the APLs. States that have refused to sign the treaty have cited the military utility of APLs as a weapon of deterrence under their defense strategy. The non-signatory states have therefore found themselves in a prisoner's dilemma where all parties suffered from negative externalities as a result of their ongoing pursuit to maximize their individual benefits. The other reason for non-signatory states was to preserve their interests in the international arms market and such interests have been largely rendered null in the past decades as many of the older types of APLs have become obsolete. These states have thus taken measures to dismantle such stockpiles and the corresponding manufacturing capabilities.

In order to quantitatively measure the popularity of the Mine-ban Treaty, this analysis will use two approaches. First is to draw a diffusion curve of that policy by determining how many states signed the treaty in the years since 1997 when the Ottawa treaty was open for signing. First, the number of states that have signed or adopted the treaty since 1997 (year 1) is plotted over a period since and ending in 2017. and determine how quickly did the countries agree to this policy. If more countries chose to sign this treaty in the first few years, it would mean that this policy has high level of popularity. Currently, the last state to sign the treaty has been Sri Lanka.

The descriptive statistics indicates that in the 18-year period since 1997, 129/198 states have agreed to and signed within the first year of the treaty (Figure A5.1). Such an overwhelming number of signatory states indicates that the Mine-ban Treaty is an enormously

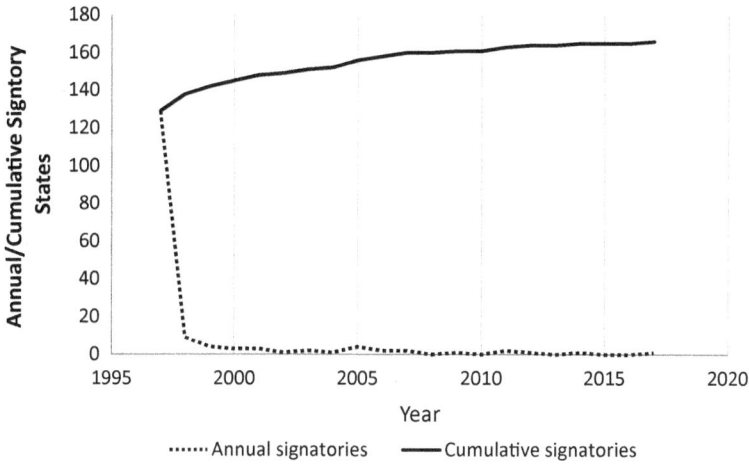

Figure A5.1. Annual and cumulative number of signatories on the Mine-ban Treaty 1997–2017.
Source: Authors' elaboration, using data in https://treaties.un.org/Pages/ViewDetails.aspx?src=IND&mtdsg_no=XXVI-5&chapter=26&clang=_en.

popular policy. Evidences from this analysis indicate that states have recognized the negative externalities of, and would much rather sacrifice short-term economic and strategic benefits to achieve, longer-term socioeconomical and reputational benefits. The results in Figure A5.1 suggest that the treaty was very attractive to the states, reaching a participation (signing) rate of nearly 65% of world countries (or nearly 78% of total signatories) in the first year. That number was kept stable until 2017 (last year for which data exist).

Once we realize the interest of the state to participate in the Mine-ban Treaty, we can attempt at explain the speed of signing by various states as a function of internal/domestic stability and governance variables (Knack and Keefer, 1986; Gray and Kaufmann, 1998; Kaufmann *et al.*, 2004). The hypothesis to be verified is that the presence of violence, instability, and governance dysfunction will cause a state to take longer time to adapt the Mine-ban Treaty.

Two measures of stability and governance were used: (1) political stability and absence of violence (Violence); and (2) the state's ability to function as an effective political entity (government effectiveness, Goveffect). These two variables are each scaled from –2 (unstable, violent, and dysfunctional) to +2 (stable, peaceful, and effective) and will serve as independent variables of the analysis.[6] Level of Violence and Goveffect will be used to explain the time elapsed (in months) since the treaty was opened for signature and the states' actual signature. Of the 166 states that signed the Mine-ban Treaty only 147 have been assigned values of Violence or Goveffect, and thus the analysis refers to the subset of 147 states. The models that were estimated are presented below with T being time elapsed (in months), V being Violence, and G being Goveffect. Both linear and quadratic versions of these functions were estimated.

$$T = f(V, G). \qquad (A5.1)$$
$$T = g(V). \qquad (A5.2)$$
$$T = h(G). \qquad (A5.3)$$

Since V and G are highly correlated, which could be expected (Correlation coefficient is 0.830), the results of the regressions of (A5.1) show high heteroscedasticity and are not presented due to low statistical significance. Results of the quadratic versions of (A5.2) and (A5.3) are presented in Table A5.1.

The rudimentary regression results indicate that there is a negative and statistically significant relationship between how many months it took a state to sign the treaty and the level of violence present in the state. The effectiveness of governance in the state has an opposite effect on time elapsed—the higher the measure of government effectiveness, the sooner the state signs the treaty. However, both variables show a quadratic relationship. That means that the effect of that variable on the time elapsed is diminished as it increases in value. This means that states that are in some level of political-military turmoil are much more eager to sign the Mine-ban Treaty. Such a result is against the initial hypothesis that linked presence of military and political hardship with slower adoption of

---

[6] NoViolence and Goveffect were found in the World Bank Worldwide Governance Indicators website https://info.worldbank.org/governance/wgi/.

Table A5.1. Time elapsed from opening to signature on the Mine-ban Treaty.

	Model A5.2		Model A5.3	
	Quadratic		Quadratic	
Intercept	10.058	(2.438)***	9.002	(2.207)***
Violence	−7.668	(−2.393)***		
ViolenceSQ	5.739	(2.310)***		
Goveffect			7.365	(2.755)***
GoveffectSQ			−12.323	(−4.059)***
Adjusted R^2	0.110		0.109	
F-stat	10.022	0.0008***	10.003	0.0008***
Number of observations	147		147	

Note: Values in parentheses are t-tests. ***indicates a significance at 1% level.

the Mine-ban Treaty. While there are numerous factors that could affect each state's ability to adopt the Mine-ban Treaty in time (as indicated by the relatively low R-squared value of the analysis), the trends from our regression results indicate that states that have gone through political and military troubles during the time of signing are much more inclined to take measures to eliminate this threat. This is further supported by the vast number of developing countries that have adopted the Mine-ban Treaty at the point of its inception. It is known that most armed conflicts have taken place in the territories of developing countries and these countries would be intimately familiar with the negative externalities of land mine uses. Hence, these states would be much more inclined to take measures to eliminate the presence of such weapons from their territories and prevent their future appearances.

A5.3 *Implementation and effectiveness*

Thus far, there are 166 signatory parties to the Mine-ban Treaty. These signatories have thus provided a working plan to eradicate the land mines as well as their production, stockpiling, and transfer processes in their respective territories. Some of the signatory states have requested exceptions to some aspects of the treaty as they need a certain stock of land mines as training tools in order to maintain their demining capabilities.

As for the effectiveness of the Mine-ban Treaty, both signatory and non-signatory states would have to bear a set of costs and benefits associated with their relative actions (or inactions) with regards to land mines. As previously mentioned, APLs pose serious and lasting social economic impacts. The direct impacts are the deaths and injuries caused to the local populace. APL-related deaths cause losses in terms of future benefits as people who were killed can no longer participate in economic activities as consumers and producers. Injuries, on the other hand, tend to have higher and longer lasting financial impacts due to both the cost of medical expenses and the long-term loss of productivity of the individuals affected. Such impact is especially pronounced in areas where most of the affected population are engaged in manual labors in the agrarian sector. Such impacts can be a measure to the potential effectiveness of the policy.

Studies on the human costs of land mines in Afghanistan indicate that land mines claimed up to 20–24 victims per day in the entire country in 1993. Over half (53%) of these victims were of working age (18–40) while adolescents account for 34% of the victims.[7] Thirty one percent of the mine-blast victims were killed while 46% suffered debilitating injuries (blindness and amputation). The medical costs and productivity loss for working age mine-blast survivors with debilitating injuries amount to over a US$11,500 over a lifetime (Andersson *et al.*, 1995; Bilukha *et al.*, 2003; MAPA, 2001; Walsh and Walsh, 2003).

Additionally, land mines hinder the rehabilitation of conflict zones as they continue to deny the area to the returning civilian population. Unidentified and uncleared minefields are unable to be used for productive purposes due to the dangers present, thus, productivity in these areas suffers. This can be seen in the Afghan case study where on average 36 farm animals would be lost annually

---

[7]Do note that because of the nature of the mine-blast incidents, it is often impossible to clearly identify the exact type of munitions involved in the aftermath of the explosion, hence the study in Afghanistan includes all mine types (anti-tank and anti-personnel) as well as unexploded ordinances (UXO).

per every squared kilometer of land with uncleared mines. Similar issues exist with residential and public infrastructures where the presence of uncleared land mines limit the availability of these resources. Such loss of productivity is reflected in the increased travel costs per kilometer on roads as well as decreased volume of traffic. In terms of residential uses, the presence of land mine would result in reduced occupancy rates.

Hence, states that choose to adhere completely or even partially to the Mine-ban Treaty through the commitment to a domestic mine-clearance campaign would realize direct benefits in the form of reduced deaths and injuries as well as increased productivity. A very limited mine clearance campaign in Afghanistan during the 1993–1997 period had reduced the daily mine and UXO victims by 50% while continued efforts to clear mines have led to 30–60% decrease in travel costs per kilometer of road and corresponding increase in vehicular volumes on roads. For residential areas, the removal of land mines has led to both a dramatic increase in housing stocks (55,400 houses with attached lands) as they were no longer being blocked by mines, as well as the increase of property values of up to $5/m^2$ in Kabul, Kandahar province (urban center), and $2/m^2$ in any other province except Kandahar (MAPA, 2001). The effects of mine removal are even more pronounced in states that have wholly agreed to and carried out the requirements of the Mine-ban Treaty. This can be seen from the case in Mozambique where it made a successful transition from being heavily mined to nearly mine-free. Longitudinal study on the economic effects of demining in Mozambique indicates that the post-demining areas have experienced dramatic increase in human activities while travel time and costs have been significantly reduced as transportation infrastructures became more accessible thanks to demining. The combined effect of increased economic activities and access to infrastructures as well as reduction of human and material losses have contributed to a dramatic increase in Mozambique's economic output (18%–25% increase in GDP per capita since demining) (Chiovelli *et al.*, 2018). Thus, states that have agreed to remove land mines from their territories have been hugely benefitting in all sectors as they reduce the negative externalities of land mines. Furthermore, it should be noted that countries that choose to phase out land mines from their arsenals have also gained positive reputations both domestically and abroad.

On the other hand, states that do not choose to comply with the Mine-ban Treaty would have to face the costs of detection and removal of land mines from their territories. This cost is divided between surveying, training, and the physical removal and disarming of mines and the costs of such activities are different based on the mode of operation (manual or mechanical) as well as whether demining is carried out at national or community level. To further complicate the issue, the effectiveness and efficiency of demining is heavily dependent upon local stability, and thus, areas that are undergoing armed conflicts may be unable to carry out such an undertaking.

Reports from Afghanistan, where mixed methods of demining have been used, indicate that the average hourly cost of demining per team in 1999 ranges from US$84 to US$199 (MAPA, 2001). Additional human and financial costs due to the dangerous nature of demining operations have also been significant. 55 de-miners have been killed and 538 have been injured in operations during the 10-year period between 1990 and 1999 in Afghanistan. Each incident with fatality would incur an average cost of US$16,210 while one without fatality would incur on average US$12,552, along with corresponding delays in work progress. Therefore, the human and financial costs of demining are significant in mine-infested areas.

Another set of costs of choosing to comply with the Mine-ban Treaty is the loss of a deterrence tool in the state's arsenal as well as the loss of export revenues for arms-producing states. These costs diminished over the years as traditional APLs began to lose their relevance as weapons of area denial and deterrence. The growing number of countermeasures that would allow a modern military to detect and safely bypass minefields meant that traditional APLs can no longer serve the area denial function against a prepared and determined enemy. This is compounded by the increased mechanization of modern armies where static minefields and their outdated placement methods meant that they cannot deter a mobile and maneuvering enemy. Additionally, the emergence of alternative surveillance and defensive measures means that the labor-intensive and maintenance-heavy land mines are no longer needed in many areas to deny an area to the potential enemies. Such decline in the military relevance of land mines led to a similar decline ion the demand for such weapons in the international arms market (Gader *et al.*, 2001).

These trends have not just reduced the actual and opportunity costs for signatory states to remove APLs from their arsenal and their territories but have also caused non-signatory states to bear a heavier cost-level for maintaining the abilities to produce, store, and deploy land mines. Landmines, like all explosive munitions, have finite shelf lives and must be stored according to specified standards and be disposed of professionally. These incur additional costs throughout the service life of the weapon and would be an additional financial burden to any state that seeks to maintain such a weapon as a part of its arsenal. The non-signatory states are now stuck with an outdated weapon with diminishing military and export value while simultaneously having to endure the negative social and economic externalities and reputational issues presented above. Such diminishing benefits of maintaining APLs and the increasing cost of maintaining such weapons have thus discouraged many non-signatory states from continuing to rely on this weapon.

Therefore, with the diminishing effects and increasing costs, non-signatory states have also been in the process of removing their own minefields as well as the stock and production capabilities of APLs. Non-signatory arms producing countries such as the United States, China, and Russia reported that they have largely dismantled their production facilities and stockpiles of APLs. Other non-signatory states such as Israel have stopped acquiring new stocks of land mines and have not made efforts to deploy mines in new areas. However, because not all states have signed this treaty, it has not become an international law of war such as the ban on chemical and biological weapons, and thus, a global ban on land mine has still not been achieved.

A5.4 *Future prospects*

While the Mine-ban Treaty has been popular since its inception, the future of this treaty faces some uncertainties. First, because not all states have signed this treaty despite the fact that each has made individual efforts to cut down on the production and use of APLs, the Mine-ban Treaty has not achieved the status of a universally recognized law of war that is applicable to all states. This means that states could adapt an egotist stance by unilaterally withdrawing from this treaty as they see fit, thus undermining the effectiveness of this treaty. The inability to elevate this treaty to the status of a universally recognized law of war meant that individual states could be placed in a prisoner's dilemma by unilaterally re-instating their mining capabilities subject to their own perceived strategic needs. This could lead other states to also return to the use of land mines as a retaliatory measure and thus erase the demining progresses made in the past decades as states re-deploy APLs in contested areas.

Secondly, the continued existence and successes of the Mine-ban Treaty is under threat from the United States's constant attempts to undermine it. The United States has, since the negotiation process, sought to replace the existing multilateral treaty that encompasses all areas of APLs with bilateral alternatives that would only encompass singular aspects of the treaty (Seldin, (n.d)). Such alternatives would undermine the integrity and the effectiveness of the treaty and were thus rejected during the negotiation stage. The United States would not sign the treaty claiming its strategic needs in the Korean Peninsula, but has made significant efforts to reduce or eliminate its stockpile of mines elsewhere. This process has recently been placed on hold as the current administration of the United States decided to withdraw from its demining commitments and authorized the military commanders in all theaters to deploy APLs as they see fit. This egotist approach to the treaty threatens its very basis as the world's biggest super-power not only refuses to take leadership in an international arms control treaty but is also taking steps to actively undermine it (Good, 2010).

Finally, recent discussions on the future of the Mine-ban Treaty began to emerge against the backdrop of technological evolution of arms. The traditional APLs have largely become obsolete and newer generations of weapons such as rocket- and air-deployed scattered munitions have begun to gain popularity. Current discussions seek to take this change into consideration by merging the treaties on scattered munitions with the Mine-ban Treaty in order to maintain the relevance of the treaty. Such discussions, however, are still in the early stages and may take years to arrive at the point where substantial changes could be made (International Campaign to Ban Landmines, 2017; Cottrell, 2009).

A5.5 *Final remarks*

The Mine-ban policy is remarkable in several aspects. First, it seeks to control a once widely spread conventional weapon due to its large negative externalities. Second, this policy was the brainchild of NGOs and has slowly gained traction among state actors in its formative process. Third, this policy took effect without the signature of major international powers but still has managed to reduce the presence of APLs in the world through other means. While this policy did not reach the ideal result of becoming a universal law of war and its future is in jeopardy due to both technological advancement and the hostile attitudes of the United States, it is still ground-breaking in the sense that it was a grassroot movement that has gained international prominence. Such a new model of formulating international treaties may, therefore, lead the way to the establishment of new international norms in the future.

References

Adachi, K., 2005. Why Japan Signed the Mine-ban Treaty: The Political Dynamics behind the Decision. *Asian Survey*, 45(3):397–413.

Andersson, N., Cesar Palha Da, S., and Sergio P., 1995. Social Cost of Land Mines in Four Countries: Afghanistan, Bosnia, Cambodia, and Mozambique. *BMJ*, 311(7007):718–721.

Bilukha, O. O., Muireann, B., and Bradley A. W., 2003. Death and Injury from Landmines and Unexploded Ordnance in Afghanistan. *JAMA*, 290(5): 650–653.

Bower, A. S., 2012. Norm Development Without the Great Powers: Assessing the Antipersonnel Mine-ban Treaty and the Rome Statute of the International Criminal Court. PhD diss., University of British Columbia.

Casey-Maslen, S., n.d. The context of the adoption of the Convention on the Prohibition of the Use, Stockpiling, Production and Transfer of Anti-Personnel
Mines and Their Destruction (Anti-Personnel Mine Ban Convention). United
Nations Audiovisual Library of International Law, https://legal.un.org/avl/
ha/cpusptam/cpusptam.html, Accessed July 28, 2020.

Cottrell, M. P., 2009. Legitimacy and Institutional Replacement: The Convention
on Certain Conventional Weapons and the Emergence of the Mine-Ban
Treaty. *International Organization*, 63(2):217–248.

Chiovelli, G., Steilos, M., and Elias, P., 2018. *What are the Economic Effects
of Landmine Clearance?* VoxDev, https://voxdev.org/topic/infrastructure-
urbanisation/what-are-economic-effects-land mine-clearance.

Gader, P. D., Miroslaw, M., and Yunxin, Z., 2001. Landmine Detection with
Ground Penetrating Radar using Hidden Markov Models. *IEEE Transactions
on Geoscience and Remote Sensing*, 39(6):1231–1244.

Giannou, C., 1997. Antipersonnel Landmines: Facts, Fictions, and Priorities.
BMJ, 315(7120):1453–1454.

Good, R., 2010. Yes We Should: Why the US Should Change Its Policy Toward
the 1997 Mine-ban Treaty. *Nw. UJ Int'l Hum. Rts.*, 9:209.

Gray, C. W. and Kaufmann, D., 1998. Corruption and Development. *Finance &
Development*, 35(1):7–10.

The Human Rights Watch, 2003. Landmine Monitor Fact Sheet. *Status of
Implementation of the 1997 Mine-ban Treaty*. http://www.the-monitor.org/
media/1419399/implementation_status_of_mbt_factsheet.pdf. Accessed on
July 28, 2020.

The Human Rights Watch *et al.*, 2019. Landmine Monitor 2019. *Concord: International Campaign to Ban Landmines*. http://www.the-monitor.org/en-gb/
reports/2019/landmine-monitor-2019.aspx. Accessed on July 28, 2020.

International Campaign to Ban Landmines, 2017. *The Mine-ban Treaty Turns
18, What Does it Mean?* http://www.icbl.org/en-gb/news-and-events/news/
2017/the-mine-ban-treaty-turns-18-what-does-it-mean.aspx. Accessed on
July 28, 2020.

JMU Scholarly Commons, 2009. *Scoping Study of the Effects of Aging on Landmines*. https://commons.lib.jmu.edu/cgi/viewcontent.cgi?article=1000&
context=cisr-studiesreports. Accessed on July 28, 2020.

Kaufmann, D., Aart, K., and Massimo M., 2004. Governance Matters III:
Governance Indicators for 1996, 1998, 2000, and 2002. *World Bank Economic
Review*, 18(2):253–287.

Knack, S. and Keefer, P., 1986. Institutions and Economic Performance: Cross-
Country Tests Using Alternative Institutional Measures. *Economics and
Politics*, 7(3):207–227.

Landmine and Cluster Munition Monitor, 2019. *Mine-ban Policy: China*.
http://www.the-monitor.org/en-gb/reports/2019/china/mine-ban-policy.
aspx. Accessed July 28, 2020.

Landmine and Cluster Munition Monitor, 2019. *Mine-ban Policy: Federation
of Russia*. http://archives.the-monitor.org/index.php/publications/display?
url=lm/2006/russia.html. Accessed on July 28, 2020.

MAPA (Mine Actions Program Afghanistan), 2001. *Study of the Socio-economic Impact of Mine Action in Afghanistan (SIMAA)*. https://commons.lib.jmu. edu/cisr-globalcwd/1078/. Accessed on July 28, 2020.

Seldin, J. *US Ends Self-Imposed Ban on Use of Landmines*, Voice of America. https://www.voanews.com/usa/us-ends-self-imposed-ban-use-landmines.

Walsh, N. E., and Walsh, W. S., 2003. Rehabilitation of Landmine Victims: The Ultimate Challenge. *Bulletin of the World Health Organization*, 81:665–670.

Wexler, L., 2003. The International Deployment of Shame, Second-Best Responses, and Norm Entrepreneurship: The Campaign to Ban Landmines and the Landmine-ban Treaty. *Arizona Journal of International and Comparative Law*, 20:561.

Worldwide Governance Indicators. *Home.* https://info.worldbank.org/ governance/wgi/.

A6. The United Nations Convention to Combat Desertification[8,9]

The term desertification was first coined in 1949 when Aubréville, a French forester, noticed 'the expansion of desert-like conditions in non-desert areas' (Sterk *et al.*, 2016: 1784). Desertification has since been linked to events such as the dust bowl and droughts in geographically specific locations such as arid and semi-arid regions (Sterk *et al.*, 2016). Between 1968 and 1973, there were severe droughts and reoccurring famines across the Sahel region of Africa that attracted global attention from both international governments, as well as NGOs (Sterk *et al.*, 2016; Bali, 1978).

A6.1 *History and original positions*

In 1978, a UN conference on Desertification was attended by 65 NGOs, 95 governments, and almost all of the UN specialized agencies. The realities of desertification, famine, and drought were recognized as well as a share in voicing opinions and concerns about desertification by different parties. Most of the information on party

---

[8]Modified from Jessica Bradford, Final Paper in the course PPBL224, June 10, 2020. Author's consent was obtained.

[9]The analysis focuses on those countries experiencing serious drought and/or desertification, particularly in Africa.

positions is based on documents as well as the declarations during the conference itself, however it was not for almost another 14 years, at the 1992 'Earth Summit' meeting in Rio de Janeiro, that a global UN convention was suggested (Biswas, 1978; Sterk *et al.*, 2016). African countries' leaders, whose states were experiencing desertification, suggested the convention to address the dangerous environmental degradation on a global cooperative scale. Originally there was some opposition to this convention by certain, less affected states, but by the end of the conference the UN agreed to establish an Intergovernmental Negotiation Committee on Desertification (INCD) dedicated to draft a Convention to Combat Desertification (UNCCD) (Biswas, 1978; INCD, 1994; United Nations Convention to Combat Desertification, n.d).

In 1993, the first of five meetings were held in Nairobi, Kenya, to determine cooperative efforts, as well as determine specific causes of desertification. Within the written convention, as well as in negotiations, the states involved were broadly separated into two distinct partial coalitions, the developing nations affected by massive desertification, and the wealthier developed nations that did not experience desertification at such a massive scale. While the convention was recognized by both coalitions as a necessary step for global cooperation, the original positions of the parties were very different as seen in the reports from the UN Conference and throughout the convention (Biswas, 1978; United Nations Convention to Combat Desertification, n.d). The convention was also attended by NGOs, who played an important role during all stages of the negotiations (Carr and Mpande, 1996; Danish, 1995).

Historically, developed countries had been providing relief funds, food aid, and other forms of support for the 1968–1973 droughts in Africa as well as to other parts of the world. It was believed that even without a global treaty they had been providing enough aid already. As Bali (2016) recognized, the United States alone donated $13 million dollars in emergency food aid between 1968 and 1971 to drought and famine affected Sahel nations (p. 271). Many developed nations referenced poor accountability of the funds already provided and deemed it a local management issue, not a global issue. They also recognized that desertification was a geographically specific issue and not a phenomenon happening at a global scale that warranted a UN global policy Biswas (1978).

The affected parties included many states in Africa, Asia, South America, and the Middle East. The parties recognized that although desertification and drought affected specific geographic locations, it was still a global phenomenon with global negative externalities that affected more than just the immediate communities experiencing desertification and food insecurity (Biswas, 1978). Some of the global negative externalities were mass migrations, such as environmental refugees, global impacts on international trade, and a myriad of social issues (Smith, 2012; World Atlas of Desertification, 2018). Besides just shared negative impacts, there was an explicit recognition that there was a collective responsibility in the actual desertification process. Their points included how unaffected/developed countries' colonial pasts had been responsible for many poor land management and cattle raising schemes that contributed to the increased desertification seen today. Developing affected nations also referenced how industrialization's contribution to global warming had affected the already harsh ecosystems and thus contributed to increased desertification (Biswas, 1978; United Nations Convention to Combat Desertification, n.d). This meant that the cost of financing, researching, aiding, and otherwise mitigating desertification was *a global responsibility*, due to both other nations' prior contributions to desertification as well as because they are still negatively affected by the desertification impacts.

Despite the different positions originally held by the parties, the UNCCD was created in a relatively short time. After five negotiation meetings the UNCCD was opened for ratification on October 15, 1994 and opened for signatures at the UN headquarters in New York until October 13, 1995. The global policy officially went into force on December 26, 1996, and to date has been ratified or acceded by 197 states out of 198 possible signatories (as only the Holy See has not ratified or acceded the treaty). Since the UNCCD's ratification there have been 14 Conference of the Parties (COP) meetings to address desertification efforts. These meetings were held annually the first 5 years after it entered into force, and then every other year thereafter (INCD, 1994; United Nations, 2020).

A6.2 *Final positions, motivations, and objectives*

As desertification was understood to be a multi-faceted problem with many contributing factors, there were a wide range of understandings and motivations behind the inception of the UNCCD treaty. Primarily, and perhaps the most explicit motivation for the convention, was that millions of hectares of land were being lost each year, especially agricultural land. By signing this convention there was a global effort to address food security in the form of land reclamation for further agricultural use, as well as reduction of famine (Biswas, 1978; INCD, 1994). This reclamation and food security would eventually decrease the annual funding developed nations provide through relief funds and programs.

Nearly every country at the conference and convention on desertification recognized that desertification was also connected to poverty. Projects aimed to educate farmers and reduce poverty rates were believed to help improve livelihoods of millions of people, as well as combat desertification. For many nations, this also meant an opportunity to address social inequalities, such as women and youth-specific programs, and ensure increased education to rural and poor children (Biswas, 1978; United Nations Convention to Combat Desertification, n.d; INCD, 1994).

At the time of this convention, there had been an increasing worldwide awareness of the devastating effects humans had on the environment and the need for sustainable development. This first ever desertification treaty was perfect for the environmentally conscious countries to stress the importance of biodiversity and climate change. The UN Framework Convention on Climate Change and the Convention on Biological Diversity had been recently taken up at the Earth Summit meeting, and the UN Convention to Combat Desertification was another way to ensure that they were followed, especially in desert-prone regions that faced a reduction in biological diversity due to encroaching deserts (INCD, 1994: 4).

In terms of fiscal aid, developed/unaffected nations agreed to increase monetary contribution and grants, although no specified amount was indicated. There was an acknowledgment that this increased obligation had to do with past colonial impacts on the landscape, as well as industrialization's effect on climate change. Beyond just direct government-to-government monetary aid, there was agreement to share technology (such as Japan's desalinization technology), increase personnel (number of US Peace Corps), and increase research efforts. There was also an agreement to favor developing countries in international trade (Biswas, 1978; INCD, 1994).

Although there was no specified amount of funding obligations, this agreement was vital for increased attention and aid for affected nations. However, although there were many gains for developing nations, they still had to make some concessions. There was an agreement that affected countries needed to share more with each other, such as successful management schemes, research, and program results, rather than just direct reliance on wealthier developed nations. There was also a process set in place to ensure that the funds donated from other countries were properly managed and accounted for, including increase of programs, laws, and progress reports to be reviewed at the COP. There was also an agreement to implement programs to help women and children, who often have to walk miles for water, and ensure there was available education to these often-remote rural areas (INCD, 1994). Positions of the main blocks of states can be seen in Table A6.1 with a breakdown of initial and final party (block) positions as well as the concessions made by each party. At the end, an agreement was reached and the final agreement and motivations are seen in the UNCCD-stated objective to:

> "combat desertification and mitigate the effects of drought in countries experiencing serious drought and/or desertification, particularly in Africa, through effective action at all levels, supported by international cooperation and partnership arrangements, in the framework of an integrated approach which is consistent with Agenda 21, with a view to contributing to the achievement of sustainable development in affected areas. Achieving this objective will involve long-term integrated strategies that focus simultaneously,

Table A6.1. A quick, noncomprehensive chart, displaying some of the initial and final positions of each party (block) coalition as well as what was both gained and conceded.

Country blocks	Original position	Gained	Final position	Conceded
Developing 'Affected' Countries	Colonial impacts at fault Global issue not just local state issue Poverty at fault Need prevention measures Needed more aid Industry impacts	Favoritism/understanding of issues in trade and market arrangements Increased financial resources from developed nations (including private sector grants) Technological information Desertification/ecological information	Agreed to implement laws, and program management. Will give progress reports on fund used Will work with other impacted nations	More accountable for funds provided Needed to show progress in reports No specific amount of funds
Developed 'Unaffected' Countries	Already have been providing funds Management issue Desertification affects global environment and climate change Socioeconomic factors at play (gender/poverty) Not a lot of affected-to-affected country communication	Formalized accountability system of affected countries' uses of funds and laws where there were prior gaps Women and youth programs Increased interaction and information sharing between affected nations Focus on UN convention of climate change and UN convention on biodiversity also being followed	Favoritism/understanding in trade relations Information sharing US increased peace corps presence	More financial aid (although not a specified amount) Recognition of Western impact/industry on desertification Information and technology given and more aid provided

in affected areas, on improved productivity of land, and the rehabilitation, conservation and sustainable management of land and water resources, leading to improved living conditions, in particular at the community level" (INCD, 1994: 4).

A6.3 *Policy structure and regulatory mechanisms*

The UNCCD is divided into six distinct sections and five annexes. The first section defines desertification, means to combating desertification, drought, and other terminology. The overall objective of the convention and guiding principles were also agreed upon and introduced within the first part of the convention, as it was crucial that all members work within the same definitions to ensure effective cooperation and successful communication (INCD, 1994: 3–5).

The general obligations of the parties (such as integrating strategies for poverty eradication and promoting cooperation between affected countries) are stated within the second part of the UNCCD. Article 5 states the objectives of the affected countries, while Article 6 mentions the role of developed countries to support efforts through 'substantial financial resources' and other forms of support. There is a note of priority for Africa and encouragement to connect initiatives from this convention to the UN Framework Convention on Climate Change and the Convention on Biological Diversity (INCD, 1994: 5–8).

The third part of the UNCCD is focused on providing a framework for national programs, regional and sub-regional action programs, international cooperation, and support for these programs. There is an agreement in this section to integrate and coordinate collection, analysis, and exchange of relevant short-term and long-term data and information. There is also a large section on promoting technical and scientific cooperation in the fields of combating desertification and mitigating the effects of drought through research sharing and development (INCD, 1994: 9–20), specifically on sharing of 'economically viable, environmentally sound, and socially acceptable technologies' (INCD, 1994: 15). Capacity-building, education, and increasing public awareness in cooperative intergovernmental organizations is encouraged as well. Article 20 specifically states the importance of financing to achieve the objective of the convention, while Article 21 promotes various financial mechanisms that could be implemented, included their own 'Global Mechanism' (INCD, 1994: 9–20).

The regulatory mechanism and institutions created to ensure that the convention is followed were specifically listed within part four. The main regulatory body is the COP that is described in the convention as the 'supreme body' meant to review the implementation of the convention, promote information exchange, establish subsidiary bodies as necessary, adopt rules and amendments, and approve programs and budgets for activities. The main subsidiary body included in the convention is the Committee on Science and Technology, which is open to all parties and made of government representatives in relevant fields of experience. They supervise, create, and implement surveys and evaluations of the networks, agencies, and institutions as well as make recommendations to improve cooperation and ensure that the stressed components of the policy are being achieved (areas highlighted in the third part) (INCD, 1994: 21–24). The year 2007 marks the establishment of the Group of Experts under the Committee on Science and Technology to provide updated and current knowledge, policy implication of previous programs, make information available to all parties, and promote awareness (World Atlas of Desertification, 2018: 15).

While none of these parties have legal powers, they are the main regulatory bodies that oversee the convention and the parties' actions. However, like most international treaties that lack legal enforcement there are three strategies that can be used to enforce compliance. Through reciprocity the potential for positive favor from participating can ensure continued compliance with the treaty, or perhaps in this case the states may receive a different form of reciprocal aid. There is also the potential for collective action, so if a state fails to hold up their part in the agreement, several states may enact a collective punishment. Although states are unlikely to go as far as war over desertification technology sharing, there can be other sanctions in economics, future deals, or other unrelated sectors.

The final method to deal with states that do not provide as much aid as they agreed upon, would be through shaming, provoking negative publicity to enforce compliance (Globalization 101, 2016).

Part five of the UNCCD is focused on communication of information and procedures, especially for affected country parties in providing detailed description of their strategies and programs, as well as their implantation. Developed nations also need to prepare a report about how/what information and financial resources were provided. There is also a brief section on conflict resolution, status of annexes, amendments, and their adoption (INCD, 1994: 24–28).

The final section of the policy focuses on the technicalities of the treaty, such as when the dates are open for signature, ratification, acceptance, and accession, as well as information about entry into force, reservations, and withdrawals (INCD, 1994: 28–30). Currently, only Canada has withdrawn from the convention, although it rejoined later in 2016 (United Nations, 2020). There are also five 'regional implementation annexes', each made for specific geographic regions (Africa, Asia, Latin America and the Caribbean, Northern Mediterranean) (INCD, 1994: 31–56), and the final fifth annex, which was later added at the fourth COP, is Central and Eastern Europe (Secretary-General of the United Nations, 2001).

A6.4 *Role of local (state) interests*

The local (state) interests in shaping the global policy can be seen throughout the convention itself, as well as the history of the negotiations leading to the convention's creation. As previously mentioned, it was the affected African countries that recognized that desertification was a serious and global issue. African state leaders brought up the topic at the 'Earth Summit', first meeting hosted in Nairobi, and were the major contributors to presentations targeted to demonstrate the seriousness of desertification as well as its global effects (United Nations Convention to Combat Desertification, n.d). African leaders were especially influential in ensuring African affected countries receive attention, with multiple sections throughout the

Convention, including the name of the convention itself, specifically calling to recognize Africa. This is seen in Article 7 of the convention, as well as the direct assurance of adding African representatives into the hierarchy of the COP (INCD, 1994).

Other affected countries were especially vocal and influential in the discussions and creation of the policy. Venezuela fought for education programs that were specific to affected populations and for local resources. Peru, which is significantly affected by desertification, insisted that there are social factors such as increasing poverty in the third world that needed to be addressed and included in funding and focused programs. India was especially concerned about prevention of encroaching desertification as that would have serious impacts on its large and growing population. It was also a proponent on insuring that programs were population-specific and based on social problems, including recognizing that nomadic groups needed to be reached with mobile clinics. Saudi Arabia, which is nearly 97% arid or semi-arid, insisted that climatic conditions caused by human settlement and industry were largely at fault and needed to be addressed (Biswas, 1978). One of the last parts that demonstrates local (state) roles in the creation of the treaty was the specifically tailored development of regional annexes that address specific issues by region (for example Northern Mediterranean annex recognizes frequent wildfires, land abandonment, and unsustainable water exploitation in the region). This incorporates weather, climate, socioeconomic status, education, economics, and other factors to address. This section highlights how local (state) actors had to be called on to highlight regional specific conditions and needs (INCD, 1994: 31–56; Secretary-General of the United Nations, 2001).

Danish (1995) demonstrates the important role of local and international NGOs, arguing that in some respects they have been the most effective agencies in the implementation of the UNCCD. It has been especially recognized that despite developed countries' fatigue and sometimes reluctance, the grass-roots demands and enthusiasm excited also the local governments in the developing countries, which added weight and pressure to continue the implementation of the policy.

A6.5 *Attractiveness, stability, and effectiveness*

The attractiveness and stability of the UNCCD can be seen in Figure A6.1. The gray line represents the annual ratification and the black line represents the cumulative number of ratifying states. As can be seen, by the eighth year since UNCCD was signed, 190 out of 198 total possible signatories had ratified the convention and that number has been kept stable with incremental increase of one state per year in certain years since. The number of states in the global policy was kept stable with only one state (Canada) disrupting the policy but then re-joining. By 2017, the Convention has been ratified/ acceded by 197 out of 198 possible signatories (United Nations, 2020).

Figure A6.1 suggests that the policy was very attractive as it quickly (8 years since being signed) reached the ceiling and is adopted by everyone (except one signatory). This figure also suggests that the policy is considered rather stable too, due to the flat level of participating states over a long period (until 2017 for our dataset) (United Nations, 2020). This also suggests that in terms of stability there is a grand coalition (compared to non-cooperation or partial cooperation) that consists of nearly all the world's states. Of course,

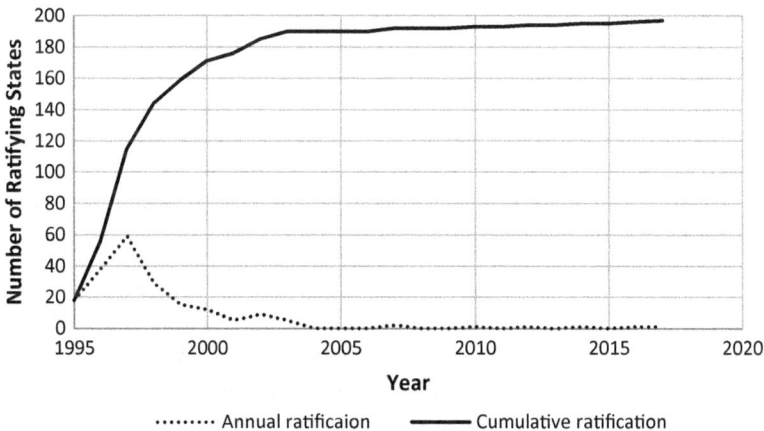

Figure A6.1. Annual and cumulative number of ratifications of UNCCD, 1995–2017.
Source: Authors' elaboration, using data in https://www.unccd.int/convention/ about-convention/unccd-history.

not every state got exactly what they had wanted, but everyone was in agreement and satisfied, assuming that the individual rationality condition was reached. The propensity to disrupt is low (since only one member left but rejoined later) suggesting high stability and the Core of agreement was superior to the *status quo*. Table A6.2 also lists the potential gains through joining the treaty, vs. maintaining the *status quo*.

While the policy itself seems both attractive and stable, yet to determine the effectiveness of the policy, it is important to look at both qualitative and quantitative measures to represent effectiveness. Table A6.3 shows that there were 75 approved programs between July 2017 and June 2019, totaling nearly $6.5 billion in total investment (GEF funding plus co-financing) that spanned across 50 affected countries. There was also a pledge to increase contributions by 10% (Global Environmental Facility, 2019: iv–v) in the 2019 COP meeting. While there was no specific monetary contribution, technology amount, or information requirements set forth within the desertification convention, there are multiple upcoming and past projects reported both in the convention's latest annual reports as well as the UNCCD website (Global Environmental Facility, 2019). In addition, there have been a rising number (over 500) of NGOs cooperating with the UNCCD with observer status, suggesting that all actors are very active (United Nations Convention to Combat Desertification, n.d).

The local and especially the international NGOs have been able to reinforce and demonstrate the importance of a decentralized participatory approach, hence the achievements of NGOs and community-based organizations. As a result, there has been increased recognition by international agencies, including regional and international development banks of the advantage of NGOs that follow a decentralized approach, compared with government agencies, which are less able to work closely with communities in localities facing difficult conditions, and the trust that these local communities have established with the BGOs (Carr and Mpande, 1996).

With all that, it is believed that since there was already funding and technology sharing among participating states, and

Table A6.2. Gains and costs of cooperation of country blocks in UNCCD.

Blocks	Potential and actual gains from cooperation	Potential cost in cooperation
Developing 'Affected' Countries	**Economic**—Increased aid from government and private sector grants, new technology for future use (example—sea water desalinization), increased information, increased productive land use, favoritism in trade relations **Environmental**—Reclaimed land for biodiversity, prevention of increased global warming, increased information of environmental issues and arid tree varieties **Social**—Job creation, better ties with other affected nations, increased research and aid in education programs **Political**—Potential less reliance on other countries in the future, attention to colonization affects, attention brought to poverty issues in developing nations; potential future aid for cooperating, increased cooperation with neighboring and worldwide affected countries, increased knowledge	Some loss of sovereignty as they have to give reports over funds use/laws made to donor countries Programs developed for local level involvement must bare the brunt of time, effort, man-power, and equipment to implement laws, controls, and programs No specified amount of funds given by unaffected countries
Developed 'Unaffected' Countries	**Economic**—Confidence on where their aid funds are going and knowledge on how they are being used **Environmental**—Global increase of biodiversity, and decreased global warming **Social**—Increased knowledge on arid and semi-arid environments, job opportunities **Political**—Increased reputation, knowledge of affected countries' attempts (or not) to influence future negotiations, potentially less immigration from affected regions, more affected-to-affected interaction and less reliance on unaffected	Increased aid in the form of funds and personnel required, even if the amount is not specified exactly Required to favor affected countries in trade relations meaning lost income Loss of information and technology superiority By adhering: potentially have to increase funds if conditions deteriorate

Table A6.3.   Investments in GEF projects related to UNCCD during 2017–2019.

Type of project	Number of projects	Total GEF resources ($million)	Co-financing ($million)	Total investment ($million)	Investment per project ($million)
Land Degradation	20	48.92	681.03	729.95	36.50
Multi-focal area	55	808.84	4,992.84	5,801.68	105.84
Total	75	857.76	5,673.87	6,531.63	87.09

Source: Global Environmental Facility (2019: iv).

the mechanisms (including NGOs) to realize the effects of such technologies, there was a large zone of agreement, and little value for maintaining the *status quo*, causing the policy to be more effective. The COP may also work as a sort of encouragement to keep states invested so as to not face collective action or shame.

A6.6   *Problems of policy implementation*

While there are regulatory mechanisms mentioned earlier that review and advice the participating parties, there are some potential technical and political issues with this treaty. One such political issue is that there is no set amount of obligations. In fact, throughout the treaty the words used are often 'suggest, to best possible, parties may provide', and 'assist' which do not necessarily restrict or oblige parties to contribute. This may not deter a country from essentially 'free-riding' as has been the case in other international environment policies (Nordhaus, 2015). By providing minimum funding, and declaring it was the best they could do, since there are many others now increasing their funding, a state can essentially attempt to give less and rely on other countries who have increased their donations. This could be done by instead reducing technological or research initiatives, or relaying on NGOs to fund and conduct research for the state instead of using government funds. Also, because of the self-reporting nature of annual reports, there could be a chance that project reports or research involvement could be exaggerated. Perhaps, instead of a 'problem' with the treaty, this was really another reason that the treaty was attractive and has been stable.

There are also a great number of technical difficulties in implementation as well. Each geographic local is different, cultures vary, and situations are vastly diverse. Just because one program works in one region does not mean it will be successful in others. Desalination technology has been shown to work on coastal deserts (Chiaramonti *et al.*, 2000), or through fracking, but this does not mean that it can be used in very situation around the globe. It may not be feasible to reach water, or there may be no reasonable aquifer to extract from. The use of some technologies may also require usually mobile groups to become sedentary, which would not be a socially appropriate technology.

A6.7 *Connection to other global treaties*

When looking toward other conventions, it should first be recognized that there were only very vague suggestions to connect the UN Conventions on Biodiversity and the UN Convention on Climate Change throughout the UNCCD. A potential option in the future would be to have a more explicit mentioning from within the treaty. For example, in the UN Convention on Biodiversity there is a specific focus on intellectual property pertaining to genetically modified plants, and yet there is a call to share technologies within the UNCCD, which may cause some conflict (Intergovernmental Negotiating Committee, 1992a,b).

The international water law treaty looking at non-navigational uses of shared water resources and obligations (Intergovernmental Negotiating Committee, 1992a) may also be a useful convention to emulate. While desert resources may be different from water (physically and in terms of demand), there are still parts of deserts that can cross borders, especially nomadic people, animals, plants, or even encroaching desertification effects. There is no explicit recognition of joint or split responsibilities between shared resources or people. There could also be a shift in other resources, such as water, if one country has more water sources or ability to desalinize than a neighboring country.

The Convention on Climate Change recognizes 'differentiated responsibilities' and 'respective capabilities' that may also be useful to the UNCCD (United Nations Framework, 1992). Although the colonial impacts and industrialization effects are briefly mentioned factors, there is less an explicit obligation made in the UNCCD compared to those stated in the Convention on Climate Change. Most likely, introducing separate donation quotas would be helpful to combat free-riding.

To summarize, the UNCCD is the first and only convention of its kind. The convention can be seen as attractive, stable, and effective. Membership is maintained by 197 signatories and over 500 NGOs focused on empowering, knowledge producing, and sharing, and based on economic, social, and environmentally specific conditions, with a focus on Africa.

References

Bali, N., 1978. Drought and Desertification in the Sahel. *International Journal of Health Services*, 8(5):271–298.

Biswas, M., 1978. United Nation Conference on Desertification in Retrospect. *International Institute for Applied Systems Analysis*. http://pure.iiasa.ac.at/id/eprint/915/1/PP-78-009.pdf.

Carr, S. and Mpande, R., 1996. Does the Definition of the Issue Matter? NGO Influence and the International Convention to Combat Desertification in Africa. *Journal of Commonwealth & Comparative Politics*, 34(1):143–166, DOI: 10.1080/14662049608447720.

Chiaramonti, D., Grimm, H.t-P., El Bassam, N., and Cendagorta, M., 2000. Energy Crops and Bioenergy for Rescuing Deserting Coastal Area by Desalination: Feasibility Study. *Bioresource Technology*, 72(1):131–146.

Danish, K. W., 1995. International Environmental Law and the 'Bottom-Up' Approach: A Review of the Desertification Convention. *Indiana Journal of Global Legal Studies*, 3(1):9.

Global Environmental Facility, 2019. Report of the Global Environmental Facility to the Fourteen Session of the Conference of the Parties to the United Nations Convention to Combat Desertification. *United Nations*, ICCD/CRIC (158)5.

Globalization 101, 2016. How is International Law Enforced? Accessed on June 4, 2020. http://www.globalization101.org/how-is-international-law-enforced/.

Intergovernmental Negotiating Committee, 1992a. Convention on Biological Diversity. *Treaty Series*, 1760:1–28.

Intergovernmental Negotiating Committee, 1992b. United Nations Framework Convention on Climate Change. *Treaty Series*, 1771:1–29.

Intergovernmental Negotiating Committee, 1994. United Nations Convention to Combat Desertification in Those Countries Experiencing Serious Drought and/or Desertification, Particularly in Africa. *Treaty Series*, 1954:1–64.

Intergovernmental Negotiating Committee, 1997. Convention on the Law of the Non-Navigational Uses of International Watercourses. *Treaty Series*.

Nordhaus, W., 2015. Climate Clubs: Overcoming Free-riding in International Climate Policy. *American Economic Review*, 105(4):1339–1370.

Secretary-General of the United Nations, 2001. United Nations Convention to Combat Desertification in Those Countries Experiencing Serious Drought and/or Desertification, Particularly in Africa. Paris, 17 October 1994 Adoption of Annex V. C.N.1490.2000. TREATIES-16.

Smith, T., 2012. Climate Change, Desertification and Migration: Connecting the Dots. *Climate Home News*, June 27, 2012.

Sterk, G., Boardman, J., and Verdooft, A., 2016. Desertification: History, Causes and Options for its Control. *Land Degradation & Development*, 27(8):1783:1787.

United Nations, 2020. United Nations Convention to Combat Desertification in those Countries Experiencing Serious Drought and/or Desertification, Particularly in Africa. *United Nations Treaty Collection*, https://treaties.un.org/pages/ViewDetails.aspx?src=TREATY&mtdsg_no=XXVII-10&chapter=27&clang=_en.

United Nations Convention to Combat Desertification. n.d. *UNCCD History*. Accessed on June 10, 2020. https://www.unccd.int/convention/about-convention/unccd-history.

World Atlas of Desertification, 2018. Part One—Introduction. Accessed on June 5, 2020. https://wad.jrc.ec.europa.eu/sites/default/files/atlas_pdf/1_WAD_Introduction.pdf

Index